WORKING ON A NEW PLAY

WORKING ON A NEW PLAY

A Play Development Handbook
for Actors, Directors, Designers
& Playwrights

Edward M. Cohen

Prentice Hall Press

New York   London   Toronto   Sydney   Tokyo

Published by Prentice Hall Press
A Division of Simon & Schuster, Inc.
Gulf+Western Building
One Gulf+Western Plaza
New York, NY   10023

PRENTICE HALL PRESS is a registered trademark of Simon & Schuster, Inc.

Library of Congress Cataloging-in-Publication Data

Cohen, Edward M., 1936–
    Working on a new play : a play development handbook for actors,
    directors, designers, and playwrights / by Edward M. Cohen.
        p. cm.
    Includes index.
    ISBN 0-13-441502-7
    1. Plays-in-progress.   2. Theater—Production and direction.
    3. Drama—Technique.   4. Playwriting.   I. Title.
PN1661.C558 1987
792'.0023—dc19
                                                                87-26469
                                                                CIP

Manufactured in the United States of America

10 9 8 7 6 5 4 3 2 1

First Edition

For Susan

Contents

Preface

I started as an actor in New York in the 1950s. I was a student at the High School of Performing Arts, and began checking out the professional scene while still a teenager.

The hottest show in town was *Tea and Sympathy*. It was a Broadway smash. There were touring companies. A movie was in the works. Anybody who stepped into the leading role of the young boy had a shot at stardom. On one of my first interviews, an agent took one look at me and said I was perfect for the part. She called Terry Faye, casting director for the producers, and said that Terry had to see me. Terry said I should come right over. I flew through the streets. An actor friend tried to stop me to say hello but I told him I didn't have the time. I was up for the lead in *Tea and Sympathy*. The poor guy turned green.

Sure enough, Terry Faye saw me. She, too, took one look and said I was perfect. The only problem was that all the touring companies were cast. Tell you what, she said. She was currently casting a pre-Broadway tour of *Saint Joan*, starring Jean Arthur. She would put me into *Saint Joan* as a page or something. That way, the producers would have me under contract so I couldn't be snatched up by anybody else. Then, as soon as there was an opening, she would move me into *Tea and Sympathy*.

I said that would be okay and went home to pack. I never heard from her again.

Weeks later, I took my heart in my hands and sat in her waiting room for hours. When she finally emerged, I popped to my feet.

"Miss Faye, remember me? You were going to put me into *Saint Joan* as a page . . . ?"

"Oh, I'm sorry, darling. That show is overbudget. I can't use any more pages in *Saint Joan*."

ix

Slam. She ran back into her office.

The following year, I was up for the lead in a CBS series about a teenage boy. I had been through four or five auditions, had been seen by every vice-president the network could unearth. The next step, I was told, was that the executive producer would fly in from California to meet me. Pretty good, I figured. I must be close or this guy would not be going to so much trouble.

The day of my appointment came. I stepped across the threshold of his office. He took one look and said, "Oh, you're too old!"

You mean, with all those interviews with all those vice-presidents, nobody ever figured that out? You mean, with all the endorsements and excitement behind me, I wasn't going to get further than that?

Sure enough, no. There was no interview. There was nothing more to the audition.

After enough experiences like that, I gave up acting for writing. It wasn't the reality I had grown to hate; it was the fantasy that was being tossed around so casually. I was building a life around promises that filled my life with joy, only to discover that nobody meant a word that was said.

It is not that everybody in theater lies; it is that the whole business is built on dreams. Shows come in; stars get discovered; people make money on the basis of luck, connections, drinks, the reviews, the weather, the gods, and also, that unfathomable essential: talent. The people on top—producers, directors, agents— survive on the brink of disaster, and everybody tries to keep everybody else's spirits alive. A torch of fantasy is passed from hand to hand, but by the time it gets to those last in line—the actors—the light has often gone out.

I hated the theater. I never wanted to see another play. I started to write fiction at the kitchen table at night. I did not tell anybody I was doing it, showed my work to no one. This was a private experience between me and the page, and nobody could stop me from doing it. I had no fantasies about success and was as content as I had been when I had first started acting.

Of course, when you are happy and relaxed and keeping your work private, you do it well. When you are doing it well, the world manages to find you. I published stories, then a novel. The surprise was that all the reviews of the book mentioned its theatricality. Once the theater has its hooks in you, it is not so easy to escape.

The book was optioned for Broadway production; this was in the late 1960s, when producers still did things like that. What it meant was that I received a little money and got taken to dinners with directors and stars, the producer's friends, and other writers; all of whom had advice on how to adapt my book, as did miscellaneous passersby, the bartender, and the busboys. Such was the process of play development in those days.

The Broadway production never came in, but I was in love all over again. I wrote another play, then another, which was done at the Eugene O'Neill Theater Center's National Playwrights Conference in Waterford, Connecticut, and optioned out of there for off-Broadway. I was right back where all the trouble started: bags packed, waiting to go on the road with *Saint Joan*.

I went through a year of backers' auditions; reading sections of my play to audiences half-bombed from the free drinks, flirting with rich old ladies, shaking hands, kissing cheeks, and smiling. I did no new writing all that year. I thought of nothing else but the waiting triumph. I was high on fantasy once again. When it collapsed, I was devastated.

My friend Corinne Jacker had been through a similar experience at the same time. Her play, too, had been optioned out of the O'Neill. My producers never even raised the money; hers raised half and vanished with it. We both needed to keep working, and we knew that we needed to work with somebody we could trust. The only one who filled the bill for us was each other.

We turned to the burgeoning world of off-off-Broadway with a project we created. Corinne wrote a one-acter for two women, which I would direct; I wrote one for two men, which she would direct. This was the early seventies, when women's liberation was making the news, and we proposed our evening as a study of the effects of a female sensibility on a male vision, and vice versa. We took it to Kevin O'Connor, then artistic director of Theatre at St. Clements, and he loved it.

Of course, he did. We had two solid plays with small casts, low budgets, designed for an intimate space, with two committed directors, and a hook for the press agent. We did them, and since we knew a lot of writers (I was a member of New Dramatists; we both were in the Actors Studio Playwrights' Unit), many came. When writers come to see a play, they don't give a damn about the script. What they want to know is: Is this director capable? Can he get a play produced? Will he do mine?

Suddenly, I was deluged with scripts. I was now a director.

The previous summer, at the William Flanagan Memorial Center of the Edward Albee Foundation in Montauk, Long Island, I had met a Yale graduate student of playwriting. I took a play of his to Robert (Bob) Moss at Playwrights Horizons, who let me direct it there. The play was Urlicht. The writer was Albert Innaurato.

I was now a hot director.

Bob Moss started sending me scripts to do. I was hired and fired by Joe Papp, producer of the Public Theater. I was getting nervous about making the same mistakes I had made in my previous incarnations, and started looking around for some place where I could ground my new career in reality.

I had a script I wanted to do that Bob Moss did not like. It was about a Jewish family, so I took it to the fledgling Jewish Repertory Theatre (JRT) and directed it there. The following season, I did another play for JRT. Then, I directed Ferenc Molnár's Liliom there. This was my first classic, and I was not able to handle the sense of style and period needed. The New York Times slaughtered me.

The day after the lousy review appeared, I had a meeting with Ran Avni, artistic director of JRT. He said, "What do you want to do next year?"

I thought to myself, "I like this guy. I like this place. I like having a home where I can fall flat on my face, get up, dust myself off, and start to work again."

At the time, JRT was mainly doing revivals, and Avni knew he had to start producing new plays in order to attract a wider audience and expand the company's repertoire. So, I offered to help. I started a reading series, formed a group of writers-in-residence, created a program designed to discover writers, nourish them, develop their plays. Soon, I was literary adviser. Now, I am associate director. As JRT has grown, I have grown with it.

I am not a star, but I have survived. I am still working in this world we all love. One of the reasons I have become an expert in play development is that I have been around for so long. Another is that, as I have stumbled through every phase of production, I have come to respect each individual's unique contribution and to cherish the magic when it all comes together on the opening night of a new play.

Introduction

Each year, new theater hopefuls descend upon Manhattan—expertly trained, thoroughly professional, experienced, talented, attractive, and confident.

The actors arrive at the first rehearsal, ready to work. The designers come to production meetings with sensational ideas. The stage manager picks up his clipboard with authority. Then, someone spots a shadowy figure in the back of the house.

"Who is that?" is asked. "Who is that dark, brooding presence?"

"Oh," is the answer, "that is the playwright."

And these confident, talented pros are suddenly filled with terror.

Perhaps it is because colleges and community groups do so many revivals that theater students get little experience with live writers. For them, including the writer in the process becomes new and, sometimes, frightening.

But off-off-Broadway, where young actors are going to work, is essentially a writer's world. Its purpose is to offer playwrights a place to learn and grow; a function the commercial theater can no longer afford to fulfill. This is also what attracts funding to nonprofit theaters, what stimulates review attention and, eventually, audiences.

Therefore, it is distressing that most young actors are so unused to having a writer in the room. At an audition, they tend to ignore him or treat him like the assistant stage manager. It is the rare bird who smiles at the writer and says, "Gee, I really liked your play."

But he is the one who knows what off-off-Broadway is all about. He understands how much clout the writer has in casting; not only of this play but of the next, and of the one that is going to move to Broadway.

And he is the one who is going to go with it.

Most commercial productions of new plays in recent years have come from nonprofit theaters, either the regionals or off-off-Broadway: *Ain't Misbehavin'*, *As Is*, *A Chorus Line*, *Crimes of the Heart*, *Da*, *Gemini*, *Isn't It Romantic*, *Key Exchange*, *Little Shop of Horrors*, *March of the Falsettos*, *The Mystery of Edwin Drood*, *On Golden Pond*, *Painting Churches*, *Pirates of Penzance*, *Sunday in the Park with George*, *Table Settings*, *Talley's Folly*, *That Championship Season*, *Vanities*.

The streets of Manhattan are lined with theaters devoted to new plays: Playwrights Horizons, Ensemble Studio Theatre (EST), Joe Papp's Public Theater, WPA, the American Place. Some, like the Manhattan Theater Club and Circle Repertory Company, do both revivals and premieres, but the new works are the ones that get the major attention.

Actors and directors are constantly running from one house to another. They do a cold reading, then a staged reading; then the writer revises and they do it again. Actor Susan Merson estimates that, in the last five years in New York, she has done an average of three readings a week and, she sighs, "I got paid for none of them." But Merson, who was in the original company of off-Broadway's *Vanities* and the Broadway production of *Children of a Lesser God*, acknowledges that, when one finally does get a job in a show, it is more than likely because of having been involved in the script development somewhere along the line.

The actors, directors, and designers who work are the ones who have discovered these simple ground rules:

1. Most of the action in New York theater centers around new plays.
2. When an off-off-Broadway house produces a hit new play, there is a chance it will move to Broadway.
3. When a show moves, the actors, the director, and the designers generally go with it.

A whole new step has emerged in the production process called *play development*. It involves the theories and techniques of taking the script from the writer's typewriter and working on it so that it connects solidly with an audience, so that the play that emerges is as close as possible to the playwright's vision, and so that the script expands and improves as it incorporates the talents of every artist associated with the production.

In this book, we shall trace the process from the moment the writer pulls the page out of the typewriter, be it the final page of the first draft, or a single speech, or a scene, or an outline. As soon as the writer shows it to another person—actor, director, agent, or mother—play development has begun.

It is crucial that the writer show his work to the right person; someone who is able to read it correctly. If something clicks, the script might end up in a director's hands, either because a producer got it there, or an agent, or an actor.

Once a director becomes interested in a script, the director and writer embark on the "living room" stage of work; intimate discussions about the play, its genesis, its vision. Important decisions are made and a course for the rewrites is charted.

As the rewrites come in, readings are held so that the writer can hear what he is doing, the director can get a firm grasp on the script, and the producer can decide whether to go forward or not. At this time, actors become involved in the process and, often, lay claims to the roles. Writers begin to rewrite with the voices of particular actors in their heads. The closed, cold reading is followed by the rehearsed reading. The open reading, often staged, invites the audience into the process. All this time, each participating artist and audience member leaves an imprint on the text.

Finally, we get to a full production and the complex contractual entanglements that all this developmental work has created. We explore the impact that the space and the budget will have on the script. If all goes well, the director's collaborative work with the designers begins.

The casting of an original play and the new rules of off-off-Broadway create new problems for actors and directors, and an attempt is made in these pages to find a logic in this chaos. At last, we go into rehearsal and follow the actors through the various stages of work, culminating in "anxiety alley": that final period of tech week, dress rehearsals, and previews when everything comes together—or doesn't.

If it does and there is interest in moving the show, there are new, somewhat more pleasant, problems to handle. And if it does not, which is more often the case, we end with some survival tactics to support the company through the lows until the next diamond in the rough emerges out of the next unlikely word processor.

Along the way, we shall hear in detail about the development of a number of plays, *Breakfast with Les and Bess*, *The Dining Room*, *To Gillian on Her 37th Birthday*, *Say Goodnight, Gracie*, *That Championship Season*, *March of the Falsettos*, *Sunday in the Park with George*, *Key Exchange*, and *Vanities*, from playwrights Lee Kalcheim and William Finn, directors Pamela Berlin and David Trainer, casting directors Amy Introcaso and Rosemarie Tichler, agent Earl Graham, actors Mark Blum and Susan Merson, and many, many others.

Play development has created a new set of experts, dramaturgs and literary advisers, with their own language and vocabulary. For example, John Pielmeier, whose first play, *Agnes of God*, started at the O'Neill, asked the Broadway producers of his second play, *The Boys of Winter*, to put a dramaturg on staff so that he had someone to turn to in rehearsals. This new trend means that actors in the future, upon arriving at the first reading, are likely to find a dramaturg seated with them around the table. How many are going to know what this stranger is doing there and how many are going to find it to be another source for soaring anxiety?

Actors have to know the steps of play development in order to shine at every level. The acting techniques for each of the types of readings are different from one another and from the techniques of rehearsing a full production. Actors should know how to behave in rehearsal with the writer in the room; what they can and cannot say, how to make a poorly written speech work or how tactfully to get it changed.

A young actor will not get cast in a Broadway show without a miracle, but he might be asked to do a reading of a new script. If he impresses the writer and director, he will stay with the project and be invited in on the next one, and pretty soon, he will be doing readings all over town—until one of the projects moves on to production.

Susan Merson put herself on the map in New York, along with actors Kathy Bates and Jane Galloway, in Jack Heifner's *Vanities*. The actors and the writer were all members of the Lion Theatre Company, which was started by director Garland Wright, and included among the original members Charles Haid, later of television's "Hill Street Blues," and Jane Alexander.

"Kathy, Jane, Jack, and I were all sitting around and Jack gave it to the three of us to read because we were the only ones out of work at the moment," says Merson. They continued to do readings of the play as it was being written, and eventually, Lion Theatre teamed up with Playwrights Horizons to do a workshop. After that, the play and the original cast moved to the PAF Playhouse on Long Island, where they did a full production. And each step of the way, the script was being rewritten, reshaped, and improved. Finally, the Chelsea Theater Center brought it back to Manhattan. Only then was it considered a commercial opening, and the three actors walked away with rave reviews.

Years later, after Kathy Bates was already an established actor, she followed the same route in 'night, Mother, first doing a reading at Circle Rep, next the premiere production at the American Repertory Theatre in Cambridge, then coming to Broadway in it and winning a Tony nomination. The point is that neither the unknown nor the known Kathy Bates got her job because an agent sent her in to read for a show that was finished, financed, and scheduled to open on Broadway. In each case, she connected with the script and the writer early, went through the developmental process of the play, and shared the acclaim when it came.

In this world, the actor's role is different from that of the college student doing revivals and Shakespeare. The words are not etched in stone. They come from a person's head, and that head is sitting out in the house watching rehearsals, going out for coffee with the cast afterward, and changing the script because of something an actor said. That head has feelings and needs and concerns about the work that the actor must acknowledge if she or he is to be included in the success of the production.

Off-off-Broadway, the writer is part of the process and the actors' functions are more than to look gorgeous and be heard, to end up human and touching and real, to get raves from the press, and praise from parents. Their function is to connect with the writer's vision and bring it to life.

That definition affects actors' attitudes from the first audition. Writers look for it. Directors look for it. And the actor who has it gets the job.

Not long ago, I was directing a workshop production of a new play at Playwrights Horizons, Beethoven/Karl by David Rush, about the relationship between Beethoven and his troubled nephew, Karl.

There was a small part open of Beethoven's valet and I was auditioning actors by asking them to read a scene in which the Master gives the valet newly composed pages of the Ninth Symphony.

A young actor walked in, having looked over the script in the anteroom. He was beaming from ear to ear, his eyes were aglow. Without even a how-do-you-do, he said, "Boy! Imagine being there when Beethoven finished the Ninth! It gives me shivers to think of it!"

Of course he got the part.

The writer loved him. I was charmed. He had talent, but that was not what had sealed the deal. The script was in rough shape, and there was a lot of work ahead of us. Here was an actor who connected to the material in an exuberant, delightful way. He wasted no time, talking about the weather or showing off his credits. He let us know immediately that he believed the core of the script, that he liked it, that he could personalize his role, that he felt the material was important, that he could make a sympathetic contribution. The writer and I both wanted him aboard.

Directors have to learn how to connect with writers early, how to spot talent, how to work on a script before it circulates. The director who connects to a script before the producer picks it up is going to get the directing job. These days, directors' résumés arrive at theaters attached to pages labeled, "Scripts I am currently developing." The director lists the plays, the credits of the writers, and outlines the plots. If the producer is interested in any of the scripts, of course, he calls the director.

The director has to know how to direct the audition reading, how to take the play through the workshop process, how to work with the writer on rewrites, how to protect himself legally so that, if the play moves, he goes with it.

With that kind of career plan, Marshall W. Mason built a relationship with Lanford Wilson that catapulted Mason and his Circle Repertory Company into the limelight. That is how Jerry Zaks first gained attention, directing Christopher Durang's *Sister Mary Ignatius Explains It All for You* in its original version at the Ensemble Studio Theatre. When Durang revised it, Zaks directed it again, first in a workshop production, then in a full production at

Playwrights Horizons. Only after the play's success there did director, cast, and play finally move on to commercial production. James Lapine also started at Playwrights Horizons. First, he did a workshop production of his play, *Table Settings*. Then it moved to a full production; then on to commercial production. When Lapine had the opportunity to work with Stephen Sondheim on a new musical, rather than Sondheim taking Lapine to the Broadway producers with whom Sondheim was accustomed to working, Lapine brought Sondheim back to Playwrights Horizons and developed the new script there. That is how *Sunday in the Park with George* started on its way to the Pulitzer Prize.

Even those perpetually aloof, nonverbal creatures, designers and technicians, have to develop a new set of talents in order to get started. They can no longer take a finished script off to the studio, work in private, and emerge with completed designs. They have to learn how to spot talent on the page, how to talk to directors and writers. They have to cover rehearsals and cope with constant change. They have to help the writer with input from their own vantage points—and they have to know how to do it without stepping on the director's toes.

All-powerful producers and artistic directors have a thing or two to learn, also. The artistic directors who have pushed their theaters into the major leagues have done so by creating new-play programs, discovering writers, developing scripts, and producing premieres.

In the heyday of the commercial theater, from the twenties through the fifties, it was, in fact, the producer who did the early developmental work. The legendary producers, many of whom became directors—Winthrop Ames, Kermit Bloomgarden, Jed Harris, Arthur Hopkins, Herman Shumlin—were men of the theater, not principally financiers, and they single-handedly controlled their shows. Broadway productions were not put together then, as now, by committees of producers, executive producers, associate producers, agents, and entrepreneurs.

Lillian Hellman was produced by Herman Shumlin. As he succeeded with each of her plays, he held the option on her next, and she, no slouch herself when it came to power and control, turned over the script when she wanted the production. They worked on it together, and when it was ready, a director was hired to "stage" the finished script. Actors were cast for the Broadway premiere. After four weeks of rehearsal, the show was taken out of town. Script changes were made in smoky hotel rooms by the powers-that-be and by play doctors.

That world is over. Straight plays have become too risky and musicals too expensive. No producer has enough power and money to take a script straight to Broadway simply because it reads well. The pre-Broadway tour for a new play is a luxury of the past. Commercial producers option plays once they have had a chance to see them on stage before an audience and, in many cases, once they have been favorably reviewed. New plays today are developed in workshops with the collaboration of actors, designers, and directors. Only when a play has been through the workshop experience does it have a crack at commercial success.

Even commercial play agents have come to recognize the way things have changed. "There was a time," Earl Graham recalls, "when you started a play in the biggest arena and you said, 'Here are the three biggest, most wonderful producers who should see this play. I will send it to them one at a time.' Well, the question becomes, do you want this play produced in your lifetime or not? I tend to treat the whole business as a great, giant rolodex. If, in fact, the world was filled with [Alfred] deLiagre and Bloomgardens who developed plays the way they did years ago, when they had an office and a staff and all that goes with it, then you could continue to work that way. Even so, you would be cheating the writer of some opportunities. Those deLiagres and Bloomgardens are all gone, sadly, and nobody has an office with twelve people anymore that I know of, except the Shuberts, and so plays usually have to come up some other way. A really polished play may need nothing more than an off-off-Broadway house where they have a classy space, understand casting, and can get the critics there. Another play might still be in the rough and what it needs is somebody who can work with the playwright so that the script becomes more realized before production."

These days it is the director who works with the writer on shaping the play before rehearsals begin. Together they define what the play is about, what the spine is, from where in the playwright's past it emerged, and what his essential vision is and how close the director's concept can come to it. The answers to these questions will determine what kind of rewrites and restructuring are needed.

This change in the director's role has created a dispute concerning the director's contract with the League of American Theatres and Producers. The director has become so much a part of the creation of the play that the Society of Stage Directors and Choreographers (SSDC) is now recommending that directors request a percentage of the subsidiary rights (television and film sales, publishing rights, etc). This is not merely a bargaining conflict but a reflection of a change in the very definition of the director's role; no one expects this dispute to be resolved with ease.

Would-be directors start in New York as play-readers for agents and theaters because it allows them to connect with writers. Not only is this a necessary part of the job, it is the best way to get directing assignments. Many new plays come to the off-off-Broadway theaters, and even to the regionals, connected to a director. Whether or not a legal agreement has been negotiated, (the SSDC has a recommended one to cover the director's contribution at this early stage), the director has discovered the script, worked with the writer and established a relationship, and pushed the play into a producible state.

In addition to the career advantage this gives young directors, they end up with a better script to work with and, as George S. Kaufman once wrote, "Good plays have a way of being well directed."[*]

The producer has been replaced in the nonprofit theater by the artistic director. The artistic director chooses the scripts, starts the process, sets the tone, asks the questions, and then allows the writer and director to find the answers. In those theaters which have the luxury to afford one, this function can be shared with the literary adviser, leaving the artistic director more time to go out and seek funding for the theater.

Whatever the title, the success of any theater dealing with new plays depends on the abilities of the person in this role. Robert Moss, founder of Playwrights Horizons, was artistic director during the early days of the organization. When Bob left to pursue a free-lance directing career, Andre Bishop, originally the literary adviser, replaced Bob as artistic director.

At the Eugene O'Neill Theater Center's National Playwrights Conference, each playwright is assigned a dramaturg, who serves to guide the playwright through the rehearsal process and to make

---

[*] Howard Teichmann, *George S. Kaufman, an Intimate Portrait* (New York: Atheneum, 1972), p. 155.

sure that communication channels between playwright and director are clear.

Of course, theater has flourished for centuries without literary advisers and dramaturgs. Writers from George Bernard Shaw to Edward Albee have claimed to know exactly how their plays are to be performed. ("I punctuate very carefully," says Mr. Albee.) But theirs was a world that permitted writers to stumble through early failure to maturity.

Even then, Tennessee Williams had Elia Kazan. Clifford Odets had the Group Theater. Several writers started the Playwrights Company for mutual support and a sense of community. Playwrights have always sought a home, and the input of colleagues they could trust. In recent years, nonprofit theater has institutionalized a process that used to be incorporated in the trial-and-error growth of a writer's career.

One of the reasons for the emergence of play development is that writers are growing younger every year. Theater has become such an unstable arena that it has turned into a way station for television and film. Even the big names that off-off-Broadway has created—e.g., John Guare, David Mamet, Sam Shepard—cannot afford to turn out play after play. For example, the Jewish Repertory Theatre opened Neil and Joel Cohen's *Friends Too Numerous to Mention*, which earned a nice review in the *New York Times* that particularly praised its humor and zany characters, and the next day the people from Norman Lear's Embassy Productions were calling from the West Coast. The writers are now working on a film, not another play.

Actors are perpetually astounded when they meet the writer and discover that he or she is a kid. Christopher Durang, when he hit New York with his first production, *Titanic*, was right out of Yale and looked about seventeen. *On Golden Pond, Crimes of the Heart, Key Exchange* were all written by playwrights making their New York debuts.

The Foundation of the Dramatists Guild's Young Playwrights Festival, which has turned out to be an excellent showcase for actors, is limited to playwrights under nineteen. No wonder an inexperienced actor can get off on the wrong foot by treating the writer like a student intern.

I sat in on a run-through of a play by one of these wunderkinds. An actor had changed a word in a line and the writer objected. The actor explained breezily that the new word was easier for him to say and seemed to create a better image. The writer's nostrils flared and he refused to allow the change. The actor turned to the director and whined, "Why can't I say it my way?"

"Because I am the writer!" the cherub announced, cutting further conversation short.

It makes no difference whether the actor's word was better or not, he clearly did not know how to deal with a playwright. Actors who want to work in today's theater must learn something about the way writers think, how they feel about their work, their anxieties, their sense of turf, and their mistrust of actors and how to get around it. Otherwise, there is trouble ahead.

The need for play development emerged once the sixties' phenomenon of the innovative director and the improvisational acting company began to run out of steam. Whatever their achievements, directors Joseph Chaiken, Jerzy Grotowski, and Richard Schechner offered little to the playwright. On Broadway, the great names of the forties were fading, but nothing was done to foster a new crop. The early bastions of off-off-Broadway, Caffe Cino, Cafe La MaMa, and Theatre Genesis, provided havens for Sam Shepard, John Guare, and Lanford Wilson, but the movement attracted little critical respect, small audiences, and almost no funding.

Once the pendulum of theatrical fashion started to swing, two organizations led the focus back to the young playwright: the Eugene O'Neill Theatre Center, and New Dramatists. These organizations were the first to define their primary interest as the encouragement and development of playwrighting talents. They were also the first to regard themselves as laboratories for writers and to invite professional actors, directors, and designers into the process. Following on their heels came the Albee-Barr Playwrights' Unit and the Playwrights' Unit of the Actors Studio. After these, came the Playwrights' Center in Minneapolis, Padua Hills Playwrights Festival (Los Angeles), Bay Area Playwrights Festival (San Francisco), Sundance Institute Playwrights Laboratory (Utah), and the Aspen Playwrights Conference. But it was at the O'Neill and New Dramatists that the techniques of play development were hammered out.

The New Dramatists Committee, as it was originally called, was founded in 1949. A young playwright, Michaela O'Hara, wrote an impassioned plea to Howard Lindsay, co-author of *Life with Father*, stating that professional theater made no provision for playwrights to test their skills before offering their plays to producers. Lindsay took up the gauntlet and got Russel Crouse, John Golden, Oscar Hammerstein II, Moss Hart, and Richard Rodgers involved. New Dramatists survives today in a former church on West 44th Street, servicing about forty talented writers at a time, and it has become a highly desirable place for actors and directors to work.

The Eugene O'Neill Theatre Center was founded by George C. White, who is still its president, and the first National Playwrights Conference was held in 1964. The organization has continually grown larger and more complex. The center now runs a New Drama for Television Project, a musical theater conference, a critics institute, and a theater training program, among many others. But the Playwrights Conference each summer is still focused around twelve young writers and the staged readings of their plays.

These twelve are chosen out of fourteen hundred—or more—who apply annually. The intense competition brings final selections a great deal of prestige. Working at the O'Neill is the goal of spectacularly talented actors and directors. Jeffrey DeMunn, Swoosie Kurtz, Marsha Mason, Ben Masters, Howard Rollins, and Meryl Streep all worked there in the early stages of their acting careers.

The month-long experience is a highly concentrated one in which actors run from the rehearsal of one play to the performance of another. Writers are either rewriting, attending their own rehearsals, or watching another play take shape. Everyone lives in a college dorm and the scripts are studied, analyzed, and gossiped about at breakfast, lunch, and dinner.

After each performance, there is a discussion limited to this O'Neill "family." The intensity and intelligence of the experience often bears remarkable fruit. Sometimes, it does not. But when an O'Neill actor says to an O'Neill playwright, "This never worked for me," everyone knows the actor is speaking out of respect, affection, and knowledge. And the writer has, at least, learned to listen.

Actors, directors, writers, and designers benefit from such an interchange, both creatively and professionally, and that interchange is what this book is all about.

1

The Writer

I can describe the shock when the writer discovers that his play needs "development" from my own experience at the O'Neill Playwrights Conference.

My O'Neill adventure started with the spring preconference weekend. The twelve whose scripts were to be produced that summer gathered in the main house of the Connecticut estate, whose rambling grounds overlook Long Island Sound, along with the plays' directors and Lloyd Richards, the artistic director of the conference.

Each writer read his play to the rest of the group, that sprawled over furniture and the floor. The writers got to know one another and one another's work. Writers and directors had a chance to talk. All were fed and fêted, and the entire group went into town and got drunk. We left, strengthened with some sense of community, which reduced our anxiety over what was to come.

After each reading, the writer had a private conference with the director to discuss script changes that might be made before the conference began in July. My play, in this early draft, took place in the living room and two separate bedrooms of a Manhattan apartment; the final scene had three duologues, one in each room. My director, James Hammerstein, said this was a major flaw. He explained that by splitting the climactic moment into three different rooms, I was losing focus just when I should be heightening it. I was weakening tension. I was making it visually difficult for the audience. At a point when the play had to glue the audience to the stage, I was creating confusion and dissipating concentration.

I was impressed by these comments and by the way Jimmy expressed them. He was asking for major changes, but was not taking over my role as the writer. He had spotted the problems, but did not tell me how to solve them. His reactions to the script were all from a directorial standpoint; he was concerned with visual impact, staging, focus, and build.

I went back to work, restructured the final scene, and eventually threw out the second bedroom altogether. I returned to Connecticut that July with a new draft, a two-room set, and, Jimmy agreed, a much tighter script. And then, I had another voice to contend with: the set designer's.

The O'Neill does not do full productions. Each play is given two performances of a fully rehearsed staged reading. The actors know what they are doing emotionally and are working at full-performance level. The play is completely blocked. The stage is lit for focus and mood. But the actors carry scripts. Only essential props and minimal costumes are supplied, and scenery is suggested with standardized modular blocks serving as furniture and set pieces. However, the designer does a full rendering of the set in order to give the actors and audience an idea of what the play would look like in full production.

The designer assigned to my script was Peter Larkin; a brilliant artist, a big Broadway name, and a lovely man. At our first meeting, he unveiled his sketch of the set, but he was not happy.

"I don't know," he said. "There's something wrong."

"What do you mean?" I asked.

"I can't explain it but, if I follow the stage directions, there is something strange about the way the people move in this apartment. It is as if there is another room that should be here but is missing."

I was astounded. I had written out all references to that second bedroom. Perhaps I had not been too careful about revising stage directions, but I had not been expecting a designer to dig so deeply into the script that he would stumble on a shadow of what had been there before.

At that moment, I had an inkling of what play development means to the writer and his script. Colleagues investigate not only the words but the intent, the impulses, the echoes of past mistakes. They discover signals the writer had not meant to include; signals, perhaps, he had not known were there. Each collaborator analyzes the script according to the needs of his individual function, and if the writer does not listen and does not respond, the flaws in the play mar the work of everyone connected to it.

Of course, there are still success stories which keep fantasies afloat and belie the need for the whole play development system. Playwright Kevin Wade tells this story about *Key Exchange:*

"I had shown the play to a couple of agents and nobody accepted it, but a friend told me about the WPA Theatre, so I walked it over there. That was on a Thursday. On Sunday, they called to tell me that they had the last slot open and wanted to do it. Five days later, Barnet Kellman agreed to direct it. He cast it over the phone, and ten days later we were in rehearsal."

Kyle Renick, WPA artistic director, confirms the amazing sequence of events and explains, "We had an open slot. The play was modest. It had only three characters. It was a once-in-a-lifetime occurrence." Mark Blum, who was in the original cast, says, "It was the most un-rewritten play I have ever done."

Wade continues, "There was no play development. Nobody asked me to rewrite, and I don't know that I could have if they'd asked. Maybe, I cut a half-page of lines throughout the whole play during rehearsals. Other than that, I didn't change a word."

Key Exchange was a hit. It was moved to an off-Broadway house for a healthy run and was eventually filmed. It established Kevin Wade, who now "spends half of each year writing for movies and television, and the one thing you learn is that nothing gets on that hasn't gone through five or six drafts."

It was only after this initial success that Wade learned about rewriting and collaboration. His next play, *Mr. and Mrs.*, went through extensive prerehearsal work with director David Trainer and was not a success. His latest play, *Cruise Control*, has followed the now-traditional process: a reading by the Green Plays Company in upstate New York, another reading at the WPA. Then work was done with director Norman René before the WPA production, and Wade is currently rewriting, once again, for an off-Broadway opening of the play.

"Rewriting," he says, "is the hardest thing to learn, and the most valuable. It's then that you become a writer. Writing is not about the flash of inspiration."

Still, *Key Exchange* emerged from the typewriter fully developed, but this can only happen when a young writer is so in tune with his inner life, writing in such isolation and unpressured privacy, that he never loses track of his impulses. Most young writers do lose their way, and it is the function of play development to guide them back.

Of course, there are play development horror stories. If a

dramaturg or director gets his hands on a play and completely misreads it, the writer can be pushed in the wrong direction. Every draft gets worse, and years of work go down the drain.

Earl Graham, the agent who represented *That Championship Season*, recalls that the play "was written by Jason Miller in his head for two years. He put it down on paper in six weeks and it was ninety-five percent there. I read it and said, 'My God, this is brilliant!' I can remember handing it to my wife at one o'clock in the morning. I said, 'You're not going to read it now?' She said 'Yes, I am,' and, afterward, she threw the script down, saying, 'This play is going to win the Pulitzer prize.' "

Unfortunately, the play went through a series of options and producers and one unfortunate situation in which the script was misunderstood and, as Graham says, "The rewrites came out sideways. I said to Miller, 'What are you doing?' and he answered, 'That's what they want.' "

Eventually, the play was dropped yet again, and A. J. Antoon, the director, brought the play, in its original version, to Joe Papp, who agreed to produce it. "A. J. Antoon worked with Jason on some reshaping," says Graham, "but no more than five percent was changed, and the other producer came along when it was on Broadway and asked, 'When did he put all that humor in?' I quietly laughed because it had been there all along." And, of course, the very same script that Mrs. Graham had read at one o'clock in the morning went on to win the Pulitzer Prize.

Play development starts when the writer takes a page out of the typewriter and puts it in the mail. Before that, everything is private and there are no rules. I can only pass on the words of Alastair Reid, the poet and travel writer, who, in an address at Sarah Lawrence College, said that he learned his greatest lesson about writing poetry when he was assistant to the chief plumber's mate in the British Navy: "Don't worry about it so long as it flows."

The first requirement in submitting material is for the writer to acknowledge how tough the road is going to be. Then, he has to figure out a way to travel and survive. The aim is not to get the first script produced, but to write the second while the first is circulating. Actors, writers, and directors have to find a way to face the constant rejection and still stay vulnerable, still keep their emotional system alive so that it can be used when the opportunity finally comes.

I know a writer who maps out a submission plan, which can cover several years, before he sends out a single script. As Earl Graham says, "I've been doing this for fifteen years and it is really unusual to have anything happen fast. Rarely does anything happen in a matter of days. Mostly it is weeks and months, and maybe even years. So many plays that I thought were fabulous have been turned down by fifty people."

My writer friend has all his manila envelopes addressed and stuffed with self-addressed return envelopes. He has all his cover letters typed out, undated. He has all the postage handy. He sends out two or three copies at a time, and as soon as one comes back, it is in the mail again within twenty minutes. The rejection has not even sunk into his psyche before he is focused on the new submission.

In the past, by waiting to prepare a new submission after the rejection came in, he was leaving a crack in time through which depression and paralysis could enter. Under his present system, that possibility is minimized, and he is able to keep hoping and writing. By the time all his envelopes have been returned, he has finished a new play. It may be self-deceptive, but it allows him to keep working, and this, in the end, is the goal of everyone seeking a career in the theater.

Writers are ahead of the game if they submit their scripts to nearby theaters. Every producing group leans toward local playwrights because they bring more publicity, more funding, more audience. Part of the learning process is hanging around, watching rehearsals of others' plays, acting, designing, ushering, going out for coffee with directors and actors. Writers who send their plays to New York straight away are missing out on this, not to mention tackling enormous odds.

For a writer who has already gone the local route, the best resource guide is the *Dramatists Guild Quarterly*, which publishes an annual directory of Broadway producers, playwrights' agents, off- and off-off-Broadway houses, regional theaters, sources of support and financial assistance, conferences, festivals, and workshops. Even those not eligible for membership in the Guild can look through a copy of the annual directory at the Guild's office or at a local or college library.

The directory offers current addresses of all functioning opportunity sources. In addition, theaters respond to a questionnaire, and their answers to the following questions are supplied:

Are you open to unsolicited submissions?

If not, what is the best way to bring a script to your attention?

What kind of material do you favor?

Do you cast with in-house actors or others as available or both?

Do your productions have any special characteristics of which dramatists should be aware?

Approximately how long should a dramatist expect to wait before getting a decision on a submission?

Are you interested in seeing new musicals?

What is the maximum number of performers you would consider for a production?

Are there any limitations—physical or otherwise—of which a submitting dramatist should be aware?

What is the best time of year to submit a script?

Under what form of Equity contract do you produce?

Do you offer opportunities for playwrights-in-residence or administrative internships?

With this information, playwrights can chart their courses of action. Scripts should be sent with a self-addressed stamped envelope or they will not be returned. A note saying, "Call me and I'll come pick it up," will not do. No one in an understaffed office wants to get trapped into an awkward conversation with a rejected playwright.

A cover letter should outline the writer's credits, previous productions, and awards. A description of technical requirements and a simple cast list should be included. The cast list should indicate each character's age and any unique physical qualities that would affect casting. Information about the character's personality and past belong in the dialogue. The aim is to convince the reader that the script fits the theater's requirements and to get the reader involved in the play as quickly as possible.

When I was a reader for Playwrights Horizons, the incoming scripts were all filed alphabetically on shelves that covered an entire wall. I often wished writers could see that wall in order to realize what they were up against. There were usually a hundred or more scripts waiting to be seen by a crew of readers. Readers were usually directors looking for projects, actors hoping to connect to the theater, and others doing it for the money. Fees ranged, depending on the theater, from a low of three dollars to a high of ten dollars per script. For this, the readers summarized the plot, recommended rejection or acceptance, and made a few comments defending their decisions.

I was reading to find plays to direct, hopefully at Playwrights Horizons. If Andre Bishop rejected my choice, I was free to contact the writer and submit the script elsewhere. So I plucked scripts off the shelf with this in mind. Scripts that readers grabbed were those by known writers, those whose cover letters listed impressive achievements, or those submitted by respected agents.

Obviously, no one wanted to read the fat scripts. They sat on the shelves for months. Any script that was unbound, or wrapped in a rubber band, or, for any other reason, was difficult to handle was left stranded. Cover letters that were poorly written, wordy, or desperate in an attempt at humor were sure signs to stay away from the play. Especially offensive were letters hyping the play in press agent lingo and insisting the play be produced. Scripts that looked as if they had already been read by every theater in town were not inviting. And why would any reader voluntarily tackle a script that was hard to read because the copy was too pale or the words ran off the page or was full of typos and misspellings?

Most of the nonprofit theaters in New York work under an Equity contract that requires some payment to actors, so plays with large casts have an immediate strike against them. As a director, I would never invest my time in a play by an unknown with a cast of more than seven or eight because it would be so hard to get a production by any reputable company. The same is true of a script with many sets or huge costume requirements or elaborate special effects. Three act plays that last four hours do not get done; there is never enough rehearsal time in the pressured world of off-off-Broadway, so directors and actors do not want to work on them.

Middle-aged men are difficult to cast. The good ones are working and supporting their families. An established middle-aged actor might do the lead in a showcase production if it offers an exciting challenge, but if the script requires a number of middle-aged men in small, unrewarding roles, the director knows he is going to end up with a supporting cast of lemons.

Plays that ignore the realities of off-off-Broadway are the last to be read, the hardest to cast, the ones that attract the least talented participants. Wonderful plays will get done, regardless, but the

wonderful ninety-minute play with one set and four young characters will get done a lot faster.

There are some instances in which play development begins before
the play is finished. Marshall W. Mason writes about *As Is* by
William Hoffman:

This play went through a development process at Circle Rep. It was
directed by George Boyd during its first four workshop incarnations. The
first was in a director's workshop at Circle Rep when it was only a
fragment—only about three scenes were written. Then it was done at the
East End Gay Organization out on Long Island and I happened to see it
there as well. George directed it a second time, and it was about
three-quarters done then. Then we said, "We want to do it at Circle Rep as
a Project-in-Progress [PIP]." So we did a fifth of it, which George also
directed. The two productions were quite different in many respects. The
whole thing about the PIP process is that you should do it very simply
without much scenery. Sometimes the actors are carrying scripts and are all
sitting onstage. This was the case at this PIP. The actors were all onstage.
There was only a cast of five, the two guys and Claris and two other men.
    There were a lot of changes that happened in the script along the way.
The character of Chet did not exist; the character of Lily did not exist.
There were no thoughts on death at the end of the play. All those things
were things that came about as a result of seeing the PIP and talking to the
playwright about where the play needed to go. In fact, even the hospital
worker had two speeches, one about a third of the way into the play and
one at the end. I said, "No, you can't do that. Take the first speech, divide
it in half and put it at the top of the show." If she was going to end the
show, I felt that we had to start with her. Dramaturgically, I helped a lot
with the play. The whole, "The first time I heard about AIDS" section was
not part of the play. When Lanford Wilson saw it out at Southampton, he
said, "As an audience member, I realized that Billy has come up with
something very important here. It reminds me of when you talk about:
Where were you when Kennedy was shot? That's going to be an important
moment in people's lives." I said, "That's very interesting," and I went to
Billy and said, "Let's get that into the play. Can you interview people? Let's
use the chorus to do that." So he interviewed people and brought in about
four pages of "The first time I heard about AIDS." We went through and
selected the ones we wanted to use and then I arranged them for the
chorus. We ended up using about four stories of the thirty we had.[*]

---

[*] James Furlong, ed., "Mason Discusses His Work," *Journal of the Society of Stage
Directors and Choreographers*, (Summer 1986).

Playwright Jeffrey Sweet started the New York Writers' Bloc, which connects actors, directors, and playwrights at weekly meetings. Writers can bring in a page, a scene, or an act, and the segment is read by actors and responded to by the group. Many writers find this immediate feedback helpful. Hearing the dialogue often tells them if they are on the right track, and they can write for specific voices that they have heard and liked.

This kind of early collaboration is also beneficial to actors, who often feel they are left out of the creative aspects of the work and are assigned to secondary roles as interpreters. Susan Merson says about the group, "A writer can come in with an idea, a monologue, and we create an environment where he feels safe enough to say, 'Okay, I've got three lines here. Where do you think they should go? I think they should go here. Will it work?' The actor is integral to the birth of his new character. It's like being an artist's model. The writer looks at us and places our arms in a particular way and then sketches the play in our image."

The actor who can connect with a talented young writer is wise to jump at the opportunity. Composer/lyricist William Finn, who went on to write the acclaimed *March of the Falsettos*, felt isolated and alone when he first hit New York, so he called three friends, unknown singers he remembered from high school and college: Mary Testa, Alison Fraser, and Kay Pesek. "I was doing temp work and wasn't very happy," says Finn. "But they were willing to meet with me twice a week so I could write for them and I could write for me and, out of that, came *In Trousers* for three ladies and a man. But no theater would give us the time of day, so I said, 'Why don't we do shows in my living room?' And we did the songs in my living room for whomever would come, and I played the piano, which was not a pretty sight."

But one of those who did come was Andre Bishop, who invited the quartet to do *In Trousers* as the first effort of Playwrights Horizons Musical Theatre Lab in their upstairs space. Eventually, it moved downstairs, starting Finn on his career and establishing Testa and Fraser (Pesek left the business), who now work steadily on Broadway and off.

From the actor's point of view, connecting to the script in its earliest stages, and having the part written with echoes of the actor's own voice in the writer's ear, cannot but help get a career off the ground. Sometimes it happens if the actor is smart enough to spot a brilliant talent and, sometimes, it happens by accident. Mark Blum tells this story about his first break in New York in *Say Goodnight, Gracie*:

"Ralph Pape, the playwright, and I had worked together in an office, selling things over the phone. I later discovered he was writing a play. Then we both quit and lost touch. Late one Friday afternoon, I got a call from a woman who had worked in the office, and she said, 'Remember Ralph Pape? He's been trying to get in touch with you. He's written this play. It's being done at Playwrights Horizons and Austin Pendleton is directing it and they've been trying to find you to get you an audition.' Ralph had been asking everybody for my number and this woman had it. Well, I was totally unknown. I didn't have a job. This was Playwrights Horizons and Austin was a well-known guy. So I went over there. It was the last hour of auditions and they didn't even give me a look at the script. 'There's no time. We're overtime already. This is the first scene. There are two characters. Read this part.' And as soon as I started saying the lines, they seemed as though they were my own. Austin and Ralph laughed at everything I said, and when we got to the end, Austin said to me in his halting sort of way, 'Uh . . . Mark . . . do you want to play this part?' From the first time I read that play out loud, I knew that was my part and I knew that this was my play. The song that was underneath the language was absolutely in tune with me. It was a character, although not identical to me, who was an extension, and a dearly attached extension, of my anxieties, of my defense mechanisms, and my sense of humor."

Here is a case in which the part was molded to the actor in the writing even though the actor did not know it was happening and, Blum agrees, the writer probably did not know it either. It happened because they knew each other, but once it was done, the writer was smart enough to recognize it and to search for the unknown actor he knew was right for the part.

Sometimes, for the writer, this process does not work out as well. William Finn explains that the path of *In Trousers* was especially bumpy because he had written with a specific voice in mind—his own.

"When the show moved downstairs, they told me I could either star in it or direct it. Upstairs, I had done both. I chose directing because I didn't want to have any fights with anyone about what it should be like, and I cast Chip Zein in the lead. Now, Chip is one of the most talented musical theater people in New York. He was a pleasure to work with, and I should have rewritten for him. It had all this idiosyncratic stuff that was written specifically for me, and I wouldn't rewrite for Chip because it had been so successful. I didn't know that I could get a laugh by just looking at the audience. I thought it was all written in the piece. But it was the actor, not the work. I was getting more laughs than the work deserved and I should have made it better for Chip. I didn't know I had to at that time."

The show opened to generally poor reviews and closed, but later, after the success of Finn's second work, March of the Falsettos, In Trousers was optioned for a California production, starring a popular, blond, handsome singer. Finn went back to rewrite and, this time, the image of Chip Zein, a short, quirky, quintessential New Yorker, had implanted itself in the composer's brain. "The part was now more Chip's than it was mine. So, I guess I was writing this time for him."

The problem was that, once again, the writer was writing for a voice in his head that was not the voice to be heard on stage. The California production was a success but Finn shrugs that off. "It won a Drama Critics Award in California. They love me in California, much more than they do in New York."

The California production was brought to New York and Finn demanded that the leading actor be replaced, convinced he could get Zein cast. But the West Coast director came with the production and, just as Finn had a picture in his head of a quirky New Yorker, the director still saw a blond Californian, and another surfer type was cast. "Here, where it was all written for him, Chip would have been spectacular."

Finn lost the battle. Matters descended from bad to worse until, at the end, the director would not speak to the writer outside of rehearsals, the show got awful reviews, the leading actor left the day after the opening, and Finn agrees that a lot of the responsibility was his. He started out writing for his own voice and was not able to rewrite for Zein when he should have. When Zein had taken over the part in his brain, Finn was handed yet another type and was writing for Zein while someone new was doing the performing. Such is the danger in writing for specific actors. "It was among the worst incidents of my life," says Finn. "It was just grotesque."

Connecting to a script still in the writing process can also be beneficial to directors. Pamela Berlin was literary manager of Ensemble Studio Theatre (EST) from 1981 through 1983. As part of her function, she conducted the EST Playwrights' Unit, which met once a week for three hours. One of the writer-members was Michael Brady, who was working on a play called *To Gillian on Her 37th Birthday*.

"Michael brought *Gillian* in in stages," says Berlin. "He had already written a full draft, which I had never seen, and he was bringing in pieces of the next draft. We didn't use actors in the Playwrights' Unit. Everyone sat in a circle and whatever the writer was working on was read by his fellow writers. The first week we didn't know where this play was going, since the character of Gillian, the dead wife, doesn't appear until the end of the first act. The third week he brought something in; all of a sudden, she appeared and we all brightened up and thought, 'Ooooh, this is interesting.' Once he had finished that draft, I suggested to Michael that we do a reading outside the unit with actors, to hear what we had. It wasn't a directed reading. We just got scripts to people and they sat around the table and read cold. Up until that time, I was serving as literary manager, but, after that reading, I said to Michael, 'I want to direct this play.' That was the first time I switched hats."

If the first essential for writers is that they have talent, everyone else's success depends on the ability to spot it. Berlin says, "What appealed to me was what it was about; dealing with a sense of loss. The theatricality. The language of the play and the delicacy. Those were the things that jumped out to me."

"An eye for a script" is a quality that producers, directors, actors, designers—all of whom invest their time for little immediate return—must develop in order to pick writers with some chance of success in the future. The decision to do it or not to do it when handed a new script can be hard to make.

David Trainer was a playwright who wanted to direct. He had no professional experience as a director but his background as a playwright had taught him how to read a play. This ability provided him with the break he needed when he was offered the script of A. R. (known to his friends as Pete) Gurney, Jr.'s, *The Dining Room*.

As Trainer tells it, "Pete and I had the same agent, Gilbert Parker, and Parker knew I wanted to direct and, since nobody thought the play was any good anyway, they gave it to me. But the reason nobody liked it was that no one knew how to read it. It had sixty-five characters and the parts weren't divided up. People would look at it and go 'Wow!' People can't keep four characters straight in a play. How can they read a play with sixty-five?

"Well, I read it and loved it, and met Pete and told him, 'It's an extensive play. It needs an intensive production,' meaning, if you've got all these people over fifty years in eighteen different households, you've got to have a core to hang onto. He agreed and we eliminated a lot of the peripheral characters; maids mostly. Then, I made a chart and divided up the characters for eight actors. But I thought, 'This is like the Long Island Railroad schedule. It has hundreds of columns and parts and it isn't rooted in people enough.' I showed it to him and said, 'Can we cut these kinds of parts and do it for six actors so it will be more intensive?' First of all, it would be cheaper to do. Secondly, six is a core group you can really identify with. Eight is a company, but six begins to feel like a family. And that's what we did and that's a huge change. It was a great piece of writing under any circumstances, but this grounded it in a more economic way."

That is a true director talking, translating the page immediately into theatrical, practical, dramatic terms; a required talent for anyone working with new scripts.

When I receive a script for JRT, there are two things I watch for. The first is the appearance of characters an audience will care about. The second is the existence of a writer's "ear." No matter how poorly structured the plot is, no matter how immature the vision seems, no matter how much cutting and reshaping is required, these two indications of talent are usually dependable.

The former is based upon subjective response and is difficult to define, but here is the way Elia Kazan described his initial reaction to *Tea and Sympathy* at a Dramatists Guild seminar.

Question: When you read this play, what most struck you about it and made you say, "I want to direct this play?"
Kazan: Only one thing: Humanity; in a word, whatever that word means. These are living human beings, and they are behaving by their own impulses and desires and ends. They are not behaving mechanically. It's an extremely well-structured play, and at the same time no one is being pushed around by the author. If you can get that, you've really got it. The

damn play is perfect, but you never feel the author is manipulating the characters. They behave naturally and simply in a modest, decent, believable way.*

One knows when one picks up a script whether the characters, or a single character, seem to live and breathe and, thereby, will engage an audience. If that element exists, anything else might be fixed. If not, all the fixing in the world will not help.

An ear is easier to illustrate. I directed a play by a talented young writer named Caroline Emmons, and I remember the moment when I decided to work with her. Her first script was a typical one about a young woman in competition with her mother. The mother was a brilliant scientist, busy with all kinds of complex experiments, leaving the daughter feeling unloved and ignored. On the very first page, a neighbor asks the sulking daughter what her mother is working on and the girl answers, "She's teaching a goldfish how to walk."

Now, that is a lovely line. It is funny. It has a strong visual image. It reveals an enormous amount, in a flash, about the girl, the mother, the problem. Good stage dialogue has compression and tension. It heightens everyday language so that we understand more than the words tell us.

In Corinne Jacker's *Breakfast, Lunch, and Dinner*, a woman describes her suicide attempt: "I got the pills down and put them in a pile and filled a glass with Tab." We certainly know all we need to know upon learning that this woman was watching her weight as she prepared for death.

The quality of compression is one of the secrets of good playwrighting. Susan Merson says, "The first thing I look at when I'm given a new script is 'How many big paragraphs are there?' If there are too many, you know this guy has not done more than one draft and you've got a problem."

Compression affects dialogue, structure, and vision and is the essence of the playwright's process; much like dreaming. In a dream, the day's events and concerns, anxieties that have been brewing for weeks, a lifetime of tensions, are funneled into one chain of events. On the analyst's couch, the result can be sorted into components and symbols, but the dreamer perceives a single story.

* Otis L. Guernsey, Jr., ed., *Broadway Song and Story* (New York: Dodd, Mead, and Company, 1985), p. 30.

In the playwright's head, many relationships and events become telescoped into one setting, one time frame, one plot. A period of years gets compressed into one night. Several conflicts merge into one. This compression gives a play tension and immediacy, qualities more crucial in drama than they are in other forms of fiction.

Just as a good dream releases repressed material, a first draft gets richer as the writer loses control. As when I had not fully erased that extra bedroom in my play at the O'Neill, a first draft should reveal echoes and feelings that the writer had not meant to include. The result is different from the play the playwright started to write, perhaps from the one she wanted to write, and the truly alive material has stuck to the page despite the author's conscious intent.

Many young talented writers do not know what they have written or why. They do not know what the play is about or who is truly the hero because the work has erupted from the subconscious, and that is the best thing that can happen to a writer. But it can make communication difficult when the time comes to discuss the play with a literary adviser.

Often, a traditional autobiographical first play will arrive on my desk about an idealistic young son who wants to be an artist and his conflicts with this horrible, boorish father who keeps telling him to go into the garment business or study to be an accountant.

The surprise is that the father is funny and alive and interesting and the son is a deadly bore. So, I will call the playwright and tell him I admire his talent and would like to set up a meeting. In essence, what I will say is that the hero of this play is the father. He is the one we identify with because he has all the excitement and energy and we can sympathize with his struggle. Perhaps, the writer was trying to reject his family by writing the play, but the truth has run away with his memory. The life on the page has emerged out of a deep-seated affection that is more moving and meaningful than angry rebellion. Now, is it possible to rewrite the play, placing the father's conflicts center stage?

The writer's eyes will narrow into slits. His lips will purse. His jaw muscles will quiver. If writers could discuss their work easily, they might make entertaining dinner partners but they would not be writers. Playwrights are dealing with material that is causing conflict; that is the reason they need to write, and it is the conflict that creates the electricity on the page.

Anyone working with writers must be honest and open; but also patient and gentle. Writers need time; they think and work in private. It is difficult to be pliable about such deeply personal matters. One must wait for writers to hear, to absorb, to think it over, to come to their own decisions.

But they are not objective about their work. They do not know at this early stage, and cannot know, and the better the work the less likely they are able to know, what is at the core of their play, where it came from, what is truly alive and what is pretense against the truth. The work emerges out of the subconscious, if it is any good. Once on the page, however, the second stage of playwrighting, which involves conscious choices to insure that the material that emerged is communicable, sets in. At this point, an outside eye can be invaluable.

Lee Kalcheim offers an excellent example of the effect of the objective eye, only, in the case of his *Breakfast with Les and Bess*, that eye was his own.

"I wrote the first draft in 1965 and there was some interest from David Merrick, only the play wasn't funny then. I wasn't writing comedies then, for some stupid reason. Merrick dropped it and nothing happened, and every two or three years, I'd pick up the script and update it. Finally, in the spring of 1979, I said, 'This is a wonderful idea for a play and you're never going to fix it by *potchkying*.' The script was 140 pages long and, when a play is that long, with the exception of *Man and Superman*, it means you have to rewrite, not just cut. I put the pages in the typewriter and I outlined the characters again and I thought, 'Now, what is this play about?'

"I had started it because I had liked those Dorothy and Dick radio shows, but it came to me that this is a play about two people who have a microphone between them. One is using it to avoid contact and the other is trying to get it out of the way. I was writing about the resistance to change and that has to be on every page. In the first draft, the play was all over the map. I also decided it was going to be a comedy and made the crucial decision to set it back in time to 1961, when I felt that the country was on the verge of a big change. People were leaving New York. It was the halcyon days of the Kennedys, foreshadowed by the doom that was to come.

"I became my own dramaturg. I was a much better playwright than I had been in 1965. My skills had been honed and I knew what to do. I had been a story editor at the O'Neill, so I said, 'Here's a young playwright who needs help and I can help him.' And I did.

I said, 'Cut the crap now. You've got a good idea. You want to do it the lazy way or knock a good play out of this? If you do, you've got to go all the way back.' "

It is usually the literary adviser who says things like that. Eventually, the director will also. After a preliminary meeting with a playwright, I will ask the writer if he has a director he wishes to work with, or I will offer to find him one. The kind of work that is on the agenda will involve a lot of talk between director and writer, in one or another's living room; talk that is essential to the future of the play and to the success of everyone's contribution to it.

2

The Living Room Stage

Theaters starting a new-works program should follow the dictum established by Bob Moss when he founded Playwrights Horizons: "If there's a page of talent, do a reading. You never know how it will pay off."

Sitting and talking to the writer, analyzing his play in an office, has little impact. He knows at once that he is not being offered a production and all he hears is the rejection. But offer a reading, turn the script over to a group of actors, seat them on a stage before an audience and let the writer hear his words; if he does not rewrite after that moment of truth, he never will.

Readings are a minor investment on the theater's part, and not only in financial terms. The play will not be reviewed. The artistic director's reputation will not be on the line. The audience will be primarily made up of the writer's relatives. But the experience can open the world to a talented playwright.

Once the decision has been made to do a reading, the first requirement is to find a director. Since producers turn over their facilities to directors, they lean toward those who know the staff, the ins and outs of the routine. At JRT there is a group of resident directors and, if one of them likes a new play, it is more likely to get done. New directors get connected to the theater when their work has been seen elsewhere. Sometimes, directors emerge out of the ranks of stage managers or play readers or actors.

The most common way for a director to get a foot in the door is to come with the play. At an American Theatre Wing seminar, Sigourney Weaver said, "The best thing about going to Yale was that you worked with all these wonderful directors and playwrights and then you all come to New York at the same time and, since nobody knows anybody else, you all hire each other." If the playwright has a director he wishes to work with—one he knows from college, one he has worked with previously, one who has already had input on this script—the theater company will usually go along with his choice, at least for the reading.

No definite commitments are made at this point. The theater asks for no assignment of rights, no options, no exclusive controls over the play. No money is changing hands. No contracts are signed. No admission is charged. No critics are invited. Publicity is restricted to a mailing of announcements, and the playwright is free to invite other producers. Neither the theater nor the writer is contracted to the director. The purpose of the reading is for everybody to learn about one another; the writer should be wary about entering binding agreements at this point.

The writer and director sit down together to talk and explore and experiment and talk some more. Israel Horovitz has revealed that he and his director read a script together, playing all the roles.

All plays are not autobiographical, but they all come from some place in the writer's life and, in this living room stage, it is imperative that that place be identified and explored. This enables the director to connect emotionally to the material and the writer to return to the original impulse when he senses that the work is going off track.

This kind of identification can only be achieved through relentless investigation. If it is not done in the early stages, the actors will force the issues but, by then, the loss will not be easily rectified.

One who is brilliant at this kind of probing is Joe Papp, who works intensely with his writers and directors during the preproduction phase. He goes over the script time and again, page by page, asking questions, first taking one side and then another. His technique is to constantly question; his talent lies in finding the right questions to ask. By asking, he forces the creators to think, revise, understand what is not right, and decide what has to be changed. Once a writer thinks he has satisfied every question posed, Papp switches viewpoints and comes up with a whole new set of queries. He shakes his writers up, but many new ideas emerge.

Eventually what happens in the living room is that the director climbs into the playwright's head, unearths subconscious sources of the material, and associates to these with his own. He merges his images with the writer's so that he understands the play on an intuitive level, and the play stretches to incorporate the director's impulses.

William Finn says that, when he started working on *March of the Falsettos* with director James Lapine, he had only a sketch of a plot about his hero, Marvin, who leaves his wife for a male lover. "It was Lapine who suggested putting a kid in it and I said, 'Can the kid be Marvin's son?' He said, 'I really don't care. I work well with children.' And you know this is true if you look at Lapine's shows, *Table Settings, Twelve Dreams, Sunday in the Park with George*; all with significant roles for children. I never would have thought to put a kid in because they always forget their lines."

Of course, the relationship between Marvin and his son became the center of *March of the Falsettos*. It gave the show its emotional depth, and it seems inconceivable now that Finn could have written the script without that child.

It is entirely possible that Lapine did not consciously realize the significance of his flip suggestion. It is also possible that he agreed to direct the show because he sensed that missing child in the sketchy script and that was what made him connect to the work. The fact is that both writer and director were working off their intuitions at this point, and because both were truly connected to the script and to each other, those impulses could be trusted to lead them in the right direction.

Usually, the director's vision complements the writer's so that there is a merging of two different sensibilities, not a competition. David Trainer describes the work done on *The Dining Room* in this stage, as Pete Gurney cut the company from eight to six:

"People go to the theater to see acting. Audiences connect to the literary meaning through the human expression. If you had six people recurring in eighteen scenes, rather than eight, everybody played an additional part. It added one more bit of color which made the roles more interesting to actors and to audiences. As we worked, we cut trivial characters. How many people can a scene in a play ever be about? Basically, plays are about tight constellations of people. Then, there are others around to decorate the edges. A smaller group of people made it more startling to see. When somebody came through that door, it wasn't somebody you hadn't seen for ten minutes. You had seen them ten seconds ago. And that's a real important part of the success of this play. It is a wonderful expression of a true vision of life, but that is true of a lot of plays. The reason that this play was successful is that it was very effective.

"What we came down to was six archetypal images, and the parts were divided so that each character was introduced as his or her archetype and finished the play as his or her archetypal character, but we wanted strong variations along the way. The types were father and mother; those were the parts eventually played by Remak Ramsay and Lois de Banzie; kids, that's Pippa Pearthree and W. H. Macy; and the romantic couple in the middle and that was John Shea and Ann McDonough. So, Pete did another draft with that outline.

"Then I divided up the parts again. I put them in columns and shifted them around so there would be the thematic character, then transitions, then back to the theme at the end. Then, I went through to see if it was technically possible to do; if it was feasible for a character to exit in this scene and enter in another. The original script had the overlapping scenes. You knew there was going to be a kind of time-lapse approach, that there were a body of people who were going to play the roles, but it wasn't worked out in the sense of how to do it. When we finally worked it out for six, we could divide the parts; actor one plays this part, actor two plays these parts, so that when we gave the scripts to actors for the reading, we would say, 'You're going to play these scenes.' "

One of the values of this living room stage is that it gives the writer and director time to establish a trust—or for the writer to escape early. Every writer, no matter how young, no matter how inviting the career opportunity, has that option. Getting involved with a director with whom there is no chemistry is not going to pay off for anyone. Whatever hints of conflict emerge in the living room will break out in rehearsal. This early interchange between director and writer allows the producer, the director, and the writer to find out if they like one another, if they trust one another, if they can find an approach to the play that is comfortable for all. If they cannot, the process stops right there.

Theater is an art form that incorporates and combines the impulses of many. The play starts as the writer's. Then, the director changes it, either in the actual word or in the structure of the production. The actors have input so that the characters also reflect their memories and emotions. When the play is produced, it has been affected by many lives and many pasts. This is the extraordinary result of the collaborative process, and in the living room between director and playwright, that adventure begins.

The most specific example I can offer of what should be happening in the living room is illustrated by a case when the process did not work; proving the old adage about learning more from one's failures than from one's successes.

The play was about a religious, literate man; a druggist who has fallen on bad times. His wife has died. He has been ill and lost his store. He has taken a job as a janitor in a temple, where he lives with his books and seethes with resentment over his painful losses. The one person he still loves is a sister, who is dying far away. He wants to be with her at the end, but cannot raise the airfare.

Since he was a druggist, he is able to steal cocaine from a nearby hospital, and then, because he does not know how to sell it on the street, he connects with a baglady and wants her to put him in touch with the local dope peddlers. This was essentially a two-character play about a fine, sensitive, bitter man who needs a gross, foulmouthed woman to complete his deal. In the process of the one long night they spend together, waiting for connection with the dealers, they share their secrets and find a common bond.

I saw it as an eminently producible script, inexpensive because the cast was so small, with wonderful roles for great actors. I knew Lee Wallace and Marilyn Chris, a married pair of respected New York actors, were looking for something to do together, and whatever the deficiencies in the script, I thought we could have a wonderful time and they would make it work; perfectly valid reasons to do a play.

The playwright lived in Chicago, so we started corresponding about the play; essentially what we did was to fill the holes in the highly contrived plot. If this druggist was smart enough to have stolen the cocaine, couldn't he figure out how to sell it on his own? Would he need to resort to the advice of a baglady? If so, would he invite her into his home to seal the deal? Once there, when she starts behaving obscenely, would he go through with it?

I had defined the play as being about the relationship, not the events, but the work I did with the writer, I see now, did not dig deeply enough into that relationship and where it came from in his psyche. We concentrated on the plot, but never got to the subtext.

So we went into rehearsal with a script in which the flaws had simply been covered up. Lee Wallace is an artist who will not make a dishonest move on the stage; not because he is temperamental, but because he is constitutionally unable to. Lee will stop in the middle of rehearsal and say, "This is not logical," in a way that is demanding and intriguing and forces the writer and director to think.

In this play, we could not get through ten minutes of rehearsal daily before Lee would say, "This is not logical!" He kept stumbling on the basic flaws in the plot construction. The minute the baglady started cursing and screaming about physical functions in a grotesque way—dialogue that was, in fact, quite funny—Lee would say, "I cannot stand here and listen to this. I would throw her out of the house. I wouldn't have it. How can I stand here without reacting? It's not logical." I was tearing my hair out but I knew the actor had hit upon an essential problem in the play that I had skated over. Each night I went home, exhausted, and tried to think of an answer for Lee.

I found it when I took the time to reconstruct the history of the play. The writer was a conventional, respected college teacher, a married father of two, who had discovered he was homosexual in his forties. As is the way with such eruptions, it blew up in his face in a particularly upsetting way and was, at first, an awful and unacceptable disruption of his entire life.

He ended up divorcing his wife, giving up his teaching career, leaving his home for another state, and out of this trauma had come a play. I knew this story but, because it was so painful and personal, because of my own awkwardness about it, I had failed to bring it up in the early stages of working on the script and had not questioned the relationship between what was happening in the writer's life and the play he was writing at the time.

But I had to have an answer for a troubled actor and the connection suddenly dawned on me. At the next rehearsal, I took Lee aside and said, "I have to tell you where this play came from. It was written by a middle-aged college professor who suddenly found out that what he wanted in life was grimy and ugly and unacceptable to everything he pictured about himself; but he lusted for it and needed it desperately. This decadent part of himself had become unavoidable. So, what we have to find is something in this baglady that attracts you. There is something about her that you need. You are in conflict about it, but the play is not about needing her for the cocaine deal. It is about needing her to fill a gap in your life." And Lee said, "My God, I think you've saved my ass."

The actor had something to play, which he went on to do, and the performances were wonderful. There was tension on the stage, electricity and humor and sexuality between the characters. The critics justly applauded them. The actors' personal reviews were wonderful, but the play was savaged.

Mel Gussow's review in the New York Times asked all the questions I had wondered about on my first reading of the script. If this druggist was so smart, couldn't he have figured out how to sell the cocaine? Would he have resorted to the advice of a baglady? Would he have invited her into his house to seal the deal? Or was the entire play a contrivance from the rise of the curtain?

Had I had the courage to insist on answers early on, we would not have faced such devastating reviews. Had I been as tenacious with the writer as Lee Wallace had been with me, I would have, perhaps, forced the playwright to write about the conflict that had created the play. The event of the play was the cocaine deal and that is what starts the motor of the play, but I should have pushed him to write about the attraction and repulsion between the characters and their eventual acceptance of what had originally been repellent to each. Had the writer and I come to terms with the impulse that had created the play, had he used that understanding to rewrite, we would not have allowed the second act to wander into contrivance and he would have had a brilliant play.

But I did not deal with this in the early stages. I thought the issue was too personal and would be embarrassing; a stupid reaction since, in the arts, nothing is secret, nothing is sacred.

My other mistake was to try to develop a play through the mail. I will not do this again, nor will I discuss changes over the phone. The play development process is not one in which the director tells the playwright what is wrong and the playwright decides whether to fix or not; the process is one of give and take in which each share responses and ideas, each bounces off the other. David Trainer says, "Pete Gurney and I did everything together [on Dining Room]. I might have made the proposals but it wasn't that he did something and I did something. We worked together on this play all along, every step of the way. That's why it worked out so well; together and happily."

The director may start the conversation with a specific complaint, but there is no knowing where it will end, and in the process, both artists connect to the material and reveal themselves. This must be done face to face, and when it happens, it can be a wonderful, eye-opening experience for the collaborators and for the play.

3

The Closed Reading

The work between writer and director will occasionally result in the determination that a rewrite is needed before a reading can be scheduled. That is up to the writer and director. If this is not the case, a decision is made as to what kind of reading to do. The determining factors are the level of the play, the experience of the writer, and the desires of the director. Generally, when dealing with a first draft which the writer has not yet heard, or with a writer who has never dealt with actors before, it is best to plan a closed, cold reading. The director will contact actors and give them the script ahead of time so they can study it, inviting them to call if there are questions. Then, all will gather around a table and the actors will read the play for the director, the writer, and the literary adviser.

It is a comfortable, private experience; a working procedure, not a performance or an audition. It is a way of starting the writer on his experience with others, and the more relaxed he can be, the better he is able to listen to his play.

If the play has complex stage directions, an apprentice actor is asked to read them, but it is wise to keep them to a minimum because they interrupt the flow of concentration. Certainly, those listening should know the play well enough to do without stage directions, but they are important where it is difficult for the actors to understand their own dialogue without them.

A good deal of the success of the reading depends on the director's ability at casting. Age is unimportant, as are physical characteristics, but a talented director is able to define the quality in each character that is necessary to the play's motor and find an actor to supply it. Beyond that, the actors must be able to read well and to respond to other actors spontaneously and honestly.

In the larger institutional theaters, a casting director is on staff with extensive files of actors, and he makes an important contribution to the casting of readings. Before the reading of The Dining Room at Playwrights Horizons, David Trainer says he "sat down with Andre Bishop and John Lyons, the casting director, and we all threw in names. Playwrights Horizons has actors, like all theaters, that they have associations with; that they are interested in. Pete and I knew immediately we wanted Charles Kimbrough to play the father and they agreed. Then, John Lyons said, 'Let's get John Shea and Ann McDonough for the romantic couple,' so we took these people. It was largely cast by John Lyons with us just basically picking names. There were no auditions or anything."

At a cold reading, it is likely that the rhythms are not going to be what the playwright desires and there is going to be an absence of subtlety. Complex interactions might get lost, but what is going to be clear is where the plot or the characters or the tension flies off the page and grabs the actors. What comes across weakly in such a reading can be blamed on inadequate rehearsal, but what is strong can be relied upon. Those moments when the play suddenly comes alive, when the actors get caught up in the story, will not vanish. If there are enough of these moments, the actors will say that, despite whatever has to be fixed, "The play works." And everyone breathes a sigh of relief.

Lee Kalcheim says, "I have had some great experiences at cold readings. Sometimes, a cold reading works better than a slightly rehearsed reading because at a rehearsed reading the actors start to think about everything. At a cold reading, they just go with it. You say, 'Give me a performance,' which is a terrible thing to say to an actor, but they gird their loins and do it. They've read the play and, if they have any questions, I'll usually talk to them on the phone beforehand. If the role is clear, they understand it. It's not going to have a lot of depth or complexity, but we're just showing people the essence of the play. Some actors won't come through if you say, 'Give me a performance.' They'll try to examine the script as they read and that's death."

At an unrehearsed reading, the actors are the ones who demonstrate to the playwright what trust in the theater is all about. They trust that the director knew what he was doing in casting them; that whatever quality it is that the director wants for their characters, the actors have it and do not need to strain for it. They also have that one important opportunity to discuss the play with the director over the phone beforehand, and in the case of an incomprehensible script, it is crucial that this opportunity be used well.

"The actor must ask the right questions," says Amy Introcaso, who took over as casting director for Playwrights Horizons when John Lyons left to form an independent casting office. "To read a play and say, 'I just don't get it,' is not enough. The actor has to say, 'What is this part about and what is that part about?' Any director worth his salt is going to give you some clues, especially in a play which isn't stated clearly. But the questions have to be specific."

Actors do not characterize at a cold reading. They do not attempt to play age or an accent or bring in props or worry about externals. They trust that the script will take them where they need to go, and if they do not determine where that is after studying the play at home, they trust they will find out in the course of the reading.

Most of all, they trust their fellow actors. Good readers develop a technique of looking down at their scripts and coming up with the line so they are in eye contact with their partners as often as possible. They prepare their scripts by color-coding their lines so this can be easily done. They decide, in advance, where to sit at the reading in order to be closest to the actor most important to them. They want to be free to look, to touch, to bounce off the other actor.

Rosemarie Tichler, casting director of the Public Theater, says that the good reader is the actor who "can make that quick decision. I don't think it's a good test of talent if an actor can read well quickly or not. I don't think they are diametrically opposed. Certain actors can only slowly build a character and don't trust themselves to make a quick decision. The gut actor who can make quick choices will, often in a long rehearsal, make a more complex choice. It's just that he can operate on both levels. Joe Grifasi, for example, is a slow worker. He builds patiently, tries a lot of things. In rehearsal, he takes a while to hone a character, but he does take a lot of chances and that is why he is good at readings. He jumps in. Al Pacino is a poor reader. He doesn't like to show the process in front of anyone. Actually, I think it has more to do with personality than with training."

Whether or not an actor understands the dynamics of her character and the play, she attempts to clue into the writer's rhythms. They are the most reliable guides to what is happening, and good writers create clear, definable rhythms for each character. Once the actor finds a rhythm, she has a sense of her character that is usable, even if it is not intellectually clear.

The actor attempts to define a through-line for her character: an overall statement of what her character wants throughout the play. The more concise this statement can be, the more usable it is as an acting tool. The more urgency the desire has, the more interesting and electric the performance will be. With a sense of the rhythm and a strong, clear statement of a through-line, the actor has a "handle" on the character. She has a starting point for the reading and can let the rest of the play happen to her.

Susan Merson says, "A cold reading is often your best reading. You've got to stay nice and relaxed, connected. Make your main choice and go with that impulse. Don't try to go too deep. Don't try to justify too many things intellectually. Stay right on top of the material. Act from your chest up, because you don't know who this person is. You don't have the background. Don't think about it too much. Place yourself in the situation and jump to it."

In preparing, it is important that actors not prejudge their characters, that they don't anticipate certain reactions and feelings. It is essential that they find something to like about their characters, no matter how villainous their roles may be. What actors need to do is lay the groundwork at home and discover the rest at the reading. The biggest mistake the inexperienced actor makes is to come to a reading with rigid expectations and then get thrown by what the other actors feed him and the direction that takes the script.

Mark Blum analyzes the differences between acting in a reading and acting in a full production:

"The luxury of a four-week rehearsal period is that you don't have to give a performance for a long time, so you can explore the parameters of the material in true laboratory conditions. You drop a little droplet of acid into the test tube. If it boils, it's okay. If it foams, that's okay, and if it blows up, that's okay too. You can say, 'Today, I'm going to play the whole scene with a tick. I'll do that and maybe it will be fine and maybe it will be stupid and maybe it will give me another idea and I'll try that one.'

"You don't have that luxury when you are doing a reading. What you have is yourself and your instincts, your voice and your energy, your sense of honesty and truth. And the other people there that you can talk to. You've read the play once or twice and you make the simplest, most straightforward choice you can possibly make. Then, go ahead and do that. As a result, the choices in a reading may often be glib. If a scene is about trying to pick up a girl, in a reading that's all you can do. In rehearsals, it may turn out that it's really about coming to terms with your mother. There's no way you can do that in a reading, nor should you try, because it will muddy what can be learned.

"The reading is primarily for the benefit of the writer; so that he can hear his words spoken out loud at roughly the speed, the loudness and softness that they are intended to be spoken. That's the actor's job. Ultimately, we may discover that a scene is more interesting when played in a whisper and actually works better that way, but if the writer wrote the scene to be done with people fighting and pounding the table, that's what you do. One of the things that the writer might learn is that the scene is too long for people to yell. It doesn't work. It's shrill. But if the script says, 'They yell at each other,' at a reading, we yell."

Some basic rules of behavior for actors doing a reading include the following:

1. Actors should arrive early so they have some time to get the feel of the room, talk with the other actors, meet the writer. The most helpful factors in giving a good reading are concentration and relaxation; these are difficult to achieve if an actor arrives in a rush, hangs up his coat, and starts to read without catching a breath.
2. Coffee and food should not be brought to the reading table. It is unprofessional and distracting.
3. Even if their roles are over before the ending of the play, actors should stay until the reading is finished, or at least until there is a break. It is distracting to the others to have someone leave the table while the reading is in process, and the sensitive writer will perceive it as a lack of interest.
4. Any questions about pronunciation should be cleared up with the director before the reading. Writers are literary creatures and mispronunciations grate on their ears to an inordinate degree.
5. After the reading, scripts should be returned to the literary adviser even if they have been marked up. This does not mean

that the actors will not be considered for the parts should the play go on. It is simply unwise to have scripts of an unproduced play circulating out of the writer's control.

6. Actors should bring pictures and resumes with them to leave for the theater's files and for the writer after the reading.

The actors are generally asked to talk over their reactions to the script with the writer after the reading, and it is helpful to their position if they have something of value to offer.

However, actors should remember that they are not being invited to serve as literary critics. I recall one fine actor saying to a writer, "The dialogue felt kind of arch." After the actors left, the writer bristled over that comment, kept returning to it and sneering at the pretensions of the actor. However good he was at the reading, he had arched himself out of the role.

Actors would not be wise to take over the director's function by telling everyone how the play should be done. Neither are they going to impress anyone by psychoanalyzing the writer. They are there to do their jobs as actors and to respond as actors; that requires their analyzing the script exclusively from an actor's viewpoint.

"It's always to the good when actors are outspoken about what they feel isn't working in terms of their characters," says Pamela Berlin. "I don't want to hear an actor talk about 'the big picture,' but once he says, 'I'm just not feeling the through-line,' or 'He wouldn't say that,' or 'Why am I doing this here?' that's fodder for the work you want to do on the script."

During the reading, actors should mark in their scripts moments, lines, or scenes that feel awkward as they play them. These specifics will lead to valid and unique contributions afterward: "I didn't believe this moment on page three" "I needed more time to get where I had to go here" "I don't understand what I meant here" "I had said this before in the previous scene."

These are not literary comments; they are points about "actable" problems and they come from saying and feeling the words, an experience no one but the actor has had. It is important that the writer listen and note these so that he can analyze them later from his own point of view. Each theater artist has his own vocabulary, but a valid insight is always translatable.

Susan Merson advises, "Say to the writer, 'Gee, what is my

obstacle here? What am I fighting against? I'm not sure what I'm after.' Make sure you ask the writer those kinds of questions and make him answer because that will make the text easier to act. Very often you can say to a writer who doesn't know what's going on in his own play, 'Look, I'm trying to track my line here. I know that I'm at this level here and why, and then I go to that level there and why. I don't know where I end up in this next scene. Can you help me with that?' Make sure you flatter the writer. Tell him it's terrific and maybe he can help you."

Rosemarie Tichler talks about the work done on Reinaldo Povod's *Cuba and His Teddy Bear* during this stage: "Rei had worked with Bill Hart for a long time in developing this play at the Public, so the writer/director relationship was very strong, and DeNiro was the first choice of both. Once DeNiro said he was interested, a two or three month process started during which they all met. DeNiro wanted to read it together with some actors, just to hear it. Afterward, he asked for certain clarity in the script. He questioned a lot of things. It was not to make his part bigger. He just would sense things. He's a very intuitive man. With an actor like DeNiro, he knows in his bones. He has a visceral response to what's good. It's hard for a playwright to trust, because some actors just don't know how to deliver. They say they can't do this speech, but when you are working with an instrument like DeNiro, you have to listen. The playwright has to stay open, not be defensive.

"Mandy Patinkin is that kind of actor; he senses it in his skin. There is a head ability and a visceral ability. DeNiro and Mandy, not that they're not smart, they are, but the instrument is so connected that they can feel when it's not right."

After the actors leave, the writer, director, and literary adviser discuss their reactions to the reading. It is at this point that the literary adviser assumes the role of the dramaturg. The dramaturg has varying functions during the play development process. The O'Neill Conference defines him as one who "advises and cooperates with the playwright from the first rehearsal through the final performance."* It is the overall function of the dramaturg to hold the playwright's hand through the process, to listen to her, to help her clarify her thoughts, to make sure she is communicating with her director.

* Dramaturgs." Eugene O'Neill Theater Center *Playbill* (Summer 1971).

Although the title of dramaturg did not exist in American theater twenty years ago, the function has always been present and has been performed by actors, directors, producers, and in the commercial theater, by play doctors and agents. Earl Graham says, "As an agent, I tend to really beat up my people. I push them and push them to go for a finished product and say to them, 'Look, if you put your play out there with a lot of loopholes, everybody, including the producer's mother-in-law, is going to have a suggestion as to how to solve it, and you are not going to like that. So do your homework!"

Robert Brustein is generally credited with bringing the term *dramaturg* from the great national theaters of Europe to the Yale School of Drama. Yale students, who might previously have become critics or theater historians, were the first to be trained as dramaturgs. American regional theater was flourishing, and Brustein saw the need for these institutions to have someone on staff with a knowledge of theater history and world repertoire, an expert who would help the artistic director create an overall vision for the theater and implement it with the choice of plays and the approach to each production.

Dramaturgs also perform the function of literary manager or adviser. They serve as script readers and work with young playwrights on development of new material. If there is any commissioning of new scripts, it falls into their domain. When working on a period piece or a classic, dramaturgs research background material and supply an overall view of the play's history. They also perform the more mundane tasks of writing program notes, paring down bios, and preparing press releases.

The techniques of dramaturgs vary according to the personality and style of the person filling the post. Some attend all meetings, frequently visit rehearsal, comment not only on the script, but on the design, direction, and acting. Others remain more distanced from the day-to-day work—unless they are specifically invited by the director or writer—and only cover the final stages of run-throughs and dress rehearsals.

Whatever the approach, the dramaturgs' main functions are to facilitate communication and provide an objective view that incorporates the overall aims of the creators in the evaluation of work at each specific level.

When they are called upon to offer advice about a new play,

dramaturgs function as trained and highly attuned audience members. They see the play with the eye of an outsider, and that is a unique vision in the play development process.

Dramaturgs can be valuable to writers if they define their responses specifically and accurately. It is not their function to tell playwrights how to fix problems, but they must be able to define their reactions, to pinpoint when they happened, and to subtly push writers to keep on clarifying their thoughts so that the play moves closer to the writers' intents. Dramaturgs take care never to get between a writer and a director and do not comment about the script directly to the actors. They remain somewhat outside the creative experience so that their vision stays objective and their role does not become meddlesome.

New Yorker magazine critic Edith Oliver, who serves as a dramaturg at the O'Neill, says that a friend of hers was describing a washing machine that was so old, it had "a crank on the side." "My God," said Edith. "You've just described a dramaturg!"

Dramaturgs respond to results, weighing them against the writers' intentions. They talk about what works and what does not, letting the director and writer figure out why. They do not say, "You must change this," or "You must cut here," or "Your writing reminds me of Edward Albee's." Their role is to supply writers and directors with a pair of audience eyes so that the audience viewpoint will not come as a surprise on opening night. As long as they stick to that role and do not assume anyone else's, they can be very valuable. The dramaturg who steps over the boundaries will be avoided. The one whose responses are vague will be patronized. The one who seems to be writing his own play will quickly be identified as the enemy.

It is a tricky trade, and writers are advised to be cautious. As a result of the dramaturgs' comments after a first reading, the writer should know whether he is in good hands or whether to smile and pretend to listen as he clicks off his brain.

At a symposium sponsored by Literary Managers and Dramaturgs of America, David Kranes, artistic director of the Sundance Institute Playwrights Laboratory, described some alternative techniques that serve to eliminate this sense that dramaturgs are focusing spotlights of external judgment upon the play. Rather, at Sundance, the aim is to "illuminate the play from the inside."

In closed session, three readings will be held of the play in quick succession. The actors gather and do a cold reading. Afterward, there is no discussion, no evaluation. They take a break and then read the play again. Once more, there is no discussion and, after another short break, they simply read the script again.

Kranes claims that sections of the play become "hot." You can see the actors physically moving toward the script in their chairs. If a section is complex, it might take more than one reading. But if a section remains lifeless and "cold" through all the readings, the playwright will spot it on his own.

Kranes often charts out a play, diagraming the entrances and exits, illustrating who is on stage and who is off, how long scenes take in relation to the whole, so that the playwright can "see" his play in a new and fresh way. Looking at a picture of a muddy moment may clarify the problem. In a different attempt to help the writer in a nonverbal manner, a choreographer can be called in to dance a troubled section of the script.

Another method that can be useful after the play is staged is to have the actors run through the entire script on their feet, very quickly describing what they are doing instead of saying the lines. "Then, I slap her face and walk away" "I try to hide my fear by turning to the window" "I light a cigarette to calm my nerves." If there are long stretches in which the actors are saying, "Then we have a conversation about this," or "Then, we talk about that," or "I tell her a story about my childhood," it is possible, says Kranes, that the playwright will realize his play is too talky.

These methods help the writer to come to her own decisions about what requires work without any outside judgment being imposed upon her. Eventually, she is going to be alone with her script, and only her own sense of what she saw and heard will refuel the rewrite.

After a reading, writers are either elated because their work has been shared, or depressed because the exposure was far from what they had fantasized. Both reactions are useless in terms of future work. The only thing that will get writers moving is a pad of lined paper and their sets of notes. In most cases, writers will have forgotten the details because the experience was so anxiety-ridden, but if they took specific notes, they will be able to get back to work.

These notes are the pathway up from depression or down from an extravagant high. For example, a writer's first note will be about a line on page three. She will go to page three and figure out what is wrong. Inevitably, that changes something on page four.

One cannot start to rewrite feeling, "The whole first act has got to go!" That is too overwhelming and undefined. A play is rewritten moment by moment, specific by specific. As William Finn describes it, "When you make tiny adjustments, you think that it's the world." Gradually, the playwright returns to private experience, becoming involved in the work once more, rather than in the response to it. Then the playwright is better able to think clearly and fix the work.

Writers who return to their desks with the voice of the director or dramaturg still in their heads are in trouble and are headed for bigger trouble once they have audience pressure to handle. They must devise ways of maintaining public personas, in order to work with others, to respond to what colleagues and audiences offer, and ways of excluding the outer world so they can dig deeply in private and find their own answers to the problems. The moment when writers first face the shock of solitude after weeks of conferences is not an easy one.

The director, also, has a moment of truth to face. Directors are used to being bosses and like to feel in control. The more authority they emanate, the safer everyone else feels and the better the work process will be. But there are moments when directors have to grit their teeth and recognize that this is the playwright's play.

They can do all the talking in meetings. They can yell and plead, wheedle changes out of the writers. As William Finn says about Andre Bishop, "He whines his way into your heart." Still, when the playwright goes home to write, he goes alone. The director cannot, may not, dare not sit down at the typewriter with him. The director is not, in the end, writing the play.

The playwright, it is hoped, is going to absorb what has been said. He ought to satisfy all valid criticism, but he is going to do it his way and in his words and he will only fix what he thinks needs fixing.

This means that the rewrite might not make the director completely happy. Most probably, he will never be completely happy with the script. Director Pamela Berlin says, "You never know when you go into rehearsal how much more work is going to get done. You want to go into rehearsal saying, 'This script is perfect,' knowing, of course, that it is not." All along the line, parties are fantasizing, negotiating, and compromising. But the director looks at the rewrite to see if there seems to be a merging of visions that justifies going on with the project.

If the playwright is trying to solve the problems in a way other than the director would have solved them, it is worthwhile also to review these problems with the director. Perhaps the director can make some trouble spot work once he gets it on its feet. Perhaps, the playwright will change his mind. The collaborators keep at it because, step by step, the trust will grow if everyone respects one another's territorial boundaries.

Directors are more experienced at this collaborative process than writers. They can be persuasive at meetings and know how to bulldoze, but the writer has one source of power: When he goes to the typewriter to fix, nobody goes with him. His work is not negotiable at the moment of creation.

When rewrites come back to the dramaturgs, they look for certain signs of hope. Nobody, after a single reading, expects to see all of the problems solved, least of all the playwright. As writer Lee Kalcheim says, "You've only heard it once. It disappears. Also, you're wrapped up in your words. If you get wonderful actors, you're falling in love with your play all over again. Sometimes, you get a sense of something wrong. You say, 'This scene is going on too long,'—just like an audience. You make a note, but you don't know specifically what is wrong or why. There are some things you just don't get from hearing a play once." But dramaturgs look for signals that the playwright has used the experience well. If so, it means that this play has a chance of getting better. If it never gets good enough, maybe the next play will.

The first time writers hear their plays, and this goes for master craftsmen as well as novices, they are going to be struck by the discrepancy between the written and the spoken word. Good actors bring new dimensions to words. They have rich voices and know how to use them, and suddenly one appreciates the subtleties of sound and texture and color and tone. There are avenues of communication available to actors other than literal significance.

The actors' tools become the playwrights' tools and writers are wise to let them assume some of the burdens of the script. If they do not, information is being communicated by two channels. The more writers allow other elements to do the job, the less they are dependent on words. Descriptive phrases are the first to go and that, to the dramaturg, is a healthy sign.

At the first rehearsal of a play of mine at the Actors Studio Playwrights' Unit, Doris Roberts, a wonderful actor, said, "I don't need that speech."

"Why not?" I asked.

"I don't have to say it," she responded. "I can play it."

This was the speech:

There's a danger in the room and you can almost touch it, but you don't know what it is. Somebody hiding in the shadows. Some awful thing you forgot to do that's right on the tip of your tongue and you know when you remember, you'll scream and scream and there'll be no consoling you ever.

All that remains, after Doris Roberts demonstrated what an actor can do, is the first sentence.

Actors like lines that express their wants, their needs, their actions. If the writer gives an actor a strong action and puts her in a situation with a strong obstacle, the collision will result in a feeling. One does not have to write descriptions of that feeling, one simply has to allow the actor to feel it.

Lee Kalcheim says, "There was a line at the end of the second act [of Breakfast with Les and Bess] which I absolutely loved and Barnet [the director] said it was not necessary. It was one of those lines which you fall in love with, and I said, 'I really want that in.' I tried it without it. I always missed it. I put it back in. Then, I took a little survey. I asked the people who were there, the dramaturg, people I respected, and they agreed more with him, so I deferred because, sometimes, you can be in love with something and be wrong. The point was to make the play better, not to keep my favorite lines in."

When Doris said, "I don't have to say it. I can play it," she was, in fact, complimenting a structure that allowed her to reach the necessary emotion so that there was no need to describe it. Once the writer allows the actor, the director, the designer to have impact on the play, the descriptive passages can go; particularly the ones the writer is in love with. These others are experts at showing what the writer would tell. And showing is what theater is all about.

At the first reading the writer faces the discrepancy between timing onstage and timing in his head. Many writers try to recreate realistic conversation by filling their dialogue with throwaways: "I mean" "As I was saying" "I was thinking" "Now, let me say." These phrases fly by in one's imagination but, around the reading table, they become annoying to hear and burdensome to actors. Everyday conversation has to be compressed and controlled in order to sound real on stage.

This sense of stage time cannot be developed by writers at their typewriters. They have to hear their plays to know what needs expansion and what needs compression. There are moments, climaxes, and discoveries that sometimes happen too quickly. There are moments that take too much time so that unimportant details overpower major events and misshape the play. These are the things actors point out in the discussions, and dramaturgs look to see that such problems are corrected in the first rewrite.

An indication that the writer is responding positively to this first exposure to collaboration is proof that some point made in the discussion has sparked new ideas in the script. Thus, the writer has not only corrected the problem but has allowed the solution to open up new channels in the play.

He has every right to reject suggestions. He can say he wants to see a moment onstage before he changes it, and maybe it will turn out that he was right. But once he starts revising, every change, every cut affects rhythm, structure, build. There should be some kind of inevitability in his rewrites.

If there is, it is a sign that the give and take is working. The writer is responding and the process is paying off. Even if the producer is not completely happy with the rewrite, even if he is never going to be completely happy with the play, he will say to the writer and director, "We are getting someplace. Let's move to the next step."

4

The Open Reading

Once the closed reading has been completed, the next step is the open, or public, reading, which can take several different forms.

The simplest is the rehearsed sit-down reading, with the actors onstage, in chairs or around a table, and a stage manager reading directions to clarify action. When the play is in its earliest stages or the writer is new to the theater, this is an effective way of introducing both to audience response without requiring a major commitment of time from the actors or space from the theater. The sit-down reading requires no more than one or two rehearsals to familiarize the actors with the text and the relationships.

This is most helpful when the questions about the script concern clarity, focus, audience empathy, the need for editing or elimination of excess characters, and plot twists. The rehearsed sit-down reading will help the playwright define his through-line, separate strengths from weaknesses, and spot repetition and overwriting. Even with this simple a structure, the writer can recognize that the play is in trouble when the audience starts coughing or squirming or, worse yet, laughing when they should be crying.

This form of reading is the kind most often used by play development programs connected to off-off-Broadway theaters. At many, such as the Playwrights' Workshop of the Puerto Rican Traveling Theatre, the Playwrights-in-Residence Laboratory at Intar Hispanic-American Arts Center, and the Actors Studio Playwrights Unit, the rehearsed sit-down reading is open only to audiences of member writers and actors.

The aim is to create a casual, supportive atmosphere in which neither the script nor the performances will be judged as finished works. The audience members are serving as co-workers, supplying writers with feedback, allowing them to see their work with some objectivity, introducing them gently to the chasm between what they have imagined and how it is received.

At New Dramatists, member playwrights are offered a progression of readings as the script develops. The first is the cold reading. The second is called the nonperformance workshop. The actors rehearse around the table with the director and writer for a total of twenty hours, but there is no public performance. After the changes from this experience have been incorporated into the script, it is put back into rehearsal for the open, staged reading.

A staged reading requires more rehearsal time but, even then, there is the simple staged reading and the fully staged one. The former is used when some essential element in the story line is based on movement or action. With some scripts, the relationships and events cannot be comprehended without visualization. Who is in the room and who is absent? Who is indoors and who is out-of-doors? Who is talking to whom and who is overhearing? Who has been introduced into the story line and who has not? In order to illustrate these essential details, the entire company sits at the back of the stage, or offstage, and only those actors in the scene occupy the playing area. Entrances and exits are staged. Locales are mapped out by groupings of chairs, and actors move from area to area. But, once the actors enter or once they have moved from one place to another, they sit for the rest of the scene and no other blocking is required. This simple staged reading is more effective in defining essential action than is the use of a stage manager's announcements, and it does not make matters much more complicated for actors in a limited rehearsal period.

The fully staged reading is more elaborate. At JRT, we call these "mini-productions" and offer them only to our playwrights-in-residence who are working on projects specifically being created for the theater. Generally, these scripts, as at New Dramatists, go through each kind of reading in succession; the fully staged reading is the final step prior to production.

In this type of reading, all movement is staged. A suggestion of a set is created out of furniture pieces or, as at the O'Neill, by using metal modules, which are adaptable and give the series a unified, sleek look. At New Dramatists, wooden cubes serve the same purpose. Often the actors carry essential props and wear bits and pieces of costumes, even though they are working with scripts in hand.

In addition, stage lighting is employed to suggest mood and focus. Music and sound can be used, although such production values are best kept to a minimum. There is a tale about a director who hissed through gritted teeth to a lighting designer that so much attention had been attached to the mood, the actors could no longer read their lines in the dark!

This type of reading requires twenty to thirty hours of rehearsal, including a technical run-through to set lights and sound cues, and involves a stage manager and crew in addition to the actors.

"I can't say I am a big fan of staged readings," Pamela Berlin admits, "but we did one for *Gillian* at EST the spring after the first cold reading and, in this case, it was helpful. You have a fantasy figure at the center of the play. There is no way of dealing with a fantasy figure sitting around the table. The play has to be staged to know if that works. And it did. We managed to get the tone of it, and the wonderful things about the play emerged.

"We used benches and a couple of chairs and, interestingly enough, the ground plan that I came up with in a cursory sort of way for the staged reading emerged as the ground plan for the eventual set. It has to be very spare anyway; a deck, the beach. We stuck in a log, which became important eventually. As to costumes, I said to the actors, 'This takes place during the summer on a beach. Let's dress accordingly.'

"We cast it with EST members, some of whom were ultimately too young, but it was more important that we have good actors who embodied the characters. It was tricky because there was a sixteen-year-old girl on stage and you had to believe that these people were her parents. The actors who read were in their early thirties, while the characters had to be closer to forty, but for the purposes of the reading, it didn't matter. Of that cast, Noelle Parker, Heather Lupton, and Richmond Hoxie went on with the play to the full production.

"We got fifteen to twenty hours of rehearsal over three days. That was barely enough time to get it on its feet, so there was little rewriting, but the actors posed questions about their problems. Actors, in that situation, offer the best feedback. After rehearsals, we would go out for drinks. There was lots and lots to talk about, and it was grist for major rewrites later.

"That was when the biggest problem with the play came up. Here you have a central character who is grieving. He has removed himself from the world and from communicating with everyone else. The others are trying to bring him back to life, and they are very aggressive about it. They are the initiators and the danger is you have a passive central character. That was something the actor immediately sensed. It was a problem that continued to be broached as we worked on the script."

Although the fully staged reading is more closely attuned to the viewer's needs, it is important to take steps to define that the play is a work-in-progress and that the audience serves as part of the developmental process.

This is accomplished by carefully selecting the people to whom play announcements are sent, by keeping the admission fee low or nonexistent, by using no advertising or publicity, and certainly, by not inviting critics so that the reading retains the air of a working experience for actors and audience. Most theaters prepare a simple offset flyer, announcing the title of the play, the names of the playwright and director, and, perhaps, a short biography of the writer. The names of the actors are not listed, since readings are generally cast at the last minute, leaving little time for preparation and mailing of the flyer. In addition, actors often drop out as their schedules change and have to be replaced, so that it is difficult to announce a cast in advance with any confidence.

In some cases, this enhances the theatricality of the evening. One of the pleasures of readings, for audiences and writers, is that it is easy, at least in New York, to get stars involved. Readings are fun for actors to do. They require little rehearsal time. They can be slipped into one's schedule at the last minute. Even the biggest stars sit around waiting for the phone to ring between jobs. If they like a script and, more important, if they can be reached without going through an agent who will automatically reject the idea, most stars will volunteer happily.

I remember the night JRT did a reading of a play called *Whispers* by Crispin Larangeira, directed by John Tillinger. The audience arrived, expecting the usual, casual, working experience. I gave my little introductory speech, explaining that this was a work-in-progress, thrown together with minimal rehearsals, mainly to allow the writer to hear his play and get some feedback.

The director came on stage to describe the set for the audience and to introduce his "thrown together" cast: Colleen Dewhurst, and out she came, glorious smile in full flower, obviously delighted to be there. And when the audience had finished gasping, Tillinger introduced her co-star, Judd Hirsch! Well, the moment had more glitz, more electric surprise than many finales of Broadway's million dollar musicals.

The not-so-remote possibility of seeing stars is one of the secret delights that brings a small coterie of regulars to readings. And the smallness is just fine. Sit-down readings are given one performance each, staged readings, two, so hordes of people are not necessary. In fact, one does not want to do a reading before a full house. That kind of standing-room-only excitement only serves to increase the anxiety of the writer and leads to disappointment for the audience. Readings are always best served if they are presented as something prepared with no effort whatsoever. Even if there is a cast of well-rehearsed stars and the script is in wonderful shape and the director expects glorious performances, everything will be more glorious if it comes as a surprise. It is a simple matter for the producer to define and attract the particular audience needed, and in sufficient numbers, for each kind of reading.

The one essential is that the audience be made up of supportive people who are familiar with the process or connected to the play. One wants a more generous response than from an audience of strangers. If this is the first exposure for the writer, the pressure is going to be new and keenly felt. One does not need viewers who are out for the kill.

The truth of the matter is that even one's family members are going to cough and rustle when they get bored. They might start out laughing wildly at every joke, but no audience can keep that up all night, and the strain will be heard. The most sympathetic cousin is going to reveal weak spots to the writer, whether he wishes to or not.

Like most off-off-Broadway theater companies, JRT maintains mailing lists for our readings—writers, directors, and actors who are part of our creative family, audience members who have specifically asked to be invited to readings, and a small group of producers, theater people, funding sources, and agents. This last group hardly ever attends but we like the New York theater community to know what we are doing, how active we are, and with whom we are working. In addition, subscribers are invited, and this is a major plus for the theater. "Invitations to staged readings, admission free!" looks great as a bonus on a subscription brochure, even for those who will never attend. Those who do grow to love the experience.

The perfect mix for a reading is an audience of the writer's family, guests of the actors, theater workers, and subscribers. It is lovely if the actors can mill around the lobby before curtain, drinking coffee and greeting their friends, and if many in the audience know one another. This immediately establishes the evening as different from a performance. The theater has been presented as a workplace. The audience has been clued into the nature of the experience and what their role in it is to be.

The houselights should be left on, perhaps at half, during the reading. If there is a printed program, it should be simple. If there is not, as is most often the case, an announcement is made identifying the actors. Always, the producer or the literary adviser makes a welcoming speech, setting a friendly tone for the evening.

This is harder to do for the fully staged reading, where the houselights must be dark to accommodate the stage lighting, the audience arrives to see some kind of set on the stage, and the actors are in their dressing rooms. One of the dangers of the fully staged reading is that it is difficult for the audience to recognize it as different from a full production.

This is the case at the O'Neill. The place has a very prestigious track record. The play selection process is highly competitive. The actors in the company are always the up-and-coming stars of the moment. At curtain time, the limousines start arriving with producers, agents, even critics, although they are asked not to review the readings. Artistic directors of regional theaters, stars, other writers, television casting directors, all come up and stay to see several plays.

Before the curtain, Lloyd Richards, artistic director of the conference, offers an engaging explanation of the play development process, preparing the audience for the fact that the evening is not a Broadway opening night. But everyone in the glittering house, aware how many careers will be affected by the performance, has a hard time believing him.

Now, we get to the truth of the matter. It is true at the O'Neill and it is true at any tiny writers' workshop; it is true if the audience consists of the writer's family and it is true if there are Hollywood producers out front: Any open reading, no matter what form it takes and where it is done, no matter how informally it is presented, differs from any closed reading essentially because of the one new ingredient—the audience.

When I am preparing a full production, after the four weeks of rehearsal, after the final dress, readying the cast (and myself) for the first public preview, I will make a little speech: "There is no reason to get nervous. There is no reason for anything to change. Tomorrow night is only the first public preview. Previews are rehearsals in front of audiences. We have two weeks of previews to fix and change before the actual opening night. Tomorrow night's preview is no different from any rehearsal."

"Are you nuts?" the actors screech. "There will be people out there!"

For the theater artist, an audience changes everything, no matter how casual the setup. The moment a stranger walks into the rehearsal room, one can feel the effect upon the cast. A courageous actor will ask with an edge in his voice, "Who is that?" If the answer is, "That's the assistant sound designer, checking out where the cues will fall," the new face will be included in the family and the work goes on. If no one asks and the director is not smart enough to provide the introduction, or if the stranger is anyone who might be seen as a judge—one of the backers, the theater owner, a reporter, somebody's agent—the actors stiffen and speak louder.

The first time I witnessed this as a director, I was not smart enough to figure out why, but I could sense that something was wrong. Moments that had worked in previous rehearsals were no longer working. Timing was off. There was a strain in the room, even during breaks. At one point, I approached one of the actors, an experienced, easygoing guy. "You seem to be having an off day," I said to him, my arm tossed intimately over his shoulder. "I can't figure out why."

He attacked like a wounded beast. "Are you kidding? The goddamn writer's wife is in the room!"

From that day on, I knew never, never, to allow guests into rehearsals for readings or for full productions.

The moment an audience becomes incorporated in the work process, it is no longer a rehearsal. It is no longer a private experience for the actor. In front of audiences, actors, like Pavlov's dogs when they heard those bells, have to perform. This can be very dangerous when the actor is not prepared for it, and wonderful when he is.

In the privacy of rehearsals, actors think, figure things out, relate to one another, make mistakes, take things over. They are working, and the process for actors is no different than it is for any other craftsman. They plan. They try. First they sketch, then they fill in the detail. They experiment and keep what works. When something is right, they store it on one side of the brain. When something is wrong, they change it. They repeat what is right until it is perfect. When a new factor is introduced, they have to change what worked the day before. They get frustrated. They worry. They look for approval. Eventually, they have established little signposts in the brain so they know what it should feel like when it is right. Once they have created a path of these, it gets easier to jump from one to the other with more courage and daring.

At a closed reading, cast, writer, producer, and director, are seated in a circle in a rehearsal room or onstage together under worklights. There is no physical separation of audience and players. There are no strangers in the room. The experience has the feel of a rehearsal for the actors and they take things easy. They try to make sense out of what they are saying. They try to believe their lines. They talk to one another, listen, react. They try to tune in to the character's rhythms. They let the script take them wherever it leads. They are acting, but they are not performing.

As soon as the actor gets onstage before an audience of strangers, energy goes up. Intensity goes up. Concentration goes up. Anxiety goes up. Things that did not work on the page, that did not work in the closed reading, work before an audience because the actor makes them work. Moments that made sense on the page become boring and repetitive onstage because the actor made them work on the page before.

An important lesson the young writer can learn from an open reading is what happens to words, what happens to actors, what happens to the entire theatrical experience once it takes place where it belongs: before an audience. This cannot be learned in a classroom or alone at the writing table. It cannot be discussed between writer and dramaturg in an office. It can only be experienced, and once the writer has done so, he will understand how the very nature of theater creates a discipline in the writing—or he will not. Only after this awful first exposure to an audience will the young writer, and everyone else connected to the play, know whether he was born to be a playwright.

*   *   *

Watching a play in a darkened theater is different from reading a book or watching television or even viewing a movie while munching on popcorn. In no other form of storytelling is the audience's role so traditional and formalized. People have made plans in advance, purchased tickets, dressed up for the occasion, hired a baby sitter, traveled a distance to attend. There is a sense of immediacy and importance in the experience that is both manipulated and actual.

Playgoers are brought to their seats by uniformed ushers, handed slick playbills, which everyone reads voraciously to be as prepared as possible. The houselights dim. The stage is brightly lit. The moment the play starts, the audience is drawn forward.

Theater audiences can be amazingly smart, quick, aware, and sensitive, because their attention is so concentrated. The same person who needs all kinds of clues when reading a murder mystery, who will happily endure repetitive exposition on a soap opera, is a fast-paced, demanding animal in a theater audience. Because his eyes are so pinned to the stage, he picks up every subtlety, absorbs every clue, decides to love or hate immediately, and most painfully, seems to have no patience whatsoever.

Katharine Hepburn, in a New York Times interview, said,

What is interesting about actors in the last analysis, is if they can arrest your total attention. Can their concentration make you concentrate enough to identify something which they're doing with something in your own life—which is why one is moved, and usually why one laughs.*

The playwright has to learn about the astonishing power of words spoken onstage by an actor. Everything becomes clearer, more textured, more vivid because of the extraordinary connection between audience and actor, the electricity in the experience.

When I studied acting at New York's High School of Performing Arts with Charles Carshon, he would often stop a scene and ask the actor what he was doing at a particular moment. The actor, usually stumped, would play it casually. "I was just checking my nails," or "I was just looking out the window."

---

* Leslie Bennetts, "Hepburn to Pay Tribute to Tracy at Benefit," New York Times, March 3, 1986, p. C11.

"There is no such thing as *just* in the theater," Charles would thunder.

Audiences demand that sense of urgency and importance in the script. Playwrights do not have the freedom of novelists to take a breath, go off on a tangent, spend an unnecessary beat, say something twice, hammer home a point. Nor do they need it.

In the living room stage of play development, the writer and director have scoured the script for every wasted word, argued over repetitions, questioned overblown phrases. The writer has insisted on some and the director has given in, for the moment. At the open reading, the writer is going to hear how every wasted phrase feels like a sag in the tent of tension between actor and audience. There is no way for the writer to learn this other than seeing his play before an audience and watching the magic an actor can create.

I once attended an evening of scenes done by students at the HB Studio, the famed acting school run by Herbert Berghof and Uta Hagen. The program was divided into classes and each teacher came forward to introduce the scenes, set the stage, identify the student actors—a standard, matter-of-fact procedure, until Uta Hagen stepped forward to perform the chore and we knew immediately that we were watching an actress at work, not a teacher. With a smile, with that voice, by the way she placed a prop here, moved a chair, the way her body found the light and her eyes glowed with anticipation, she drew us to her. We wanted to hear what she had to say. We were eager to see her students. With the strength of her concentration, she imbued the moment with importance.

Such star quality is both a gift to the playwright and a responsibility. He does not have to work so hard at seducing his audience with fancy words, at creating pictures, psychoanalyzing characters, or describing feelings. All the playwright has to do is to get Uta Hagen onstage in a situation that equals the power of her personality. The problem is that, since she has this magical ability to draw the audience forward to hear every word, those words have to equal the buildup.

I directed a reading at the Hudson Guild Theatre some years back with Jeff Daniels as a member of the cast. Jeff was then starting out in New York and only had a supporting role. One scene required the leading lady to give a long, intimate speech to Jeff, and I remember arguing with the writer about that speech, insisting that it be tightened, given more urgency. The playwright claimed that he just wished to clarify the relationship between the two. The speech was to be casual and low-key, as it would be in reality.

But one of Jeff Daniels's brilliant talents is the way he listens. Onstage, he drew his body toward his co-actor, listened with every muscle. There was such intensity in his interest that the audience drew forward with him and the speech that followed was an enormous disappointment.

"There is no such thing as just in the theater." If the playwright is going to give an actor a page-long speech and her co-actor is to listen without interruption, that speech has to have enough drama to justify his reaction.

Seeing the play through the outsider's eye in this way is going to be an amazing, perhaps infuriating, revelation to the writer. The audience is going to lean forward at the least expected moments, laugh when they should not, fall in love with a subsidiary character, grow bored with the main story line, figure things out before they should. Time and again, dramaturgs say it: Nobody knows the truth about a play until an audience gets involved. After an open reading, the writer believes it.

Even after the open reading of The Dining Room, which was an unqualified smash, director David Trainer says, "There were a couple of scenes that, for one reason or another, didn't suit us. Pete and I had a long talk and he was quite angry because I told him three or four things I didn't want. His attitude was, 'Who the hell are you? This was a great success of a reading so why change anything?' Now, I don't want to set myself up as saying to Pete Gurney, 'Do this. Do that.' It was always a discussion, but any discussion between an author and a director about script changes has tension. Authors tend to like what they've done and the director sometimes has to say, 'You've got to rewrite that or we're in trouble.' Pete Gurney never does anything that he doesn't want to do. He is responsive to an intelligent argument. He will always listen and he never scorns what he hears, but then he does meditate and he made these changes that we had talked about. He may have been angry when he heard about them, but they eventually took hold in his mind. There are subsequent points when I would say that something had to be changed and he would absolutely refuse. Or he would come in with a rewrite and he would say, 'Dave, forget it. That's it. You got it. Do this.' My theory, based on my experience with him and subsequent experience, is that whoever puts his or her foot down hardest is probably right. Similarly, when I would badger and badger and badger, he would somehow hear that this guy is not going to shut up until x, y, or z got changed. The rule that I operate by is: 'When you hit that wall, feel that it is the wall and assume that it is the right answer.' In any event, it is the answer if you are dealing with smart people, which is what I always try to do. Anyway, there was rewriting before rehearsal started, more than Pete expected was necessary."

The open reading is of great value to the other creators involved in the future production as well. Designers who have seen an open reading of the play are many steps ahead of where they normally would be when handed a new script to read. And they are able to make a strong contribution to the script development. They have been alerted to where the audience looks, what they see, how they respond. They know where the center of the stage should be. They know which scenes are funny and which are not. Working on new plays offers designers the opportunity to have greater influence on the production early in the process.

Jeffrey Schneider, one of the resident designers at JRT, attended the open reading of Susan Sandler's Crossing Delancey, which went on to great success. In its earliest stages, the script was somewhat unfocused and spread over many locations. At the reading, Jeffrey keyed into the scenes that received the strongest response, where the major action seemed to be taking place. Seated in the audience, he sketched a ground plan giving two areas, out of the many in the script, the central placement. He showed the sketch to the writer and director and they immediately saw the play differently. He had divided it for them into foreground and background. They knew which scenes had to be sharpened and which could be diminished. The drawing was as much a sketch of the structure of the play as it was of the set, and the rewrite was built around the ground plan.

The best demonstration of the value of the reading to the designer is when the designer has not been at readings. There was a production of a play by the splendid young writer, Jeff Wanshel, which failed primarily because of a misconception about the lighting.

Jeff writes in short, sharp scenes, which should travel through the viewer's brain in chaos until a mosaic is formed. But they are not blackout sketches. Jeff purposely does not write punch lines. The scenes seem disjointed and pointless; more like scattered links in a chain than consecutive scenes with a beginning, middle, and end.

The production was done as a series of blackouts, and this was a big mistake. The scenes did not justify the emphasis the lighting gave them. The audience felt gypped and confused at each ending, as if there had been a gag which had not worked. The play lurched from one ineffective blackout to another and never came together.

Long after the disaster, I mentioned the problem to the writer. He agreed at once. He, the director, and the lighting designer, all spotted the mistake at the first public preview. "But you know how things are at that point," Jeff went on to explain. "We would have had to restage all the set changes. We would have had to rewrite all the light cues and had another tech. There seemed like so much else to do and there is never enough time. So we didn't change it."

In the golden days of the commercial theater, Jeff's play would have been taken out of town for four weeks prior to its opening. There would have been time to analyze the audience's reaction and rectify the error. Such a luxury is not possible in nonprofit theater, and hardly ever even on Broadway these days, and major problems in design, like this one, often cannot be corrected late in the game.

If the lighting designer had attended an open reading of the play and been privy to the way an audience was supposed to respond to the short scenes, or if there had been an early demonstration of the way the play was intended to flow, visually, then there is a chance this awful mistake would not have been made and the play could have been saved.

Other individuals who would benefit from attending readings are would-be designers, writers, and actors. After all, here is an occasion that is informal, easy to get into, and free of charge. The artistic director of the theater is going to be there, as are the literary adviser, the writer, and the director of the play. They are all going to be identifiable, delighted to have an audience, and accessible to whomever wishes to talk to them. That is the point of the evening.

Instead of putting a script in the mail, a young writer might find out where readings are being held and bring his script with him. Afterward, he might approach the literary adviser, express admiration for his taste, and hand him a manila envelope. There is no guarantee of success but, as any garment salesman will tell you, the product has a better chance if it can be connected to a familiar face. This is certainly true for a young actor. Many a smart kid has come up to me after an open reading to say what a wonderful play I have just directed. He has reached me at a vulnerable moment. I am seeking response, so I am going to pay attention. If he goes on to say he really admires my work and wants to work for me in the future, I am not going to be annoyed. If he hands me his picture and résumé and says he would be willing to read stage directions next time I do a reading, I am sure to keep it for future reference.

Finding someone to do that chore is always a pain in the neck. A director cannot ask an established actor to read stage directions; therefore, that smart kid is going to find himself onstage at my next reading, before an audience filled with other directors and writers. Reading stage directions is not going to reveal his emotional range, but the audience will hear his voice, get a sampling of his presence, and if he has a twinkle in his eye, it will come across. Whatever else results, as that wise garment salesman will tell you, the kid has his foot in the door.

The open reading is the first meeting between the two forces that are going to shape the play: the artists and the audience. If everyone comes with his own agenda, that is as it should be. And if everyone walks out with something gained, that's good too.

5

Actors and Readings

After working so long in solitude, after picking the script apart in the living room with her director, after sitting in judgment of the actors in rehearsal, the writer arrives at the theater to find herself powerless, just another figure in the darkened house. And every other audience member is focused on the actors, delighted with them, impressed by them—as if they were making up the words themselves!

In the final analysis, the actors are the ones onstage at the crucial moment. The costume designer knows that the actors must be happy with their clothes. The lighting designer's first responsibility is to make sure their faces can be seen. And the writer finds that the actors are his partners.

In *Tennessee: Cry of the Heart*, Dotson Rader quotes Tennessee Williams on the subject.

You know, playwriting is a funny kind of art. It's both a solitary thing, and it is a group thing. Many people contribute to the writing of a play, whether you want them to or not. Performers can be enormously valuable in suggesting line changes in a play. I mean, if they're intelligent performers. Geraldine Page. She's very intelligent, and she's a genius at acting. Being a genius at acting, and being intelligent aren't always the same thing. I've known more dumb actors than you'd believe. Geraldine would suggest line changes. She'd say,"I find this line difficult to read."I think most of her suggestions were good, although she's not a writer. So I'd make the changes to satisfy her. I often do that with actors, if they're intelligent and care about the play.*

The statement reflects Williams's patronizing attitude toward actors, which is a very common one among playwrights. Actors and

* Dotson Rader, *Tennessee: Cry of the Heart* (New York: Doubleday and Company, Inc., 1985), p. 285.

writers are like creatures from different planets. Their inevitable relationship is one of curiosity and mistrust, if not outright hostility. They come at the world from different vantage points. That is what makes them dependent on one another to create an artistic whole. The writer aims to give shape to internal experience so that it can be communicated. The actor has to reinternalize that communication and recreate it emotionally. Their processes, their tools, their talents, their approaches, are exactly reversed.

When I was a young actor in the 1960s, I studied with Herbert Berghof, and the young Sandy Dennis was in my class. At one session, Herbert was teaching the techniques of cold audition readings. He handed out "sides," two pages of a script which offered no hint as to the story of the play or the background of the characters. The actor's job was to make the scene work without knowing where it came from.

Sandy was my partner and we got up before the class to read. In a flash, anyone could have predicted that I would become a writer and she would become a star. I sat. I tried to make sense. I leaned over the script and knitted my brow in thought. I was searching for a logic in the scene and my reading was therefore cautious, perhaps intelligent, certainly dull.

Sandy, on the other hand, had clued into something in the lines, some hint of a desire in her character and, whether it was correct or not, she flew with the impulse. After two seconds, she was out of her chair, circling me in desperation. Then, she was down on the floor at my feet, pressing her head to my knees. I stared down in embarrassed horror. What in hell was she doing? Did it make any sense?

Who cared if it made sense? It was wonderful. The audience felt for her because she felt something, and nobody looked at me. For all the intelligence in my writer's approach—the maturity, the search for logic, the caution—onstage, her way worked.

The writer takes some long forgotten pain and tries to control it by giving it shape and sense. The actor blasts through the control and returns to the core of the pain. That is why writers frequently hate actors. They are threatened by them. They are mystified. They sneer at them and call them children. But the playwright's work is in the hands of these "children" and, in the process of the open reading, they give the playwright an opportunity to learn how they work, how they think, how they live.

It is likely that directors, when casting a reading, will offer roles to actors they know, without auditions, and writers will have no input. This might be upsetting to beginning writers, but they would be wise to go along.

The essential problem is that actors are paid very little for readings, if at all. Some nonprofit theaters in New York pay actors carfare for their services; the smaller ones pay nothing. At the Public Theater, which is the largest nonprofit theater in New York, actors get paid fifty dollars, for which they rehearse two afternoons and work the day of the reading.

Actors do readings because they want to connect with the writer, they want to work for the director, because it is better to keep busy than to sit about the house, because they like the play and want to get a toehold on the role. These are perfectly respectable reasons, but it does mean that their services are available only until a paying job comes along, or an audition interferes. The busy actors, the ones every director goes after, cannot always donate an enormous amount of time.

Money, or the lack of it, affects everyone involved. Nobody has signed any contracts. The director is generally not being paid. There is no budget to cover the minimal sets, costumes, or props needed in a staged reading. Rehearsals are planned around the schedule of the full productions; therefore, they get very little stage time. In many workshop groups, the writer has to supply his own script copies.

One of the shining exceptions is the O'Neill, where everyone gets paid and readings are the reason for the program's existence. But that is what makes the place so unusual and why so many actors, writers, and directors want to work there.

Generally, readings are put together very quickly, and the director wants to cast actors he knows. For a full production, he might cast an actor far from the role because the actor is so talented and there will be time to work on the problems. There is no such time when doing a reading. The director has to find actors with demonstrated ability who can come through for him; actors who will work quickly, who will not be difficult, who are close to the role, who will do a great deal of work on their own, who can perform under pressure. The only way he can be sure of all this is if he has worked with the actor before.

Traditionally, actors are not asked to audition for readings. Since they are not being paid, it is demeaning to ask them to audition, and actors with any kind of reputation will be unwilling to do so. If the director wants to cast actors with known qualities and solid experience, he is going to have to offer the roles to them without allowing the writer to check them out at auditions.

Casting director Rosemarie Tichler explains, "In a profession where actors have to put themselves on the line for everything, we feel they are doing us a favor, so we would never think of asking them to audition for a reading. If it's a very young role, we'll often read people. Where there is no body of work to base a decision on, we don't think it's taking advantage."

This means that the writer might have to settle for actors in the reading who are not physically right or who are the wrong age. All the director looks for is an actor who can make the words come alive with the essential qualities of the character.

There is no point, in a reading, in casting an actor with a dark, moody quality for a bright, fast-talking comedic role. A good actor might be able to play both kinds of roles, but there is no time for that kind of experimentation. The director is going to look for the essence of the character, and if he knows what he is doing, that will serve to bring the core of the script to life.

One of the advantages of this casting procedure is that it gives the writer a chance to find out if the director does know what he is doing. The director may be a good talker and seem to understand the characters in meetings, but if he brings in someone totally wrong for a leading role, the writer gets an early signal that he is in trouble and that more meetings are called for.

It is also a way for the producer to evaluate the director. Any director who has done enough work, and successfully enough so that actors want to work with him again, should be able to cast a reading from his own files. The more impressive the people he is able to recruit, the more solid, it may be assumed, is his reputation around town.

Consequently, the director who wants to make an impression goes after "names." Of particular worth in a reading are actors who are in the producer's "stable." Joe Papp has actors he casts over and over again. So does the Manhattan Theater Club and Playwrights Horizons. If a few of these favorites are in the reading, the producer feels reassured and the play is more likely to go on to full production.

Writers, at this stage, always get nervous and want to have input. They wish to suggest actors or bring in their friends, but they would be sensible to let the director do his job. This is a golden opportunity to check out the director's abilities and choices and connections, and for the writer to experiment with the emotional impact of stepping aside and letting the director take over.

Obviously, this closed system of the casting of readings creates a problem for unknown actors. Readings connect actors with directors, yet directors will only use actors they know. How on earth does one get started?

Like any system, this one has its loopholes. It is never difficult to find reputable actors to play the major roles. The problem is filling the smaller ones. What working actor wants to put in the time, for no pay, to do a rehearsal and a reading for a tiny role? Directors cannot ask their actor friends to do the smaller parts for fear of insulting them. Yet, the director, who is not getting paid, does not want to spend the time auditioning actors for the smaller roles. And the producer, who is preoccupied with a full production in rehearsal, is not willing to give the director space for auditions, even if he were willing to conduct them.

Casting a reading is always a hectic experience for the director. Generally, there is no stage manager, so the director ends up dropping off scripts for actors all over town. Actors accept, then do not like the role and drop out. Actors develop schedule conflicts or get paying jobs and have to be replaced. The director has to contact the next actor on his list, drop off another script, and wait for a response. Because of the lack of money, the whole process takes place in the cracks of everyone's professional lives. If there is a tiny role in the script, the director will turn it over to the first person he can think of who seems eager to do it. All he really needs is a body up there, but this is the young actor's chance to break through the barrier.

The director might ask a casting director to recommend a talented young actor. He might ask one of the other actors to suggest a friend. He might remember a kid who introduced himself after a reading the director did recently. He might have seen a kid read stage directions at someone else's reading. The kid had a good voice. What the hell, he might give him a call.

A young actor is not going to step off the bus in New York and get hired for a Broadway show. Here is the way full productions are cast—that is, at a small nonprofit house like JRT, not a Mike Nichols blockbuster.

The director turns over his cast description to the casting director, who sends it out to agents, and to Equity (the actors' union) with dates for the Equity Principal Auditions (EPAs).

The EPAs are required by Equity as part of the union's contract with the theater. Any Equity actor must be seen, either doing a monologue of the actor's choice or reading from the script. The problem is that the system is a farce.

The casting director, or sometimes the stage manager, runs the EPAs. The director rarely attends because it is such a time-consuming, tedious experience. Equity sends over a monitor to assure that everyone is seen in turn, as well as to keep out the non-Equity people. Actually, nonmembers of Equity are allowed to be seen, but only after all the Equity people have auditioned.

At JRT we usually get over 600 actors at an EPA. The hallways are lined with actors. The wait to be seen is often several hours. The auditions go on for two or three days. The casting director gets bleary. Who can tell anything about anyone, seeing 600 actors, one after the other, day after day? Do the actors really understand that they have virtually no chance of getting the roles?

For my last show at JRT, the casting director was terrifically impressed by about a dozen people out of the 600 she had seen at the EPAs. Of the twelve photos she showed me, I was interested in seeing one actor. He was a young actor who she claimed was the best she had seen, who was physically perfect for a role, and whose credits were substantial: an M.F.A. from Yale and a season at the Williamstown Summer Festival. I saw that young actor; yet, even though he was as talented as he had been trumpeted to be, the role went to somebody whose work I knew.

With these odds, why do actors waste so much time on EPAs, which are, if anything, auditions to get an audition? The real auditions take place for the director once the EPAs are over. They are scheduled by appointment for the people submitted by agents, actors with whom the director has worked before, actors seen and liked in other productions, actors who have already worked at the theater, and of course, the actors who did the reading of the script when the play was being considered for production. Rosemarie Tichler says, "If an actor has done well in the reading, he'll usually get the role if the play is done. If there is a question, we'll, at least, ask him to read."

Of all the avenues, attending readings is the best way for young actors to crack the system. Young actors should find out which theaters around town do readings regularly, and should attend them as often as possible. If there are audience discussions afterward, they should make their presence known. They should try to connect with the directors who do them. They should concentrate on meeting young writers.

There are plenty of writers' workshops, most of which are formed by the writers themselves; they meet in living rooms and read plays to one another, or get actors, usually friends, to do the readings. Actors can visit the Dramatists Guild office to look through the Guild newsletter, where such groups advertise. They can then contact the groups, which are often desperate to find actors for readings, and offer their services.

Actors can also contact playwriting teachers or directing teachers and offer to read scripts or work on scenes in class. Actors can become play readers for theaters, and when they find a writer with talent, they can put a note in the mail, introducing themselves. Taking a playwriting or a directing course may also prove fruitful.

It's a good idea to meet young writers and directors because those on the way up do readings, one after the other. For each production that finally gets produced in a single season, there are dozens of readings of scripts that are dropped along the way.

Because there is so much activity, because it is all done so frantically, with so little financial support, this is the area in which the unknown actor has, at least, a chance to get a part. If he offers to read stage directions, if he is willing to do the smaller roles, if he approaches the rehearsals with energy and responsibility, if he is easy to work with, if he has talent, if he comes through, he might become a member of the exclusive club of actors who do readings over and over again.

He might soon be running from New Dramatists to Playwrights Horizons to some writer's living room. The parts might get better. He might connect with a script which will move on. He might end up, finally, in a full production with the New York Times drama critic out front.

And next day, on his dressing room door, they might hang a star.

*   *   *

As crazy and chaotic as the system seems, it works for everyone, and the reading gets cast.

The writer comes to the first rehearsal to greet a room full of strangers who, in one rehearsal for a sit-down reading (and maybe three or four for a staged reading), are going to bring his play to life. How is this miracle going to happen?

Actors are creatures with extraordinary access to their inner lives. The emotions are their tools, and a certain kind of everyday repression that exists in most adults is missing in the actor. This does not make life easy. To go to the supermarket with such a ready availability of pain or rage or joy is not the most efficient way to exist and is probably the reason actors are given to rocky relationships and stormy lives.

The process of rehearsal is the process of controlling the externals so the actor's inner life can explode safely. Movement is preplanned. Lines are learned. Rhythms are defined. Furniture is spiked. Props are set. Once a good actor has found a moment in rehearsal that feels right, he will repeat it, often without knowing he is doing so, down to the exact angle of his head on his neck, the placement of the intake of breath.

Ironically, this does not make the performance stale and artificial. When the outside world is absolutely predictable, the actor can allow his feelings to flow unchecked. The amazing result is that, if the externals have been worked out with logic, if the intellectual ground plan has been carefully drawn, if the actor has reached a point in rehearsal when the mechanics have become so ingrained that he does not have to think about them, the connections in his psyche will always lead to the same emotional responses, which will always be appropriate and always be spontaneous.

When working, actors find themselves in an external setting that makes use of their particular internal structures; then they are secure and happy. Actors who perform nightly spend all day, on some level, preparing, conserving energy, awaiting those few hours onstage in a perfect world. It is then that the gates to their inner lives can be fully opened. Ordinary life must seem drab in comparison.

Young Melanie Mayron worked at JRT as the star of *Crossing Delancey*. All through the rehearsal process, she emanated confusion, shyness, and self-doubt. She is a tense young woman who tends to walk with burdened shoulders, limp hair covering her face, her clothes always in disarray. At the first read-through, the other actors threw themselves into the bright comic script with confidence, but Melanie, the best known of the cast, seemed frightened and overwhelmed, her voice barely more than a hesitant whisper. She often appeared miserable and worried, curled in a chair in the corner, going over and over her lines, figuring things out, making notes in the margin of her script.

But on opening night, even her hair came alive with joy. It sparkled under the lights and found a shape and strength it never before appeared to have, unveiling enormous eyes which had until then been hidden by glasses. The girl acted with her elbows, her wrists, her fingers, her knees. We are not talking about any proper work processes here, nor training, nor experience; we are talking about talent. And talent is directly related to the actor's ability to release his inner life on stage. It breathes life into the role. It brings a history and a texture to the words. It enables the actor to believe on stage with a more concentrated energy than one experiences in life.

What the director has to do in rehearsal is make the ground clear and safe and defined enough so that the actor's inner life can flow. This can be achieved in the one day it takes to do a sit-down reading, the three days for a staged reading, or the four weeks for a full production.

It is a matter of defining goals, establishing priorities, and eliminating choices. In three days, actors cannot work toward the complex goals they would endeavor to obtain in four weeks. But if the goals that are established can be achieved within the time allotted, actors will reach that point of safety.

The trick in directing a reading is to cast the actor with the required quality and allow her to go with her initial impulse. The actor does not have the luxury of exploring various possibilities, of questioning her impulses, of trying different things. The good reading actor gets a handle on something in the character that she can relate to, like Sandy Dennis at that long-ago acting class, and flies with it. The good director allows her the freedom to do so.

There are some actors who simply cannot do this. There are actors who have vision problems, or hearing problems, or reading problems, or whose inner rhythms are innately too slow to accept the speed with which readings are done. There are actors who have anxieties that get resolved in the longer rehearsal situation but are aggravated under pressure. There are actors who take a long time to relax, who are awkward and inhibited at first, who do not easily trust the director or the other actors, who need an enormous amount of information and background before they come alive. These are not the kind of actors who work well at readings.

On the other hand, there are many actors who are absolutely brilliant readers. They work quickly, get a characterization in a flash, jump right in and fly by the seat of their pants, and enjoy working that way. Yet, these actors might have difficulty sustaining inspiration, repeating it, and controlling it. They have a brilliance that is quick and spontaneous and will always be there for the one or two performances of a reading, but if asked to go through four weeks of the drudgeries of rehearsal and maintain the same level of inspiration and then repeat it nightly, may not be able to do it. An actor who can come through in a reading is often quite different from an actor who comes into his own in the longer rehearsal period for a full production.

The good reading actor makes an impulsive choice that frees him; a rhythm, a voice, a look. This supplies an immediate definition of the character and a mental image to start with. Then, he lets that take him where it will. Director David Trainer talked about an actor who was dropped from the cast after the reading of *The Dining Room*: "I didn't feel he had the technique. He was like rubber. He didn't hit his choices hard and clean."

Directors want actors with an innate trust in their impulses, courage to follow them, and an affection for other actors. These qualities might come out of early improvisatory training or they might come out of a happy childhood. Some actors have them and some don't. Some actors, like some people, have to test the waters before they jump.

Broadway is rife with legends of how Laurette Taylor was awful at the start of work on *The Glass Menagerie*, how Shirley Booth mumbled through rehearsals of *Come Back, Little Sheba*, how Dustin Hoffman was nearly fired from *Journey of the Fifth Horse*, the show that established him in New York. These actors would not have done well at readings.

It may be true that the slower approach leads to greater work. It may simply be a different but equally valid approach as that of the impulsive reading actor. It may be that there are different techniques required for different situations and some actors can do it all.

"What gets some actors into trouble at open readings," actor Mark Blum points out, "is that either they are trying to act or they are rehearsing, and neither of those is really very helpful. Certainly, rehearsing the play in front of an audience is not helpful because you are not giving the playwright and his group of friends or colleagues, or strangers who fill out cards, what they want. You are not allowing them to hear his play, his voice as he hears it. And if you try to give a real performance, you will not succeed. One of the hints I can offer about staged readings is, don't do anything that might make anyone in the audience think that you are trying to give a performance, because it won't be a good performance. It will only be a bad performance. If you are sitting in your chair and reading the play, you can give a good reading and, the less you give anybody the impression that you are trying to act, the better you are. Because it's not really acting. You are trying to read the script persuasively. What actors have to bring to the experience is a certain amount of ability to make a primary choice, simply and with energy and integrity and to manage to say all the words in proper sequence. Respond to the other actors. Make some connection to the other people so that what happens is a scene; not in any sense a fully explored scene, but an accurately impersonated blueprint of what the play intends to have at that point."

Most directors recognize that there is a danger for actors in doing too many readings of the same play. Often a script, going through development, seeking a production, has reading after reading in theater after theater over a period of years. Sometimes an actor seems born to play a role. She is called back for each reading and is always brilliant. Finally, the play gets a production commitment and enters into a standard four-week rehearsal period. The actor finds herself stuck with choices made too early, stuck with reactions to actors who are no longer in the cast, stuck with a performance that came too quickly. In the longer rehearsal period, she finds that the ground has been so cemented under her feet that she cannot crack through and dig deeper. So, she repeats and repeats and ends up with a shadow of something that was once spontaneous and wonderful, but is no longer capable of growth.

There are dangers in every art form in the quick and easy approach. The very same talents that make actors wonderful in readings can be traps when they want to move on.

This often happens to soap opera stars or actors who are

successful in television commercials; areas where time is of the essence and those who work are the ones who come through quickly. The qualities that were once fresh and engaging become mechanical and no longer related to the actor's personality. The constant use of the same approach becomes draining. If the actor never explores, never digs deeper, never takes risks, then that way of working becomes the only way. The use of the glib and superficial becomes a dependency and, with terrifying speed, the talent grows stale.

But there is always the exception, like Swoosie Kurtz. When she started at the O'Neill's Playwrights Conference, she was brilliant at readings, skimming the surface of her ability and coming up with unique choices, a wide range, an unwavering honesty, a wonderful energy. When she moved on to television situation comedies, she was somehow able to absorb the pressures and her work got even sharper. When she became a Broadway star, in *Fifth of July* and *The House of Blue Leaves*, she unveiled depths of her talent that had never been touched before.

The rehearsal process for a sit-down reading has clear aims. The mechanics must be defined. How are the actors to get onstage? Who sits where? Which stage directions will be read and which will be ignored?

In addition, the director must deal with each actor, resolving the questions we all learned to ask in Acting One. Who? What? Where? Why?

Who am I?
What am I doing?
Where am I doing it?
Why am I doing it?

The actors need to understand what the play is about, who the hero is, what the author's intent was. They might need help in getting a handle on their characters—some quick fix, a rhythm, an image, a history. They need an idea of who the others are and what their relationship is to each one. They have to have a sense of how the play builds; the passage of time, the cause and effect of events, and what the function of each scene is in terms of structure.

All these questions can be dealt with in one careful read-through followed by a discussion. Actors will mumble their way through one reading just to get the ground plan clear in their heads. They need to find out who is playing which role, to whom they are talking and when, what kinds of vibes the other actor is sending, and how the play seems to drive them. Actors are like finely pitched tuning forks. They get a sense of the emotional groundwork of the play very quickly and then they know what to do.

The director will then attempt to define all this intellectually. She will talk about the play's structure, characters, through-lines, and the writer's intent. The actors will respond with questions. The director will answer and, wherever possible, allow the actors to interact. In so doing, the actors connect with one another, grow comfortable, and improvise on their relationships in the script.

Then they will read again, and the play will start to come alive. Only the most elemental issues have been touched upon, and only in general terms, but if the director's analysis has been clear and on target, if the actors are smart and responsive, and if the atmosphere is conducive to concentration and collaboration, then that is all that is necessary for the actors to understand the basic story line and to play it.

Since actors must make choices without dealing with complexities, it is the directors' function to lead the way. They should deal with the basic issues of the play, expressing themselves succinctly. They should not go off on tangents to show off their wisdom, but should define each character in a nutshell. By introducing no elements that will confuse and muddle, good directors will sacrifice subtlety so the actors have a clear and playable story line. Just as there are specific talents actors need for a reading, good reading directors excel in clarity, decisiveness, and communication.

The most important questions directors have to answer for the company are:

Who is the central character?
What is his or her conflict?
How do the other characters contribute to this conflict?
Is the conflict resolved happily or tragically?

Each actor, after reading the play at home, will come up with a different answer to these questions, from the viewpoint of his own character. Therefore it is the director's job to define these points so that the play has an overall vision. Once done, all other individual decisions will fall into place. Each actor will know how his character fits into the scheme of the play, what his purpose is, and what he needs to contribute in order to make the play work.

These are the same questions that are dealt with in the rehearsals for a full production. However, in that situation, the director will allow the discussion to wander, permitting the actors to explore various possibilities. Such free-flowing talk can be beneficial to the actors and may give birth to many new insights that the director can use. However, there is simply no time for such an approach when preparing a reading. The director draws upon the searching and open-ended discussions that were shared with the writer and comes in with clearly defined conclusions. The actors, aware of the limited rehearsal time, are grateful for this. The most common statement an actor makes at a reading rehearsal when he is in the hands of an inept director is, "You're confusing me." The smart actor says it for his own protection and the smart director picks up the clue at once.

In order to limit the possibility of confusing the actors the writer should say nothing. The actors cannot deal with input from two experts. It is essential that they trust the director and that they all see the play from a single viewpoint. Playwrights who have had no training as actors or directors do not have a grasp on the vocabulary, and do not understand the kind of statements actors need to do their job. Playwrights tend to bring up too many complexities for the purposes of a reading. The playwright has had ample opportunity to talk to his director, to convey to him his insights and information, to check out his abilities. When the time comes for the director to deal with the actors, the playwright has to let him do the work.

If a director is able to describe what he wants from a particular scene, even if it is not fully written, or if it's sketchily written or badly written, the actors should be able to give him what he wants. They play the subtext, not the words.

In her first draft of *Emma Rothstein*, Leslie Brody had written two wonderful characters with two separate plot lines, but the play never came together because it was not clear what they had to do with each other, why they were in the same play, or what the play was about. I was directing the play, and I asked her to write a confrontation scene for the two women, but the new scene was confused and ineffectual. Leslie was discouraged and wanted to cut the scene, but I was convinced it would lead us to the core of the play, if she ever fully wrote it.

In our meetings, she was able to express what she wanted to happen in that scene, what she felt was the connection between the two women, what the impact of the scene should be in the play. She simply could not find the right event and dialogue to bring it about.

"That's okay," I said. "We'll play what should be. Not what is."

And we did. At the rehearsal, I communicated Leslie's intent for the scene to the actors, and they traveled under the dialogue, which was uninspired, and played the actions. Perhaps the audience did not understand what was going on, but Leslie could see how the scene fit into the play. She could feel what should be happening between the women. She was reassured that the scene was necessary and right and only after the reading was she able to write it.

If the purpose of a reading is to define the center of the play, to find out whether the dialogue is actable, to see how the audience follows the story, it is reasonable to ignore some questions which might have to be answered later. In a reading, the director and actor must learn to deal with first things first.

David Trainer describes the rehearsal process for the open reading of The Dining Room: "We all got together on a Thursday afternoon to rehearse, then had a read-through scheduled for the following morning, then were to read the play to whomever came on Friday afternoon. And the first time everybody read, they played an attitude. They all acted like lockjawed Protestants and it was ghastly. So, I stopped them and said, 'Look, there's no need to characterize. Pete has characterized the people sufficiently. Play the action and don't characterize any more than you have to in order to deal with the realities. If you play a very old woman, you can't hop around like a little bird, but don't characterize as to type. Let the people speak in their own voices.' So they immediately stopped with this lockjawed characterization and it was wonderful. What was coming through was simple humanity.

"And a second thing that we changed was that Pete and I always wanted a scene at the dining table where the grandfather would be played by the youngest actor and the little boy by the oldest actor because that was the most striking reversal of roles. We got to that scene and the kid could not play an old man and Charlie Kimbrough was wasted as the young man. So, I said, 'Switch parts.' Right when we were doing it. Now, it's interesting that when we did the production, I again went back to our original plan. Remak Ramsay played the young boy and Bill Macy played the old man for the first day of rehearsal, and again they couldn't do it. I remember they ran through the scene once then walked off, and there was a long silence and I walked into the wings and said again, 'I'm wrong. Switch parts.' And that scene, where the little boy comes to get money from his grandfather to go to school, is one of the most effective scenes in the play. In the beginning, we had this idea that everyone should play strongly against their type but this scene never worked that way.

"So, that is what this reading was like. When I made a mistake, I could see it and not think, 'I'm going to beat you over the head until you get this right.' Instead, I said, 'I'm wrong. Let's switch parts.' If someone wasn't clear about an action, I would clarify it. If they were playing an attitude, I would say, 'Drop the attitude and play the action.' Another important thing that I contributed at this time was where they sat and how they sat around the table. This is the simplest kind of staging, not staging at all, but it does have to do with how people are working off each other.

"Generally speaking, I don't talk a lot when I direct. I think that talking is baloney, basically. I say blue, you say blue. Better you should smear a blue down and I'll smear a blue down and we should see if it is light, dark, navy, or turquoise. Talk is not always the best way to find out what is going on. But I did have a clear idea of how it should be cast and to get people to embody those values and to have a script that was very supportive of actors. Working on it was trying to let individual character, human character, inform the writing rather than have the writing shackle the individual.

"Pete did very little rewriting during those rehearsals. He may have cut a little but basically nothing changed. There wasn't enough time and it wasn't for that. What we were doing was testing to see what we had accomplished at this point. The job was to make this work and we did. The reading was a triumph. It was fun and effective and people cried, people laughed. You knew you were in the presence of something special and, the minute it was over, Andre Bishop agreed to produce it at Playwrights Horizons."

· * * *

For a staged reading, the approach to the blocking should be the same as the approach to the text; simple, direct, defined. The director blocks for clarity of the text. He needs to get the actors on and off the stage. He defines relationships physically. He follows the writer's stage directions wherever possible, removing the necessity of having them read.

At this point, the decisive director is the most effective one. The actors need mechanics which can be easily absorbed so that they can forget them and relate to one another. This can be accomplished with one blocking rehearsal, at which time the actors record the movement, and then another to make them comfortable with what has been done.

"At a staged reading," Susan Merson advises actors, "the main thing to remember is to learn your blocking, not your lines, and read the script. Do not try to act the script—read it. You are not ready to act the script. The more you feel comfortable in your surroundings in terms of knowing where you are, walking around, the better you will be. Make contact with the other actor, but also make sure you keep your eye on the text so you don't screw up the rhythm of the scene.

"Here are the things you're going for in a staged reading: You want to make sure that the externals are apparent. You want to make sure the rhythm of a scene works. You want to make sure the basic character content is revealed. You want to make sure the arc of a scene is there so that the playwright can see whether or not he's got something. Sometimes actors will make a script better than it is on the page. For a staged reading, I would suggest—always make it better. For a closed reading around the table, never make it better. Let the playwright hear it fail. Let him see there is no arc in this scene, no conflict in that one. But once you get into a staged reading, it's your ass up there. If they've agreed with your initial choice—and they must have or they wouldn't have put you in the part—then go with your initial choice. Read the words clearly. Make sure the structure of a scene works: where it begins, where it must peak, what the climax is, where you have to come down."

One of the most valuable bonuses of a reading performance is the spontaneity. The central aim of the lengthy rehearsal process for a full production is to get the actors to the point of believing that this play is happening to them for the first time. This takes weeks of breaking down the script, absorbing mechanics, relating to the other actors, adjusting to sets and costumes. Only after all this has been achieved can actors forget it all, look and listen and truly respond.

At a reading, the story is new to the actors. They have to be open and available and intensely involved because there has been so little rehearsal. Therefore they really listen. They come on stage with no set expectations. They can be taken by surprise. If they are relaxed, they will respond deeply and honestly; often a reading can reach a level of intensity and emotion that would take weeks to reach in the normal rehearsal process.

Since the work is spontaneous and undefined, it cannot be repeated, but that is not one of the requirements of a reading. The director does not try to create stage pictures or work toward a sense of place. There is not enough time to achieve complex ends and, by trying to gain that kind of control, by overrehearsing so that the work becomes routine without reaching below the surface, the actors gain nothing and lose the sense of newness.

Readings should be fun. The actors' pleasure in the experience, in the script, and in their colleagues comes across to the audience. Since there is not time to achieve this kind of comfort among strangers, directors will often try to cast actors who know each other: husbands and wives, former colleagues, friends. One of the essentials is trust, and actors who start with a past shared experience are ahead of the game. That awkward stage of getting to know one another is eliminated, and actors appreciate the effort. The first thing an actor will ask, when invited to do a reading, is, "Who else is in it?"

Another important aspect of a successful reading is scheduling. For a sit-down reading, many directors like to hold a single rehearsal just before the actual performance, with only a dinner break in between, so that the momentum is unbroken, the bond between actors is maintained, the energy and excitement has no chance to diminish.

Others prefer to rehearse the day before the reading, giving the actors a chance to work on the script on their own. They will come in the following night with new ideas, a richer grasp of their characters, and do things on stage that will surprise and engage the other actors.

Even if only one actor in the company has found something new overnight, the other actors will perk up and scramble to his level in response. The result will be a sense of discovery and a true interaction among the actors that will bring life to the script.

The other advantage of the overnight break is that it gives the playwright a chance to make revisions and cuts, solve some of the problems that emerged in the reading's rehearsal and discuss with the director any points that seemed muddy or wrong. Whatever changes the playwright makes can then be given to the actors the following night and included in the reading.

Staged reading rehearsals have to be spread over several days and should be kept to three or four hours at a time. It is more convenient for the cast since actors can then keep casting appointments, see their agents, and earn a living. In addition, since so much is covered so quickly and in such a concentrated fashion when a director blocks an entire play in such a short time period, actors often get tired and lose concentration, and after too many hours of intense work, reach a point of no return.

No matter what the schedule, the director must insist that one rehearsal, or part of a rehearsal, or a half hour before the reading be spent on the stage. This is true for a sit-down or a staged reading, and the director often has to fight for this privilege. The stage is usually in use for the full production scheduled, so the producer will shove the reading into a back room to rehearse until the final moment. The director must insist that the actors be given some time to adjust to the actual space in which they will ultimately do the reading.

If actors have rehearsed in one room and then are asked to perform in another, they must have a chance to adjust to the different sound, different echo, different chairs, different lights. These factors affect the actors' comfort, their concentration and their ability to relax and let loose. It is awful if, with good, concentrated rehearsal, clarity of purpose, and a sense of relaxation, the actors get thrown at the final moment by some technicality.

One common unforeseen problem is that stage lighting has a tendency to bounce off white script pages. The director might be assured that there is plenty of light on stage when, in fact, there might be too much light. If the actors have not had a chance to work in it, they may find themselves blinded by the glare when it is too late to make the necessary changes.

Another problem is that gelled lights can blanch out the actor's color-coding and script markings. Imagine the actor's horror if he has not had a chance to rehearse in the lights and walks onstage to discover that all his clues as to where he should be, when he talks, when he enters and when he exits, are simply wiped out!

The writer has two responsibilities. One is to supply a well-written script. The other, and at this stage, equally important one, is to supply a properly typed one.

The standard forms of script preparation are created for the actor's use. The needs of the book buyer are different; preparing a script for publication has requirements that the writer may, or may not, need to learn about later. For a reading, the script has to be regarded as a tool for the actors. Information they need must be clearly stated; information they do not need must be eliminated.

The character's name should appear above the speech, in the center of the page, set clearly apart from the dialogue—not on the same line as the speech, in the left-hand margin. Names are always capitalized above the dialogue and in the stage directions. The balance of the stage directions are not capitalized, so that the names clearly stand out. Because things move so rapidly and there is no time to waste in a reading, the actor must understand immediately that he is being called upon to say or do something. If his eye has to scurry over the page to find his character's name, he is likely to miss it.

Scripts should be double-spaced so actors can read them easily. Stage directions should be set off from dialogue, indented on the page and placed in parentheses. If they are not, some actor, in the rush of emotion, will inevitably read his dialogue and continue right on into the stage directions before he realizes what he is doing.

The margins on both sides of the page should be wide. Scripts are always bound so that actors will not have loose pages to deal with, and will not lose pages or get them out of order and find themselves, onstage, in the middle of the wrong scene. Writers who type scripts from one side of the page to the other without margins to allow for binding are going to regret it.

Speeches should not continue from the bottom of one page to the top of the next. If there is not enough room on a page to complete the dialogue, it should be started on a fresh page. Actors should not have to turn a page in the middle of a speech. It breaks their concentration, forces them to deal with a physical and visual distraction, and reduces their ability to relate to the other actors. If the script does not allow the actors to do their job efficiently, the play will suffer.

The first thing many actors do with a new script is to cross out acting instructions, such as "John (gently)" or "Sarah (lovingly)." If the play works, the writer will get what he wants. It won't happen because he asked for it in the stage directions. Such instructions might be helpful for the book reader to understand the play, but they can only block the actor or force him into artificiality. The writer might use such acting hints at selected, extremely ambiguous moments, but if the script is littered with them, the actors will ignore or delete them.

The script should be typed uniformly and always on the same typewriter. When the actor is working at high speed and with high concentration, it is distracting for him to turn the page and adjust to a new format.

In addition, the script is a guide to the director for scheduling rehearsals and knowing how long material is going to take to prepare. Ordinarily, a page takes a minute to a minute and a half to play. The variation depends on typeface and format. If these are not consistent, the director will have a hard time predicting how long scenes will play and how rehearsal time is best used.

The pages of the first act should be numbered separately from the second. The first act starts with 1–1 (act 1, page 1). If the act is divided into scenes, 1–1–1 is used (act 1, scene 1, page 1). Act 1 is then numbered consecutively and if the final page of act 1 is 1–3–40 (act 1, scene 3, page 40), the second acts starts with 2–1 (act 2, page 1).

This reduces the confusion of renumbering when pages are added or deleted. It means that any changes made in act 1 will not affect the numbering of act 2. Scripts are working, living organisms and are meant to grow, expand, contract and change. If the basic numbering is kept intact, there is less likelihood of confusion in rehearsal.

When pages are added, they are identified alphabetically after the last numbered page (7a, 7b, 7c). When a page is deleted, the numbering is not changed. If page 7 is cut in its entirety, the actors are instructed to throw it away and write on the bottom of page 6, "Go immediately to page 8."

When the writer revises and retypes a page, he makes note of that fact in the numbering (1–3–35, revised Aug. '87). This identification guarantees that all the actors are working from the same revised page. If it is not done, time can be lost in rehearsal, figuring out which actors have the correct new page and which do not.

These problems are easily avoided if the script is typed according to standard formats. It is surprising and dismaying that so many scripts are circulated that are not. Actors and literary advisers are always dubious when handed a nonstandard script. It either means that the writer is a rank beginner who has never had a reading, or failed to learn anything about the actors' needs in the process.

Rewrites, cuts, and revisions are part of the nature and the purpose of a reading, and writers should not be afraid to make them. Good actors can incorporate changes easily and quickly. After the rehearsal, the writer and director share their reactions and decide whether revisions are needed. If they are excessive, the director will call another rehearsal, immediately preceding the reading, to go over the changes.

If the changes are simply cuts, they can be given to the actors without rehearsal. Actors have an enormous ability to absorb changes when their concentration and energy are high. The writer should never resist making changes because he is afraid of throwing off the actors. It is part of the function of the process, part of the actor's job to accommodate him.

The greatest enemy of the reading experience is anxiety—something that is true about theater at every stage but is particularly obvious in a situation where so much is left to chance.

Sometimes the signals of problems appear in rehearsal, and directors can take actors aside to find out what is wrong. More often, however, an actor's anxiety will not emerge until it is too late. Actors are fine when they are relaxed and enjoying themselves, but onstage before an audience, anxiety may possess them. They stop relating to other actors, they stop listening, they push and force and, if theirs is a major role, can sink the show.

The most obvious sign of anxiety is the retreat of an actor. The actor backs off and gives nothing to the others. The actor slumps in the seat and denies his body the possibility of life. This creates barriers to connection with the other actors.

I have seen actors develop accents at readings that make them incomprehensible. I have seen them suddenly chain-smoke so they are barely able to get out their lines, their co-workers turn away, coughing. Some yell so that instead of reaching for the other actors, they push them away.

This type of behavior may be the result of some physical discomfort which has upset the actor. Or the director might have introduced so many variables and demands that, at the crucial moment, the actor becomes frightened, begins to mistrust his impulses, to question what the other actors are doing, and to perform for the director's approval.

Reading actors should get onstage with a firm hold on the basic story line, a comfort in their surroundings, a script they can follow, a trust in their fellow actors, and the freedom to allow their inner lives to lead them.

David Trainer's advice to his *Dining Room* company, as they faced their first audience, was: "Tonight, we take on a new partner. We don't know what they're like. We didn't rehearse them. We don't know what they think of this. Let's do our show. If they laugh, don't let that distort the show. If they don't laugh, don't let that distort the show. Let's play what we decided we were going to play, simply and truly and strongly and they'll get it. . . . But they are not contractually obliged to get it."

If actors throw themselves into the story and believe in it with total concentration, the emotional core of the script will bubble up and be communicated to the audience. In that case, the writer will have found out what he needed to know about the play and the reading will be deemed a success.

6

Audience Response

The audience is seated and the reading has begun. The writer, director, producer, and dramaturg should sit apart from one another. Plays look different, everything feels different from different sides of the house. If those there to evaluate the play sit together, they tend to reinforce one another's reactions and the decisions already made. Nothing is more annoying to the unknowing audience than a back row of insiders, laughing at lines that nobody else finds funny. If the act comes to an end and the audience sits silently, it does no good for the director to start the applause and cover up the problem. Observers should observe, not lead the way.

From the open reading on, the major changes will be dictated by the audience. The most valuable help that anyone can offer is to pinpoint correctly audience response. The actors can say, "When I got to that speech, I felt like I had them in the palm of my hand" or "Why didn't I get this laugh?" or "Did you hear them gasp when I said this? They hated me then." Afterward writers will go back to figure out what was happening and why, but at readings, their role is to chart the vibes in the audience as accurately as possible.

Plays have important philosophical levels, psychological insights, and poetic subtleties that might go right by the audience while at the theater and then hit them on the way home. But theater is designed to work in the auditorium in front of the audience. The perpetual cry of the director over some treasured moment that needs to be cut is, "It doesn't work!" A necessity to hold the audience in the immediacy of the theatrical moment is what makes playwriting different from other literary forms.

At the Actors Studio, Lee Strasberg once grew impatient with an actor who started a scene by making a cup of tea, which took five silent minutes on stage. She poured the water into the pot, heated it, searched for the tea bag, sliced a lemon, and spooned out the sugar. Apparently, she was making some major statement about the loneliness and despair of the woman's life, but the audience found it deadly.

After the scene, Strasberg asked the actor calmly, "What is the primary function of the theater artist?" She had a dozen high falutin' answers: "To be moving, to be meaningful, to enrich the lives of the audience, to make a statement about humanity." Strasberg finally cut her short. "Darling," he said, "it is to be interesting!"

That is the lesson the playwright must learn from the open reading: whatever the intent, if the moment does not hold onstage, it needs to be reworked. Audiences will always let you know which moments these are.

The audience response inevitably pushes the play toward the dramatic. Explanations, descriptions, offstage events drop by the wayside and are incorporated in action. Gradually the subtext gets hidden under events. Playwright Corinne Jacker once said, "My first draft is usually all subtext, and as I rewrite, my job is to cover it up."

As the play unfolds, its interior life is revealed; the second act reveals the subtext of the first. In the beginning, the audience wants to know who is who, what they are up to—and the audience wants to figure out why by themselves.

And they want this information quickly. In the twenties and thirties, when life was more leisurely and the three act play was in fashion, playwrights were taught that the audience "gave you" the first act to introduce the characters, set up the plot, charm them into caring. Today, Broadway wags claim that the audience makes up its mind in fifteen minutes. If the playwright has not hooked them by then, he has lost them for good.

The concentration spans of today's audiences are molded by television viewing. They know how quickly, or slowly, a plot should unfold. They expect a climax at a certain point. They sense, rhythmically, when the plot is being resolved.

Their antennae are highly tuned. Freud has clued them into the mysteries of the unconscious, and they are able to pick up clues, motivations, and complexities in a flash. Today's sophisticated New York theatergoers talk rapidly, absorb like sponges, listen to three conversations at once. That is why simultaneous dialogue has become so accepted in the plays of Lanford Wilson and the films of Robert Altman. Audiences have become deluged with stimulation and they have adjusted their response mechanisms accordingly.

Lee Kalcheim says, "Barnet Kellman and I have this running gag about how many times you have to say something to an audience before they get it. As a playwright, I think it's forty-six and, as a director, he thinks it's once. He's usually right. There were some questions about the top of Les and Bess. We kept trying to get the play off a little sooner. It used to start with the daughter and son-in-law coming in early in the morning. They've just been married. They sneak in and look around the apartment and she drags him off to bed and a couple of minutes later, Les and Bess wake up to do their radio show. I thought it was essential to establish that the kids were married and Barnet thought that the play should start with Les and Bess [radio stars who broadcast from their breakfast table] getting up. They go on the air and this absolute stranger appears. I thought we had to see him earlier. 'No,' Barnet says, 'why can't the audience feel the same way they do? Why do they have to know who this is? "Who the hell are you?" "I came with your daughter." They didn't have to see him before to learn that he had just married the daughter.' We tried it before an audience and Barnet was right."

Audiences tell the writer and director when a laugh is needed to relieve tension, whether a line was meant to be funny or not. They tell them when a small gag is killing the reaction to a bigger one coming closely behind it. They tell them when a breathing space is needed after a big scene, when a scene is over and it is time to move on, when the play is truly resolved even if the poor actors have pages to go. They tell when a beat goes on for too long; when a scene, no matter how unique it appears on the page, is a repetition, emotionally and rhythmically, of information previously conveyed; when two characters serve the same purpose and can be compressed into one; when an intermission is needed and when it is not.

These are not questions that deal with the core of the play—the theme, the psychological truths, the kinds of questions discussed by the writer and director in the living room stage. These are questions that deal with how the play works. In that regard, the audience is always the expert.

*   *   *

The postreading audience discussion has become a popular practice. The writer and, often, the director join the literary adviser on stage. Sometimes, the writer makes an opening statement describing his goals, posing specific questions. Then, the literary adviser opens the discussion to the house.

Everybody likes to be heard in a public forum, everybody is an expert about one's own reactions, and most audience members think they have the potential to write or direct or act. People vent their opinions all the time in Broadway lobbies; it is an accepted part of theater-going. Nonprofit theater has offered the public the invitation to do it inside the house, and audiences accept eagerly.

There can be no doubt that these discussions are worthwhile for the producer. They are an effective way of introducing audiences to new plays, of offering them a role in the creative process, of making them feel like members of the family. Nonprofit theaters throughout the country have inaugurated these discussions because they offer something that film and television cannot: active involvement, a connection with the artists, friendship with other audience members, a sense of intimacy, a chance to be heard.

The discussions bring audiences to readings. Since readings are available only to subscribers, they increase subscriptions. They help connect audiences to the thought processes of writers and encourage the production of riskier new plays in a subscription series.

Sometimes these discussions can be helpful to the writer; sometimes they can be damaging. After all, the writer is being placed in an uncomfortable position at the worst of all possible times. He is either in a state of euphoria or misery; most probably, exhaustion. He is confused and overwhelmed and needs time to figure out his own reactions. He is a human being at a vulnerable moment and he is going to respond either by putting up defenses against attack, making it tougher for any real words of wisdom to get through, or by believing so happily in what his mother proudly declaims that he will never fix what is wrong.

A great deal of the success of the discussion depends on how the moderator, usually the literary adviser, sets it up. Certain ground rules should be announced, and it is the moderator's role to protect the writer by seeing that they are respected. The ground rules are as follows:

1. The literary adviser, writer, and director are interested in specific responses, not opinions. If the audience was bored, they want to know when. If something was difficult to believe, they want to know what it was. If the audience found a character unappealing, they want them to pinpoint the moment when it started to happen.
2. The goal is to get the playwright talking by asking questions. In his efforts to explain to the audience, he will explain to himself.
3. The audience is not allowed to write its own play. Statements such as, "What should have happened is . . ." should be cut off before they are finished. It does not help a writer to be told he is like another, more famous, writer; nor to be criticized because the material has been treated elsewhere. A writer should not be stopped from working on familiar material but, rather, encouraged to dig deeply into the familiar so that he comes up with something unique.
4. It is important to tell the writer what was enjoyable about the play and why. Once he understands what works, it is easier for him to deal with what does not.

Wise writers will do some preparation and take a hand in controlling the situation. In an opening statement, they can state specifically what they wish to learn. They can pose questions that will rule out material they do not wish to discuss in public and that will discourage the show-offs in the audience from monopolizing the floor.

Who was the person you most cared about?
When did this affection begin?
Did it ever stray to another character?
Can you trace your attention and let me know when you were most concerned with one character and when your focus changed?

As a general rule, playwrights should remember that criticism is not going to be helpful if there is no basic affection for the play. They should quickly turn off when they sense antagonism and lean forward when they sense warmth.

It is always generous for the actors to stay and listen to the discussion. One of the aims of the play development process is for the relationship of the collaborators to grow stronger as they go through the steps together. Not only are the actors making a statement about their concern for the play by staying, they might learn something that will make their work easier on the reading of the next draft, or on the playwright's next play.

Here is an opportunity for actors to bridge the gulf between playwright and actor, only part of which is due to the writer's innate mistrust of actors. Some of it is due to the actors' resentment of the writer, who seems to be, and often is, sitting in constant judgment.

Most actors refuse to see writers as frightened and needy artists like themselves. However, if they just sat in the audience and smiled, spoke up in support when the writer was attacked, and complimented him afterward, they would be astonished at how grateful he would be.

This sense of affection and support is the most positive element at the O'Neill, where the discussions are limited to members of the working company and guests who attended the readings. Because everyone attending knows the writer, has had a meal with him, or has lived across the hall from him, there is a friendly concern built into the situation.

The writer is up there with his director and dramaturg for support. The discussion is moderated by Lloyd Richards, who is paternal and kind and knows how to cut off destructive comments with a glance. In the audience are writers who have been, or are scheduled to be, in the same hot seat, so they are careful about what they say. A good chunk of the audience has been actively involved with the play.

The dramaturg and director outline the history of the script, describing the problems the work at the conference focused on. Setting the critique within such a context is helpful to the audience and the writer. Usually, valuable comments come from the people who have made a commitment to the material, struggled with it, and can analyze the problems from their own efforts. An actor could not believe a certain moment. A designer felt a scene disrupted the visual flow. The other writers, who heard the play read at the preconference weekend, are in a position to compare the drafts and comment on what has been lost and what has been gained.

The critique takes place on the morning after the final reading; therefore, some thought has gone into everyone's remarks. There have, often, been changes between early and later readings and those who have seen both can address the development of the script.

The morning critique is often held outdoors, in the O'Neill's loveliest theater, The Instant, under an enormous, sheltering tree. Even nature offers the writer protection.

At Playwrights Horizons, according to David Trainer, "There never is an audience discussion. Andre [the artistic director] has a discussion in his head with himself."

At JRT, we do not put the writer through the trauma of an open discussion either. After the reading, the writer goes out with the cast and his friends. The director goes out with his guests. I, the associate director, go out with mine. The artistic director has talked to the subscribers during intermission. In this way, we all have a chance to gather information from the audience. It is simply not done as a public ritual with the writer in the spotlight. The next day, offering all a chance to absorb what has been said, we meet for a private postmortem to share the feedback and discuss our individual reactions. In a closed room, after a night's sleep, the writer is better able to absorb criticism, to take in suggestions, and to think about revision and a future for the play.

New Dramatists has developed an effective program of panel discussions after the readings. The panels consist of theater experts and other member playwrights who attend the reading and then meet with the writer in closed session. Once again, top priority is given to the protection and privacy of the writer.

Playwrights learn from sitting in on discussions of one another's plays. It is clear when something has to be cut, when the center of the play is foggy, when a character has not been fully written—as long as it is not your play. Writer-panelists have a chance to learn about the art of revision, which might make it easier when it is their turn at bat.

There are some dangers in relying on the audience's response, and they should be noted.

There are plays that can be successful at a reading which will fail in full production. This is because, as Martin Gottfried once wrote in a review of an adaptation, "Basically, a book is directed for the mind, happening there, and a play is directed for the eye—it is physically seen."*

One summer at the O'Neill, one of the plays was an enormous chunk of work filled with excessively stylized use of language, long descriptive speeches, and complex metaphorical material. The writer was considerably talented, and at the preconference week-end, we were all impressed with the play. Seated in the living room with the writer reading for us, we were able to close our eyes and focus on the words. There was a sense of leisure instead of the compressed concentration one feels in a theater. Surprisingly, this interesting work in the living room turned into an unending bore onstage.

Once there was movement, once actors added other emotional layers, it became clear that the language was much too rich. The writer had not given the actors room to breathe. He was manipulating his characters at every moment so the audience could never escape his presence and relate to what they were seeing onstage.

After the first reading the writer demanded that all the staging, all the props, all the developmental work be discarded and the actors simply sit and read the play. So, for the second staged reading, the audience arrived to find five folding chairs on stage. No question about it, the second reading was more interesting than the first, and once again, the play seemed impressive. The audience could focus on the words. Their concentration was not dissipated. There was no emotional pressure.

The writer was pleased but I do not think he got the true message. In each case, the sit-down readings served to cover-up the problems in the writing and were not accurate guides to the stage-worthiness of the script.

Actor Mark Blum tells this story: "A woman I know sent me a play. She had gone to college with the playwright and she now lives in Montana. 'He wrote this play about me,' she said. 'Do you like it?' I did. It was a nice two-character play which was indeed about this woman's relationship with a man. I told her I liked it and she said, 'I'm coming to New York. Why don't we read it somewhere?' So, we did a reading of it at Ensemble Studio Theatre and she read the

*Martin Gottfried, *Opening Nights* (New York: G. P. Putnam's Sons, 1969), p. 54–5.

part of herself, except that she is older now than the character is. It was a great reading—a really hot, alive thing. Barnet Kellman was there and he said, 'Let's do it! Come on, let's do it!' So we got all excited and went to lawyers and began the process of optioning this play. There was a production of it already promised to the Hartman Theatre Company in Connecticut, so we went up to see it, figuring we could learn something. Within five minutes, it was the most excruciating thing I'd ever been through. The play was bad, the writing was bad in a way we never dreamed it was bad. If you had just walked into the theater, you would have said, 'This is the worst play I have ever seen.'

"We left at intermission, and we had a long train ride home, trying to figure out how much we were wrong about the play and how much it was this production. So we immediately called the lawyers and said, 'Don't do anything. Stay where you are.' We put together another reading and got somebody really perfect for the girl. The woman about whom the play was written was back in Montana, anyway. We did this reading in Barnet's loft and it was mediocre; all right, but nowhere as exciting as it had been, and Barnet and I had to sit down and say, 'Now what exactly happened? What went wrong?' The best I can figure it, the first time we did it, this woman and I had a connection. We had known each other for fifteen years. There was chemistry between us. It was her real life and she played it with an urgency that was not like acting. It was raw and kind of scary. The reading had been an event, and it gave us a false sense that the play was stronger than it was. We liked the essence of the script but we discovered that many of the actual lines and the structure of the play were not really successful. We were blinded by the pure visceral excitement of the human event and the reading simply fooled us."

It is important to keep in mind that different theaters attract different audiences. When the audience becomes part of the collaborative process, the same old question arises—the one that has also been posed about the director, the producer, the dramaturg: is this the right audience for this particular play?

That is not to say that good plays do not have universal appeal. They do. We are talking here about plays and writers going through developmental stages and audiences coming to the theater without being influenced by powerhouse critics. In this instance, it is essential that there be a basic affection between play and audience, or the work is going to die before it has a chance to blossom.

Our audience at JRT is middle class, somewhat older and more conservative than the traditional off-off-Broadway crowd. They are sophisticated and lifelong theater goers, but they are not avant-garde.

They love musicals. If they walk into the theater and see the music stands and piano out, the air ripens with excitement before the curtain even goes up. Our audience is much more giving to this particular theatrical form, and as a result, we have been very successful with new musicals. We have been able to experiment and fail, and our audiences have still supported the work. We have been able to say some shocking things and deal in a courageous way with material in musicals the audience never would have accepted in straight plays.

When audiences are responsive, actors love to get onstage. In previews, performances bloom and grow. It's easy to fix and change in such an atmosphere. It's easy for material to improve, and expand. Happy actors will adjust to any changes and eagerly try something new for the betterment of the show. Unhappy actors will grumble and resist. A play previewed for the wrong audience misses its chance to get fixed. The actors feel waves of hostility floating toward them. Instead of the good moments expanding, the whole work sours. This might have been avoided had the play been previewed before a more sympathetic audience.

If the producer says to the writer after the open reading, "I love your play but my audiences won't go for it," he is, in fact, doing the writer a favor. It would not be helpful to present the play to an audience that could not accept it.

So, once the reading has been a success, the writer has learned a lot, the producer says he loves the play, all that remains is for the writer to connect with the right audience.

Another question that emerges at this point is whether the play is right for the space. The shape and size of the playing area, the seating capacity, the look and feel of the house, the relationship of the audience to the stage, all have an immense impact on the play.

The Broadway hits of the 1940s seem out of place and poorly written in our small black box theaters. They are filled with grand dramatic moments, bravura speeches that require a large distance between audience and actor if they are to work, star entrances, and exits designed for applause. None of that is believable on a tiny stage, under a low ceiling, with the first row just a leg's stretch away. Many interesting and well-crafted plays are meeting rejection off-off-Broadway because they were written for a space that no longer exists.

Sidney Kingsley's docudramas, Lillian Hellman's melodramas, Maxwell Anderson's historical epics, William Inge's slices of life would be more successful these days as films. The theater cannot recreate reality the way movies and television can. Audiences have grown sophisticated and demanding about the look and feel of sets and locations. The theater cannot duplicate the external world, the spectacle, the mob scene, and historical detail the way cinema can.

What off-off-Broadway offers is intimacy. Successful modern plays deal with the inner life, interpersonal relationships, fantasy, spiritual and personal crises; the subjective vision instead of external reality. The world gets smaller, the humor gets subtler, the pace gets quicker.

The small-cast play has become popular, not only because of the lower costs and higher rewards to a small house, but because only a few actors can fill the stage. In a Broadway production, the two-character play might seem skimpy. In a small theater, the audience is so close to the actors that, even if the script is short on event, they fall in love with the characters.

Lanford Wilson had been experimenting with simultaneous dialogue for years, and it paid off in The Hot L Baltimore, which originated at Circle Repertory and became one of off-off-Broadway's biggest hits. This play was specifically written to be done in Circle Rep's original home, a tiny theater-in-the-round on upper Broadway. Wilson's simultaneous dialogue techniques worked like a charm because, wherever you were in the house, you caught a heightened fragment of the dialogue. The very playing space gave the language a shape. This play almost never works as well when produced on a proscenium stage.

The mini-musical is a form that has been created by off-off-Broadway. The Fantasticks, March of the Falsettos, Little Shop of Horrors, Ain't Misbehavin', and JRT's Kuni-Leml are all short and fast. The book is minimal, staging is cinematic. The orchestra is tiny and often on the stage. There is no chorus and very little dancing.

In a small house, choruses are not successful because there is such a connection between audience and cast that everybody on stage has to be an identified character. A group of smiling strangers who have no place in the story strikes an artificial note, unacceptable in an intimate setting.

Also, because these houses have low ceilings, leaps, jumps, and elaborate dance numbers are limited. In a large Broadway house, the chorus offers visual excitement and color. Off-off-Broadway, it merely makes the stage look crowded.

Because there is a strong connection between audience and characters, elaborate, realistic sets are not necessary. As in *March of the Falsettos*, one movable door and a couple of chairs on wheels can create any number of believable sets.

We've come a long way from *My Fair Lady*.

The one-person play has become popular because it is economically feasible, it tours easily, and it works so well in a small space.

It is, in fact, a play about the relationship between the actor and the audience. In the process of watching, the audience falls in love with the character and/or the performer. The actor, like the cabaret singer, tells his story, plays the action, remains honest, but also relates directly to the audience. The actor has to be able to take internal moments and open them up to include the audience. The form offers the public an experience desperately missing from modern life and mass entertainment—an intimate relationship.

Susan Merson, during her first long run in *Vanities*, made use of the time to create a one-woman show, *Reflections of a China Doll*. "It started out at Ensemble Studio Theatre. I was thinking about my life and started putting some incidents into story form. The reason *China Doll* worked was, not because I was a writer, but because I was a good actress. What sells the actor's solo piece is his soul. No one else can play that piece and make it as interesting because the text won't hold up. The combination of the human being and the text makes it work. In a really great play, the actor might not make such a difference, but a deeply personal play needn't be great if the actor can make it work."

Another theatrical form that has developed out of a small space is improvisational theater. Starting with Chicago's Second City Company, it has produced such celebrated graduates as Alan

Arkin, Barbara Harris, Elaine May, and Mike Nichols, has made itself felt in the plays of David Mamet, and the comedy of Eric Bogosian, Whoopi Goldberg, and Lily Tomlin.

These artists have been given the opportunity to develop because their work is so related to the economics of today's theater, the available space, and the needs of the modern audience.

Every talented writer thinks that his play will work in any space, for any audience, but he is wrong. Many a script has been a smash at a reading and, still, the producer has turned it down. Writers should not lose faith. What they need to find is the proper audiences for their plays, the moment in time, and the right space in which they can come alive.

7

Agents, Money, Unions, and Contracts

Provided that none of the previously mentioned problems exist, and that everybody involved is now happy with the prospects for the play, the producer should make a commitment for production.

This does not mean that the play is completely ready to go. Another rewrite may be required, incorporating what has been learned from the open reading, but at least, the playwright, director, and dramaturg are in agreement about what needs to be done. Nor does this mean that the producer will offer to mount a full production. Another developmental step is available: the workshop production.

As far as the work processes of the actor, director, and designers are concerned, a production is a production. When a play is fully staged, set, lit, and costumed; when the actors are off book (i.e. the lines have been memorized); when there has been a rehearsal period of three to four weeks; when there is a run of at least a few performances—*that* is a production.

The differences between a workshop and a full production fall in the area of money, exposure, and size of the venture, but the most crucial distinguishing fact is that a workshop is not reviewed. It gets neither advertising nor press attention, and is generally seen only by subscribers and friends of the company. It is most valuable when a work in development needs to be seen in full production, yet is not ready for critical attack, and, most especially, when the project involves star names who are going to attract the big guns before the work is ready.

Playwrights Horizons has done workshops of such works-in-progress as Wendy Wasserstein's *Miami*, William Finn's *America Kicks* up Its Heels, and, most prominently, Stephen Sondheim's and James Lapine's *Sunday in the Park with George*.

Amy Introcaso describes the process: "There had been a couple of readings of the script; one reading of the first act in which we just got actors. We didn't necessarily need actors who sang so we had actors who we thought would be best for the parts. And then another reading, just for Sondheim and Lapine, at which Sondheim played some of the music. The first time I heard 'Color And Light,' I heard Mandy Patinkin sing it. Sondheim had written the part for a baritone, but the only person we could think of for the role was Mandy, so Sondheim needed to hear him sing before we would cast him to see if he could rewrite the part for a tenor. Mandy came in and actually auditioned with 'Color and Light' and it was magical.

"*Sunday in the Park with George* is an example of a script that was deeply influenced by the actors, because Lapine was the director as well as the playwright. The script was all coming together in the workshop. He did a lot of improvisations and the actors told him what they wanted to see. Mandy started out very introspective. He starts from inside and works out, and by the time it came to Broadway, he had found a way to make George introspective and still play out. Danielle Ferland, who played the little girl, came in wearing glasses. We decided to cast her and she said, 'Oh, I'll take my glasses off,' and they said, 'No!' and wrote that into the second act. 'I want my glasses.' So she actually influenced a lyric.

"Christine Baranski made up that woman (Yvonne) and, ultimately, in the Broadway production, Dana Ivey changed her. But Christine defined a sort of interesting, different kind of character. Then, she was doing *The Real Thing*, so she didn't move to Broadway with *Sunday in the Park with George*.

"We did a fully staged version of the first act and did the second act for only three performances. We didn't open it for the press, and even those subscribers who only saw the first act got their money's worth. They put a lot of new songs in at Playwrights Horizons and changed things. Then, before it moved to Broadway, they wrote a whole new second act."

Some off-off-Broadway houses, like many regional theaters, have "second stage" spaces that enable them to produce plays on a smaller scale and take advantage of this step in the developmental process. However, many theaters do not have a second performing space. If they have a rigid schedule imposed on them by subscription sales, the only option, after the successful staged reading, is to take the play on to full production.

If the reading has gone well and the producer asks for another rewrite without offering a production of any kind, the writer had better take a good long look at what is going on. Artistic directors' jobs depend on play selection. This can make them indecisive, resulting in a habit of toying with writers and extending the play development process seemingly without end. No one in theater can predict what is going to be a hit, and there is a point at which a commitment is required, even if the producer has no gilt-edged guarantees.

It took David Kerry Heefner, then artistic director of the Hudson Guild Theatre, a year and a half, after two readings with two different all-star casts, including James Broderick, Darren McGavin, and Charlotte Moore, to commit to do Breakfast with Less and Bess. Lee Kalcheim says, "One day, I called David and he said, 'I'd love to do it but can you get me that cast?' I said, 'David, I've given you two separate casts. The play has worked both times. They are wonderful actors, but it's the play. If I get you another cast it will be equally good. You want to do it; make up your mind now or hold your peace.' So, finally, it was scheduled for that coming season. He obviously liked it enough, but most theater people are jugglers, and understandably so. They all sit around waiting for the Holy Grail to walk through the door and present itself so they can guarantee their subscribers a hit. They don't really know, so they always wait for the last minute."

This is one of those moments when artists must protect themselves. If the producer says, "Let me see the rewrite and we'll talk" or "If you could get me a star, I'd feel more comfortable" or "I'm worried about money so cut it from seven characters to five and let me take another look" writers are in trouble. They cannot continue to rewrite on the basis of vague promises and declarations of affection, no matter how sincere. It will damage their work, eat away at their self-esteem, stall the progress of their plays, and adversely affect plays to come. The ambivalence of producers is one of the traps facing theater artists. They must be prepared for this and, when such a situation becomes dangerous, get out.

*　　*　　*

If an offer of production is forthcoming, it presents a good time for the writer to contact an agent. Playwrights' agents are not eager to spend their time circulating plays off-off-Broadway. They are not in business to seek out opportunities for beginning playwrights nor to hustle for productions that are going to earn them minute commissions. The unproduced playwright looking for an agent will not get much response.

However, playwrights with a commitment from a theater are likely to hear "Send in the play and let me read it." Such writers are full of potential. They have some evidence of their talents. They should use this moment to strike. If the production never comes off, if it is a disaster, at least they will have gained an agent and be one step ahead of where they were when they started.

A playwright needs an agent to negotiate the contract. The theater may be tiny, the royalties may be minuscule, but there are bound to be clauses that could turn out to be costly. Most contracts for off-off-Broadway require some future participation in the play. This can mean that the theater has an option on the play for a period of time after the production closes, and controls the move to commercial auspices, or it gives the theater a piece of the writer's royalties from any subsequent productions, either for a limited time or in perpetuity.

The contract can tie up a portion of the playwright's future income from film, television, cable, or publishing rights to the play, or its ability to be adapted to another form (i.e., a musical) or to be produced in another country in another language. It may call for an option on the writer's next play or several future plays and his exclusive services. It may dictate the creative controls to which he is entitled.

These days, even the smallest nonprofit house will hand playwrights a standard contract form. This is nonsense. There is no such thing as a standard contract; still, it always intimidates playwrights. Every contract must be negotiated and any one for any kind of production can include clauses that writers might not fully comprehend without the experienced eye of an agent or an attorney.

Even without an agent, everyone should have some sense of the bottom line. William Finn says that when he was offered the Playwrights Horizons Musical Theatre Lab production of In Trousers, "We were doing it as a lark. They expected it to die and we expected it to die. There was no money for anything. The set was a piece of cloth. We could only rehearse after the performance downstairs, so we worked from eleven at night to three in the morning. I went over to Michael Starobin, the orchestrator, who had only just left Bennington, and I said, 'Will you orchestrate the show for thirty-five dollars?' And he said, 'I won't take anything less than fifty!' "

One of the best ways to find an agent is for the writer to approach one who represents other playwrights close to his style and sensibilities. Of course, it helps if a mutual acquaintance or a client makes a recommendation. But if the writer has something solid to sell—an upcoming production, an invitation to a reading at a first-rate house—a good query letter, even coming in cold, will catch the agent's eye.

The *Dramatists Guild Annual Directory* lists agents, together with the plays they have represented each season. The membership desk of the Guild has information on writers' agents. The Society of Author's Representatives will make membership lists and addresses available to inquiring writers.

The first approach to the agent should be by letter. "I ask for a letter of inquiry because it will eliminate the crazies," Earl Graham explains. "It will eliminate plays that don't interest me or seem unsalable from the description. For everything else, I answer saying, 'Send it in with a self-addressed stamped envelope and allow six weeks.' " If several agents are being approached simultaneously, they should be so informed, as some agents will not be willing to read a script on that basis.

If the agent responds positively to the script, a meeting will follow and, from then on, the scenario depends on the needs and tastes of the agent and the writer. Some writers wish to be informed about the status of every submission. Some only want to be involved if there is a sale. The legendary agent, Kay Brown, told Earl Graham, years ago, "Don't put writers on a roller coaster by telling them all the moves because you'll make them crazy."

Everyone agrees that having an agent does not mean that writers can stop hustling on their own. "A lot of times," says Graham, "an author can hang out and get to know the people in a company and he can get a production of his play. If you have an author who is able to get his ass on the street, it makes sense to let him do that." Writers should continue to enter their scripts in competitions, submit them to festivals, and attend conferences. Agents might take over submissions to commercial producers and regional theaters, but writers must continue to seek out additional available opportunities on their own.

Some agents require a written contract. Others will proceed on the basis of a handshake. Large agencies have "agency papers." Graham explains: "When an agent negotiates a contract for a play, he gets locked in as the agent for the play for time immemorial. Agency papers, which specify that you represent everything a writer writes over a period of three years or so, are used mostly by large agencies because an author's agent often gets fairly close to the client, and if he is with a big agency and he either gets canned or quits, he takes the client. So that that can't happen, the larger agencies have papers which are signed by that agent and usually three others at the company. The client is bound to that agency unless three of the four signatories for the agency leave the company, in which case there is a release. Most of the independent agents don't have that because you are talking about a long-term thing and if it works, it works. Working on a new play is so involved, it would be very hard to work with an author you don't feel comfortable with."

The one indisputable fact of life is that wherever a group of playwrights can be spotted huddled over a bottle of Scotch, they are not talking esthetics, they are not sharing inspirations—they are complaining about their agents.

The Dramatists Guild minimum basic contract only covers first-class productions, and in certain cases, off-Broadway. Unlike the actors, writers are not protected by their trade organization when they work for an off-off-Broadway, workshop, or showcase producer.

Any writer who is not represented and is entering into a production agreement can call the Guild for advice. The minimum basic contract can be used as a guide to any contract in any situation.

At a Dramatists Guild symposium on authors' rights, Executive Director David E. LeVine advised playwrights as follows:

One might divide all the contractual rights into seven categories, five of which should be in any contract you make for any production, and the other two of which have to do with compensation and perhaps should be omitted in various kinds of workshop productions. Of the first five, the most important is the artistic integrity provision guaranteeing that no changes, alterations, or omissions will be made to a play without your consent. You should never not have that clause. You should never permit that clause to be diluted by the words "not to be unusually withheld" or "by consultation rather than approval." You own that play, and that clause should go into every contract you make for its production.

An important flip side of that clause is a clause insuring that any incidental ideas or contributions made by other participants in the production become your property the instant that they are made. Second in importance is a clause guaranteeing and specifying that you own that property and that you are granting a particular license for a particular production only; and that you reserve all other rights. If there is to be any additional participation by the producer in any of the ancillary rights, it is to be very carefully spelled out and limited.

This brings me to the fourth category of the five I mentioned: You shouldn't grant a lot of rights together. You should grant either first class or off-Broadway or resident theater. You may want to grant a rider which permits the producer subsequently to pick up another of the rights, but you shouldn't enter into a contract which permits him to produce the play in various places—on and off Broadway, in a roof theater, etc.

The fifth is a kind of miscellaneous pickup clause. Every contract should have a clause prohibiting the producer from assigning rights he may have been previously granted; you want to know who's going to be producing your play and whether he gets a billing credit. You want a guarantee that if you select an agent, that agent can represent you. You want a guarantee that any dispute arising from the production can be settled by arbitration. It's neither cheap nor quick to settle anything by arbitration, but it is much cheaper and quicker than going to law.

The other two clauses you may include, particularly in the case of a larger production, guarantee you compensation. You should get an advance. You should establish a relationship dealing with the kind of royalties and/or fees that will be paid to you for the use of your play. Obviously, you should try to base your compensation on a percentage of the receipts taken in by the producer. This not only protects you from loss due to inflation but it also makes you more secure in that you will not be connecting yourself to the producer's bookkeeping or his break-even figure as it passes through bookkeeping.*

---

*David E. LeVine, "Authors' Rights: A Review of the Dramatist's Standing," *The Dramatists Guild Quarterly* (Winter 1982).

Certainly, when the writer is working off-off-Broadway, where his aims are not primarily financial, he should make sure that he is well protected in all other areas. Those clauses that touch upon career advancement, creative controls, ego boosting, and incidental perks are all the more important in off-off-Broadway contracts because that is all the writer is getting.

As well as the protection offered by the artistic integrity clause covering changes, alterations, or omissions, writers should have mutual control with producers over the choice of directors and casting. They should be protected in the area of billing; their names should appear in all publicity, press releases, advertisements, and flyers in type no smaller than anyone else's. The house complimentary ticket policy should be spelled out: writers ought to receive at least, free tickets for themselves to all performances, for any professional contacts they wish to invite, and for a specified number of personal guests for each week of the run.

The off-off-Broadway production is intended to be a learning experience for writers, and that education includes all aspects of their profession. Even if they have an agent, they should read their contracts carefully before signing, ask questions, insist on clarification, and ensure that their rights are protected.

The relationship between the Actors' Equity Association (AEA) and off-off-Broadway has been a long and complicated one. In order to understand it, some essential facts have to be clear. First of all, the Dramatists' Guild and the Society of Stage Directors and Choreographers are not unions; they are trade organizations of self-employed workers. Therefore, they have no obligation to protect their members in every area of their working lives, and certainly not in nonpaying areas.

Equity, however, is a union. It was formed to protect the working conditions and wages of its members, who are always employees. Even off-off-Broadway, writers own their plays and are protected by the copyright law. Producers negotiate contracts with writers; therefore, writers' rights are defined. But Equity members are working without salary or employment benefits, and the union, from the beginning, has had a responsibility to see that such work was compensated and to prevent actors from performing under unacceptable conditions. This is why directors and writers have always been able to volunteer their services off-off-Broadway, but

Equity members had to be covered with a contract of some kind.

Because there never was a body of nonprofit producers, because the writers and directors were not represented by their respective organizations in this area, because Equity regarded its members' work for no salary a subsidy, the Equity off-off-Broadway contracts were not negotiated through collective bargaining. They were unilaterally prepared by the actors' union and are subject only to the approval of Equity's council and membership.

This lack of any negotiating process led to years of disputes, confusion, and legal hassles. Even today, the SSDC and the Dramatists Guild have no jurisdiction over off-off-Broadway, the producers have created no central negotiating body, and Equity contracts are still unilaterally created. The Equity codes covering off-off-Broadway comprise a body of rules governing conditions under which union members may work. Equity solely determines whether and to whom a code contract should be issued, what kind of contract that should be, and if any of the provisions are violated, abridged, or modified, Equity may withdraw the contract without notice and without legal proceedings.

At present, there are several Equity contracts covering off-off-Broadway.

The Basic Showcase Code allows union actors to appear in exchange for carfare reimbursement, provided the production budget is within certain limits, the number of performances is limited, the seating capacity of the theater is below one hundred, ticket prices are controlled, and any outside financial support or funding is minimal.

The Funded Nonprofit Theatre Code is available to nonprofit seasonal producers whose earned and unearned incomes fall below a certain point annually. Under this code, the actors are paid anywhere from $72 to $600 for the entire rehearsal and playing period. As the nonprofit theater's box office and funding grows, the theater moves from tier to tier, with the actor's remuneration growing at each level. This code also controls the number of performances, the seating capacity, and the admission prices of participating theaters.

One step above these codes is the letter-of-agreement, available to nonprofit seasonal producers who have grown beyond the code limitations, yet who still fall within certain Equity-established guidelines. The letter-of-agreement is written for each theater individually and calls for payment to actors of minimal salaries on a weekly basis.

The mini-contract pays salaries, plus contributions to the union's pension and welfare plans, for rehearsals and performances, although the salaries are scaled down for theaters with less than one hundred seats. It is designed along the lines of the contract covering off-Broadway productions. There is a differential between the salaries paid if the run is a limited one, as in a subscription series at a nonprofit house, or an unlimited one, as in a single production in a smaller house.

Copies of the standard contracts can be obtained from Equity, and actors should study them and learn their rights. Such areas as casting procedures, rehearsal conditions, performance schedules, publicity, and advertising are spelled out in detail. Actors should be aware of the clauses specifically written in recognition of the fact that they are not getting paid. Rehearsals, for instance, are supposed to be scheduled "at the actor's convenience." An Equity member may leave the production at any time during rehearsal or performance. The actor's photo must be displayed in the front of the house. The program must include a biography. The actor's name must be included on all flyers, posters, brochures, invitations, etc., and if any names are used in paid newspaper or broadcast advertisements, other than the names of the theater, play, and author, then the names of all Equity members of the company must be included also. The producer must supply complimentary tickets to franchised agents, bona fide casting directors, professional producers, choreographers, and directors. Paid-up members of Equity are to be admitted, at no cost, on a standby basis so the actor can be seen by all his friends.

Every contract calls for the election of an Equity Deputy to protect the actors' rights and report any alleged infringements to the union. The deputy is elected by the union members of the company at a meeting during the first rehearsal. Young non-Equity actors can be cast in a showcase code production. However, only Equity members can sign the mini-contract, and if a nonunion member is cast, he is immediately eligible for membership.

These contracts are all written on a "most favored nations" basis, which means that all actors receive the same remuneration and rights and "where any person is engaged in any capacity for a single Code production and receives remuneration, all AEA members shall be likewise compensated." For this reason, actors who know their rights do not need agents to negotiate union contracts for them.

The conversion rights clause has been an important part of the off-off-Broadway contract since its inception. Equity has claimed that actors, working without salary or employment benefits, are entitled to this form of compensation. Since the showcase production allows the playwright to revise and improve his play, to expose it to commercial producers, and enhance the possibility of future productions, the actors have a right to share in those benefits.

Accordingly, the code states that if a new play, originally produced as a showcase, is subsequently produced under another Equity contract, those actors who participated in the showcase are entitled to an offer to perform the same role in the commercial production or to receive a "buy-out." (Originally, this was three weeks salary. It has increased with each revision of the code.) The code calls for a similar obligation to the actors if the play is subsequently produced in another medium (e.g., motion pictures, television, videotape, etc.).

In the beginning of off-off-Broadway, Equity's thinking was that only the playwright could assure such a commitment to actors. After all, the showcase producer did not own the play. In the early days, he did not normally participate in the play's future and had little control over what happened to it after the showcase production. The eventual commercial producer was not a signatory to the showcase contract and so could not be held legally responsible. Therefore, Equity required the playwright to be a party to the showcase agreement between producer and actors, and it was the playwright who could be held responsible to see that the obligations to actors were met. The code stated that "the [showcase] Producer and Author [must] acknowledge a lien against the play, generated as a result of services rendered by AEA members rehearsing and performing the play in the Code production."

This caused a great deal of friction between actors and playwrights and, as some saw it, left those who should have been responsible—the producers—off the hook. Since code contracts are granted at the discretion of Equity, the union had ways of enforcing its rights. If the playwright refused to sign the code, the production was threatened with cancellation, often after rehearsals had begun and shortly before the first performance, when both the writer and producing organization were most vulnerable. If a production moved and the original actors did not recieve the compensation due them under the conversion clause, Equity would not process the bond, thus not allowing the actors to begin rehearsals, unless either the playwright or the commercial producer came up with the buy-outs required in the code. Equity could refuse to allow future showcase productions of a delinquent writer's plays.

The conflict came to a head in 1980 when Equity added regional theater productions to those covered by the conversion clause. As far as the writers were concerned, this extension seriously impaired the marketability of their plays. Regional theaters often have resident companies on annual salaries. Many theaters could not afford to produce a play burdened with the requirement of importing New York actors, paying their transportation and living expenses, or paying them salaries for not playing the roles. This meant that the writer would have to come up with the buy-outs for the entire showcase company if a play was to have any life outside of New York after the original production. Writers bristled, refused to sign, demanded to be heard. Equity refused to negotiate and the conflict ended in the courts.

Six playwrights (James Childs, Barbara S. Graham, Romulus Linney, David Mamet, John Olive, and Michael Weller), supported by the Dramatists Guild and the Society of Author's Representatives, brought an antitrust suit against Actors' Equity Association, involving Equity codes for showcase productions of plays in off-off-Broadway and similar theaters.

In December 1981 a consent judgment and settlement agreement was announced. The judgment prohibited Equity from requiring playwrights to assume obligations for conversion payments. It also imposed a four-year limitation period on the obligation required of showcase producers for conversion payments. The settlement agreement also called for the creation of a committee of actors and playwrights to consider possible ways to handle conversion payments, including those with regional theaters.

Since that time, an Equity–LORT (League of Resident Theatre) Subsidiary Rights Trust Fund has been created. Under the current showcase code terms, the code producer is required to contribute a specified amount to this fund, which will satisfy the showcase producer's obligation in connection with a subsequent production of the play at a LORT playhouse.

*   *   *

The Society of Stage Directors and Choreographers has no collective bargaining agreement covering off-off Broadway, and directors and choreographers are free to work there on whatever terms they can get. SSDC does supply members with two sample agreements to be used as guides for their own negotiations.

The first sample agreement is a letter to be signed by the writer. It is intended to protect the director who comes on board early in the process, perhaps before a production contract has been offered. It assures the director that his contributions to the development of the script will be compensated, as follows:

In addition to the terms and conditions in the Agreement with the Producer, it is agreed that in consideration of your services and your contribution to the production, you shall have first option to direct any further production of this play.

In the event this play is subsequently moved or produced in a Broadway, off-Broadway, or middle theatre, it is agreed that you shall receive no less than the minimum compensation then prevailing as established by any agreement or regulation of the Society of Stage Directors and Choreographers, Inc.

In the event this play is subsequently moved or produced in a theatre where the Society of Stage Directors and Choreographers, Inc., has no jurisdiction, agreement, or regulation, then you shall be compensated under such terms as are mutually agreed upon.

However, playwright Terrence McNally, vice-president of the Dramatists Guild, who is opposed to writers executing this type of agreement, wrote:

The implications of a Guild member signing such a letter of agreement with a director are enormous. If the director became unavailable or you no longer wished to work with him on your play, it could cost you a lot of money. The letter of agreement is with the director, not with any present or future producer of your play. You will absorb any royalties to be paid to the original director out of your own pocket. A play encumbered in writing with the services of a director may have difficulty in finding another director or producer.

Do nothing until you have spoken with the Guild.*

*Terrence McNally, *Dramatists Guild Newsletter* (January 1985).

Since the SSDC has never attempted to enforce this agreement and the writers have never consolidated their objections, the matter has never come to a head. Most of the time, directors are expected to do readings and work on plays in the living room stage with no guarantees and no payment, much the same as actors and writers do. Only when the writer has signed a production contract is the director covered with an agreement between himself and the theater.

The SSDC model off-off-Broadway agreement between directors and producing organizations calls for a fee to the director, plus royalties should the play be extended beyond its announced run, plus payment to the SSDC pension and welfare program. It also guarantees the director first option to direct any subsequent production in which the original producer continues to be a participant or, if replaced, the full fee applicable is to be paid. It also guarantees the original director a percentage of any subsequent film or television production, provided the original producer is involved.

Lighting designers, set designers, and costume designers are members of United Scenic Artists, Local 829 of the International Brotherhood of Painters and Allied Trades. This union has no basic agreement covering off-off-Broadway, nor does it restrict its members' work in that arena. However, if a member negotiates a letter of agreement with an off-off-Broadway house and files that letter with the union, the union will support the designer if there is any default on the producer's behalf. In addition, the designer can ask the off-off-Broadway house to contribute the required percentage of his fee to the union pension and welfare fund, which also covers crucially important health insurance. This is useful to most designers since there is a minimum fee requirement of $1,000 per quarter which they must accumulate in order to be covered by the plan.

A designer drawing up an agreement on his own behalf should see that the following areas are covered:

1. The fee and how it is to be paid
2. Pension and welfare contributions
3. The designer's rights if the production moves
4. Billing
5. Out-of-pocket expenses

6. In those rare cases where it applies, traveling and per diem expenses

In the end, Earl Graham points out, the writer of the off-off-Broadway play that attracts commercial interest, "is going to pay dearly for that showcase production. The first thing a commercial producer says is, 'What are the strings? Who has to be paid off?' The writer has a property now that carries a mortgage to all the actors that appeared in the play, the director, the designers, to the showcase theater, which has a percentage. You have to take into consideration all those arrangements you've made and the more strings you've got, the harder it is to do. For example, a lot of showcase theaters ask for billing at a specified percentage of the title in every program forevermore. I look at that and say, 'Wait a minute. I've got to be saddled with that on every contract I negotiate on this play.' It makes sense that, if the play goes to Broadway within a period of time, the Broadway audience should have the benefit of knowing that this showcase theater helped the playwright. But if you are talking about a Broadway production twelve years later, and four other theaters have produced it in the meantime, are you going to give them all credit? The writer has to remember that there is going to be a lien against this property after the showcase, and if the baggage is too great, the commercial producer is going to say, 'I'll pass on that play and do some other play.' "

It is important that every artist working off-off-Broadway know his rights, define them in advance with the producer, sign a written contract, use the resources and guidance that his trade organization or union offers. Not only will he get whatever everyone else in the field gets and whatever there is to be had—which may not be much—but he will lay the groundwork for whatever success is ahead.

"The Dining Room," says David Trainer, "was a perfect example of a show that nobody thought anything was going to happen to. Andre Bishop claims, in retrospect, that he knew at the reading we would have a great success, and that may be true. I always thought it could be wonderful, but a hit is another matter. Nobody should pretend they know what is going to be a hit. Good, I can tell you. Successful, that's something else. But, in fact, contractually, it was all arranged so that when it started to roll onto success, there was no discussion about who was to get what. It was all arranged ahead of time."

Inevitably, this approach contributes to more creative work. The artist will feel better about herself. The producer will respect her more. And there will be less energy lost in feelings of resentment and deprivation. From the onset, the artist must prepare herself for the creative problems ahead. They can be more easily resolved if there is no chance that the waters will be muddied with matters that should have been handled on paper at the beginning of the process.

8

Preproduction:
Directors and Designers

Once the script is ready to go into rehearsal, a production date has been set, and contracts have been signed, the director hires his staff: set designer, costume designer, lighting designer, sound designer, and stage manager.

Usually, the director leans toward people he has worked with before, but the theater's artistic director has some say in the matter and he will push for designers who have worked for the theater before. For a young director on his initial assignment at an off-off-Broadway house, where budgets are limited and there are always hidden problems, working with designers who know the space and the routines, who have connections with the administration, is not a bad idea.

The design process for a new play is the same as it would be for a revival but with some important considerations. There is no precedent. There are no previous productions, no past designs, no recordings of old ground plans, no historical texts or photos to help or limit the designers' imaginations. The director and designers all come to the conference table with only the script to guide them.

The playwright will be present at the meeting. What he has written is new and unique it is hoped. Perhaps his vision is difficult to comprehend or his execution faulty. The designers will need to lean all the more on the director for guidance, and the playwright will learn about his play as the designers work. Sometimes, the design changes the play. Sometimes, the designers lead the director to new levels of comprehension of the text. Sometimes the uniqueness of the writer's voice leads the designers down uncharted paths in their own work. Always, the collaborative nature of theater is such that, if there is a chink in the foundation or a sloppy piece of work anywhere along the way, the entire structure can collapse.

The foundation of everyone's work is the writer's story line. If that is strong, valid, and clearly defined, it will guide the director to a production concept that will come out in the designers' work.

The writers of Fiddler on the Roof might say that their play is about a dairyman who needs to marry off his daughters and deals with the conflict between his traditional desires for them and their desires for themselves. In the end, the conflict enlarges the dairyman and enables him to confront the changing world. That is a solid, succinct story line. It indicates who the hero is, what his conflict is, and what change emerges from the experience.

It will lead the talented director to a production concept that makes a more general, perhaps metaphorical, and potentially strong visual statement. Jerome Robbins, the director of Fiddler, has stated that he thought the play was about the dissolution of a way of life.

If the designers then take the writer's story line and the director's concept to the drawing board, they find some specifics with which to begin. They know they have to establish a world first; they know in the end it has to be dissolved. They have a sense of movement and direction. The very word, dissolution, gives them a clue to tone. They know the vision is nostalgic and full of longing. Still, the hero will overcome the conflict and that controls some of their artistic choices.

In his concept, the director has defined for the designers the nature of the characters' relationship to the outside world. Is it a benign world? Is it a hostile world which the characters are battling? The stage directions might read that the play is set in Central Park, but Central Park on a Sunday afternoon to lovers is different from the park at dusk to the lost stranger who finds himself alone and threatened.

Since the production concept attempts to lead the designers to thoughts of textures and colors and resonances, the director's language will suddenly fill with adjectives and visual images. (And the playwright's jaw falls in shock. All those overblown phrases the director made him cut, everything that was ruled out as too descriptive, gets passed on to the designers.)

Set designer Janice Davis tells about a director who wanted a room to look like "a cluttered costume jewelry box." She knew immediately what to do. She had worked for a director of *Hello, Dolly!* who asked for a set which would remind the audience of old sepia prints. She designed a production of *Carnival* based on a director's request that the landscape look like a Corot painting. Certain visual images reveal what directors want without telling designers how to give it to them.

It is important for the director to tell the designers what the play is about, who the hero is, what happens to that hero, what the point of view is, and what the tone of the evening should be. Designers want pictures. They want a sense of progression. They want to hear adjectives. The adjectives the director uses to describe the script can also be used to describe the set. *Company*, which is cool, hip, urban, cynical, and modern, was brilliantly designed by Boris Aronson in a shining chrome and glass structure with a now-famous working elevator. *Oklahoma* would be described as romantic, rural, soft; those words lead to the colors and tones of the set, costumes, and lights.

The designers can help the director by pushing him to talk in these terms. The set designer does not ask, "What color do you want this sofa?" Instead, he asks, "Where do these people shop? How much money do they have? What is the room used for? How do they feel about it?" The lighting designer does not start the conversation by asking how many follow spots are needed. She wants to know whether this play is set in reality or in memory, through whose eyes we see the experience, whether the vision is loving or harsh.

In fact, the designers are doing to the director what the director did to the writer at the beginning of the play development process; they are asking questions to get the director to describe what he wants, probing beneath the text to uncover pictures, using the playwright's words, the director's images, and their pencils to arrive at the production concept.

This is done in a series of meetings, initially with the set designer alone, at which the talk about the script should be as far-ranging, informal, and interactive as were the meetings between writer and director in the living room stage. Once there is a merging of minds there is time to talk about mechanics: the director's blocking plans, which will create the ground plan (or vice versa), set changes, sight lines, storage space, prop needs, etc.

*   *   *

What happens when there is a clash of visions between director and designer? They work it out, just like the director and writer did. This is a collaboration, not a boss–employee relationship.

I once worked on a script that took place in a basement apartment. The central character constantly referred to it as a cell, and to his life as a prison. The set designer immediately grasped these images. He arrived at our first meeting, bubbling with ideas and loaded down with sketches. That was his first mistake. Designers should never get committed to ideas, and certainly should not talk about them, until they have heard the director out. They should never, ever, arrive at an initial meeting with sketches.

The designer pictured a set that was the image of a cell. It would be an abstract suggestion of the basement room constructed out of pipes and bars. The stage would be perfect for the bleak, despairing world of Samuel Beckett.

I was horrified. The prison the character kept referring to was internal. If the real world was a duplication of the inner world, there was no conflict in the play. More than that, there was a great deal of humor in the play; how could you be funny in a set like that? I wanted the actors to have lots of business with real coffee cups and bags of garbage. I wanted the audience to have a firm hold on the real world so that the character's pain could be seen for what it was. This design left no room for the play. A set is supposed to establish an expectation which the actors will then fulfill, not give away the punch line at first sight.

Both the designer and I left that meeting in despair because we seemed so far apart. In a few days, he returned with a design that was brilliant: a room filled with the clutter of books and props, an actual kitchen unit with working sink; everything I needed to stage the play. However, he created the room out of three utterly straight walls, as opposed to the jutting corners, angles, arches, curves, nooks, and crannies designers eagerly use to make the set more interesting. By wiping out all that detail and angle, the designer created a realistic room which had the underlying quality of a cell.

It worked splendidly for the production, was related to what he saw in the play, taught me something about the script, and was a far better set than either of us could have come up with independently.

*   *   *

Once the set designer has something down on paper—rough sketches, drawings, research photos, fabric swatches—he meets with the director again. Then he does a rendering and, if the use of space is complex or there are elements hard to visualize, a miniature model.

With these complete, all the designers (set, costume, light, and sound) are invited to a production meeting. It is imperative that the designers coordinate their efforts early and form a visual team. This can only be achieved through interaction. They must all hear the director define his concept, explain the story line, outline the movement, discuss the set. They must all share reactions and impulses.

A successful production looks, feels, and seems like it came out of one head; that effect can be achieved only by the merging of images and the chance to bounce ideas off one another around the table.

If the production concept is sound and clearly outlined, it will control all the work that is to come. It will guarantee that all the designers are working on the same play and protect everyone from mistakes in moments of crisis.

We did a play at JRT called *Unlikely Heroes*, based on three short stories by Philip Roth: *Defender of the Faith*, *Epstein*, and *Eli, the Fanatic*. The evening consisted of three separate one-acters, but the secret to making the production work was to find a through-line so that there was a connection between each act and a cumulative build. The adaptations stayed close to the stories. Each play was narrated by a central character who, from time to time, stepped out of the dramatic action and addressed the audience. This allowed the script to retain Roth's own voice, but it made it difficult for an audience to relate to plays that were still in story form.

Defender of the Faith is about an army private who gets his sergeant to bend the rules of basic training by manipulating the sergeant's guilt about his lapsed Judaism. *Epstein* is about a man who has lost his son and dives into a comic midlife crisis. He has an affair with the widow next door, which results in an imaginary sexual disease, which leads to a real heart attack. *Eli, the Fanatic* is about an assimilated, suburban Jew who feels strange stirrings toward the past when his wife becomes pregnant. As she goes into labor, he assumes the clothing of a Hasid his embarrassed neighbors have been trying to evict.

All three plays are about paternal relationships, and in each case, the father figure starts off removed from his past. Through the acquiring of a son, or the loss of a son, he connects with his tradition, his identity, and his soul. Thus, we have a workable story line; it tells us who the hero is, what happens to him, and how he changes.

Taking this one step further, the designers and I decided that the play was about the alienated man who bonds with his heritage and, in so doing, his inner life becomes richer and more colorful. That certainly offers clues about the growth and changes required in the look of the plays and the links connecting them.

As it happens, *Defender* is cool and cynical. *Epstein* is manically funny, and *Eli* is passionate and heart wrenching. So there is an emotional and dramatic progression, which justified what we wished to do visually, and would also help the audience grow comfortable with the storytelling form of the evening.

We decided to allow the production effects to grow with the inner life of the characters and the dramatic progression of the stories. The first play was done on a virtually bare stage, before black drapes, with colorless lighting, and no music or sound. The actors were costumed, but the play required only army uniforms so the color palette was prescribed. It looked like a reading and allowed the audience to accept the narrations. It would start the evening on a low-keyed note that, we hoped, would vastly increase the dramatic impact at the end when Eli dons Hasidic garb.

For the second play, we introduced more furniture and sound effects. We got a little richer in our colors and more fanciful in the costume design. And the third play was a visual blossoming. An enormous set piece was added to the stage. Incidental music was used throughout. Lighting was rich and, of course, the dramatic climax of the play dealt with an exotic costume. By that point, we expected the audience to be so used to the narrative techniques that they would not be jarred by these more theatrical effects. The evening would have a visual and dramatic development that emerged from the story line.

We were pleased with our work and each designer went off to his individual task with a confident picture of the whole.

Just as a solid story saves the writer in moments of crisis, so the good production concept works for designers. Our moment came the first time we rehearsed *Defender* on the unfinished set. Nothing was painted. There were no costumes or lights, and the actors arrived to find a bare stage, hung with still-wrinkled blacks, a desk, and a chair.

"That's it?" they muttered. "That's what we've got to work with?"

Immediately, there were whispered complaints about working off-off-Broadway where there was never enough money to do things right and it always looked like amateur night. The set designer and I, seated in the house, could not defend what we saw with enthusiasm.

"It's not finished," I apologized. "The floor still has to be painted."

"How's the floor going to be painted?" asked one actor.

"Black," wisecracked another.

The designer curdled in his seat. The rehearsal went miserably. After the actors left, he and I stared at the bare stage in silence.

Finally, he said, "You know, I saw some panels in the shop. I could paint them and hang them here and here . . ." He was on the stage, pacing, dressing the set. Actors have moments of panic. So do directors and designers. When writers panic, they throw everything but the kitchen sink into the script, but that never solves the problems. The designer was doing the same thing. It only lasted a second.

We stared at each other with the identical thought: "Wait a minute. We've got a concept here. We know what we are doing. Let's not start adding panels and set pieces. Let's not fix until we know we've got a problem."

And the strength of a solid production concept saved us from making a major mistake. Once the floor was painted beige, a sharp contrast with the curtains, the actors popped into the forefront. Arden Fingerhut, the noted lighting designer, claims that there is nothing more theatrically effective than well-lit actors in front of blacks. In *Defender*, the audience had a lot of faces to see, a lot of words to hear, a lot of information to deal with. They did not need more visual stimulation. Once the actors were costumed, once the stage was lit, it looked perfect for the cool quality of that particular script. And it certainly paid off in the context of the entire show.

The strength of the concept gave me the confidence to better deal with the actors. Actors need to know what is going on, what is expected of them, what the total picture will look like. I was so frightened by my first look at the set I had answered them with evasion. Once I renewed my own confidence, I told them what the design team was doing. It made sense and even clued them into a progression of acting styles that would mesh with the production concept.

Everything eventually came together. Of course, as is the way off-off-Broadway, we got one nice review in the *Village Voice* and then faded into oblivion. But I still relish the triumph over that moment of crisis.

All this only happened because we had worked so well as a team. The production concept represented a uniting of visions. The set designer was confident enough in the work of his colleagues to leave spaces in the design for them to fill. No single designer overwhelmed the process, and the director served as a conduit and mediator once he established the basic concept and essential needs of the production.

And what is the writer doing during all this? Director Pamela Berlin says, "Every show dictates its own rules, given who the writer is and the needs of the production, your relationship with the writer, and all sorts of things. There are no hard-and-fast rules about how much the writer gets involved on the nitty-gritty level with the design elements. In the case of *Gillian*, Michael Brady didn't, and he felt comfortable with that. I've worked on other shows where I've absolutely wanted more of the playwright's input or shows where the playwright demanded more input.

"In this particular case, I picked Michael's brain about what he imagined. He always had it in his head that the house would be glassed in, and some of the inside of the house would be onstage too, along with the porch and the beach. Among other things, the space precluded doing that, and to tell you the truth, it would have been wrong. It would have been too solid. So we just had a suggestion of the house. From the staged reading on, it was clear to me what the set would consist of, no more and no less, and that is what it became."

The writer is certainly a member of the team. He is invited to all the production meetings. He listens, he watches, he takes notes. If he has any problems, he meets with the director afterward to talk them over. But the truth of the matter is that, if a successful physical production is to be unified by a single vision, it will be the director's not the writer's. The writer may find this a difficult adjustment to make, but his play is out of his hands. The director serves to blend all points of view, and the writer represents only one of these. His vision is restricted to the pictures in his head, which can limit everyone else's possibilities.

The director must be free to make mistakes. He must be free to try ideas out on his colleagues, follow them in any direction, ask questions and spontaneously respond to the input.

What works onstage is not necessarily what is true or real. Things look different onstage, under lights, and designers know it. Platinum blond hair, which might appear tawdry and harsh in daylight, glows with innocence under stage lights. A dress made out of cheap fabric, with no frills and nothing to recommend it offstage, looks elegant and expensive onstage because the line is so dramatic and the color works so well on the set. The designers are well trained in this regard. The writer must learn to trust them. The specifics rooted in his imagination may have helped him to write the play, but they will only restrict the design.

One of the most difficult adjustments facing designers of new plays, and their primary responsibility, is to comprehend the playwrights' sense of the world and the spaces where plays are now premiered. These two, as we have seen, are usually related.

Massive box sets filled with architectural detail, patterned wallpaper, arched entrances, and grand stairways, do not work off-off-Broadway, where stages are tiny, ceilings are low, audiences are close, and seating capacity is one hundred or less. The taste for such sets grew out of the 1940s' Broadway sensibility, and they were designed for houses with lush lobbies and massive hanging chandeliers, and one or two balconies, that had enough distance, height, and size to give them perspective. They were right for playwrights and audiences who hungered for the replication of a very different reality. The Broadway set for John Van Druten's *The Voice of the Turtle*, for example, was such an accurate recreation of a Manhattan apartment, complete with working kitchen and foldout bed, that the zealous press agent reported that if the phones were connected so they could order groceries, the actors would never have to leave the stage.

No matter how good that design would look today, when the

actors arrived, the stage would seem cluttered. The audience in a tiny house would be dwarfed and intimidated. The lack of height and distance would make the actors seem too tall for the walls. The script would be overwhelmed.

More than that, the world of John Van Druten and Lillian Hellman and Robert Sherwood was one in which right was right, wrong was wrong, real was real, and in case anyone was still in doubt, the central character explained it all before the final curtain. Sure, such plays demanded solid superstructures for sets. The designers' visions were attuned to the writers' perspectives.

But writers like Christopher Durang and Wendy Wasserstein and David Mamet see the world differently—full of cinematic edits and flashes and dissolves. They hear in abbreviations and speak in shorthand. Their world moves rapidly. Nothing is stable. Relationships are transitory. Surfaces are deceptive. The differences between right and wrong are vague. Reality can go up in smoke in an instant.

Designers must be able to key into the writer's sense of the world. There must be a relationship between the writer's vision, his rhythm, his ear, and the way the play looks. Modern writers deal with suggestion, hints, and ambivalence. The world they see is not solid. Their plays are done in small theaters, and the writing has been affected by the space.

For the designer, texture, color, and detail can do the trick. Walls can be outlined, architecture simplified, furniture reduced to essentials. One chair can create a room in the mind of today's audiences, provided it is the right chair. An ankle bracelet reads in a tiny house. The scenery has to change at the writer's pace. The lights have to be controlled by the rhythms of the script. The costumes have to make their point quickly.

Writers whose plays get produced are in sync with today's space, time, and audiences. Designers who wish to work with these writers must abandon the sensibilities of a previous era.

David Mamet's *American Buffalo* was a success in its off-off-Broadway premiere at the Theatre at St. Clements. It was a success years later in an off-Broadway revival starring Al Pacino. Yet the original Broadway production, despite a brilliant performance by Robert Duvall, was a failure. It was not the fault of the script or the acting. A big part of the problem was the set.

How could the director and designer have imagined that this

play could have worked in a set, supposedly a junk shop, which was filled from corner to corner, from floor to ceiling, with huge tires, planks of lumber, discarded furniture, rusted machine parts? The set was massive, the texture was rough-hewn, the colors were dark, the hold on reality was firm and strong.

Yet, the essence of the play is its smallness. The characters' dreams are petty. Their relationship is casual, specifically denying each other importance. The plot they are hatching requires secrecy. The dialogue is based on their inarticulateness. Their hold on reality is tenuous.

The set had no relation to the writer's vision. One of the obvious clues to the misconception was that, in the midst of all this junk, the entire play was blocked around one desk and two chairs. Clearly, that was all the playwright needed.

If the director is unable to tell the designer how the actors will use the set, it is a sure sign that the set will end up as background and not an integral part of the production. This is an indication that the play is being done in the wrong space, that the production concept does not emerge organically from the writer's story line, that the design is going to sink the script. At that point, the designer or the director or the producer should stop and wonder what is going on, and figure out how to get back on track.

David Trainer describes the design process for The Dining Room: "Playwrights Horizons gave me Frances Aronson to do the lights because she knew the technical resources of the upstairs studio. Most of the lights were actually headlights in coffee cans. That's how rudimentary it was. There were a few specials and a few actual theater instruments, but Frances knew what was there and what could be done and Andre wanted her because of that. I chose the set and costume designers and I had a strong sense of what I wanted it to look like—not so much specifically, though eventually it was very specific. I knew how I wanted it to feel. The image I kept using was that the set had to be a speck of dust in a mote of sunlight. Glowing, was the word I used.

"I called some people that I knew and asked them to recommend people. Eight set designers brought their portfolios in, and Loren Sherman was clearly the most talented, but I sort of passed over him the first time because he seemed disagreeable. His idea originally was that there should be a Plexiglas table that came down out of the flys. So, I went back to him and said, 'I would really like you to do the show. I think you're wonderful but we're going to do it my way. Right?' He said, 'Yes, of course.' And then he was wonderful to work with. But he came from Chicago and he kept doing these models that had this timbered lakefront look to them. Pete grew up in Buffalo and I grew up in West Hartford, Connecticut. The play could take place as far west as Milwaukee, but it wasn't Chicago lakefront timber. And no matter what I'd say, I couldn't get him to see quite what it was. So I came home one day after arguing with him and called my mother and said, 'Ma, get the Polaroid camera and stand in the middle of the dining room and shoot all around the room.' Two days later, I said, 'This is the set,' and he said, 'Oh, now I see.' And that's what he did, took these Polaroids of my mother's dining room with the arched doorway and the sconces and the sideboard. Everybody in a certain kind of life has the same dining room, and my mother's house was a perfect example; the style, the relationships, the proportions.

"Also, Loren and I had agreed before that, even as we were trying to get the particulars, that we both loved Joseph Cornell boxes and the set should duplicate that sense of peering into something that held artifacts and looking at the implements. We basically used my mother's dining room and a Joseph Cornell box. The set had a little frame around it, a lip at the edge of the stage. If you looked through the frame, the walls were wider than the proscenium, which is one of the characteristics of a Cornell box. You look in and it is wide behind the frame. And the side walls were blank. They floated back from this frame. Only the back wall of the set was decorated and it had no paintings, just sconces and a mirror. What was interesting was that, when the reviews came out, people wrote about seeing ancestral portraits on the wall, when it was just a square box. We didn't want to illustrate the room. We wanted to do a room that suggested all rooms and knew the audience would project into that space.

"That was true of the costumes, too. They were simple generic clothes, and this was all intentionally worked out. I'd take a set of notes on every department and I'd give all the notes to everybody, and I'd use reference points to make sure what I said to the set designer was consistent with what I'd say to the costume designer. I'd work out the theory and they'd give me the particulars.

"Another image that I had was that, at the end of the play, I wanted everyone in the audience to want to come down and sit at that table. You should want to go back into that room. You should feel that comfortable there. I didn't want to overparticularize because particulars make it about 'them' not 'you.' There were certain people who were going to like The Dining Room no matter what you did, but I was concerned about the people who wouldn't like it, who don't like families, who don't feel comfortable in this world. We didn't want to exclude them. The director's job is to find the most common meeting ground. That goes back to the acting style. We wanted interesting human beings that the audience could connect to. We didn't want to overcharacterize the people. If the actors simply played the action, everyone would see their own grandmother or their father.

"The play appealed because everybody who had ever had dinner with their parents understood what was going on. It was a basic human experience; eating with your parents and being instructed about tradition and life."

The other designers key into the set and the director's concept and their work flows from these. Lighting frames, focuses, controls the mood. "To Gillian on Her 37th Birthday was a tricky play to light," says Pamela Berlin. "It's somewhat episodic. You have lots of different scenes and you have to bridge those scenes. You had a very spare set. You had to work in that space, which can be problematic. And it was up to the lighting to catch the texture of the play. It is a realistic play, but it is also very lyrical. Bob Thayer, the set designer, and I immediately went to Edward Hopper as a prototype in terms of the look and feel of the set. But it was Allen Lee Hughes's lighting and the music by Robert Dennis which made it miraculous."

With the minimal space and technical facilities available off-off-Broadway, sound design has become increasingly important because it provides information quickly and inexpensively. Music can create a place, a season, a tone much more efficiently than a new set can. It is often more subtle than lighting or costumes can be, and with modern writers who switch gears so rapidly, who are unafraid to mix reality and fantasy, subtlety and speed are essential to the designs.

In Caroline Emmons's When Petulia Comes, which was produced at Theatre Genesis, we had to deal with a fantasy figure who strolled in and out of scenes. She had to be defined as a fantasy, yet there was a reality scene continuing on the stage. A change of set was uncalled for, even a lighting change would have damaged the play's ability to work on two levels. We did not have a follow spot. We could not fly her in as we might have done on Broadway. And what was most ironic about the writer's touch was that this fantasy figure had a greater sense of reality than the other characters had, so to have dressed her in gauze would not have worked either.

The sound designer came up with a simple, exquisite solution. Every time the figure appeared, she was accompanied by the sound of wood chimes in the background. It was subtle. It was lovely. It was even funny. It did not disrupt the reality scene, yet it took the play into another dimension.

Sound can also help solve one of the perpetual problems of designing off-off-Broadway: working without a front curtain. Set changes, getting the actors on and off the stage, ending the scene, starting the show, all have to be solved in the design concept.

Actually, handling the final picture or the boffo curtain line is not such a problem and is a perfect example of the way the art form changes with the space. Most young writers, never having seen a play with a front curtain, do not write for them anymore.

In the forties, theater comedy was based on predictability and repetition. The seed was planted, and two lines later, there was the payoff. The gag was repeated and got a bigger laugh. At the end of the act, it was brought back to get the curtain down. Comedy was based on punch and the curtain line often needed the physical drop of the curtain to make its point.

Today's humor is based on unpredictability, is much slyer and sharper and off-the-wall. Humor is less designed to bounce off the startled faces of the society matrons serving as straight men, less dependent on the blackout or the burlesque drummer's roll to punch the gag home. When doing a revival of a forties comedy at an off-off-Broadway house, the lighting designer feels the loss of a curtain because nothing he does closes the act with such finality. But this is not a problem with plays by modern writers who write for fades and cross-fades, isolated moments, and quick glimpses. These can be underscored by lighting better than by a curtain.

The absence of the curtain has also been turned into a design asset in the emergence of the pre-set as part of the concept. Since there is no way of preventing the audience from seeing the set the moment they enter the theater, they may as well see something that prepares them for the play to follow. A great deal of thought, mainly the lighting designer's, goes into how much of the set is seen, what is focused upon, what the tone of the stage should be in the pre-set. Of course, that wonderful moment of surprise is lost; that moment when the curtain rises and the audience sees the fully lit set for the first time; when it gasps and applauds. Sorry, designers, that chance for glory may be gone forever; theater is changing.

Pre-show music has emerged as an asset, especially if the play is set in the past, or in unfamiliar territory, or is to be seen through a distinct pair of eyes. It is frequently played at a low level so that the audience can talk, and they usually do, but the effects are subliminal. If the same music is repeated at intermission, the audience will listen and, if they liked the show and the music comes up again after the curtain calls, they go out humming.

Music is also used to cover the awkwardness of set changes in full view of the audience. As off-off-Broadway audiences have grown more sophisticated and directors more demanding, it is less acceptable to have a stage manager in jeans appear between scenes to set the props. Directors often require that set changes, prop changes, furniture moves, be incorporated in the design scheme so that they can be handled by actors in character, thus not disrupting the audience's suspension of disbelief.

Getting the actors on and off the stage without a curtain is always a problem. Blackouts in tiny, ill-equipped theaters are dangerous. Sometimes the director and designer agree to establish a pattern that the audience learns to accept: they go to black at the end of the scene, then to blue allowing the actors to move on and off, then to black again before the next scene. If the director does not like that, or a similar scheme, and insists that the actors move in the dark, he had better allow plenty of time at the tech rehearsal, and the lighting designer should have some blue gels in his back pocket for an emergency call.

When budgets are limited, innovative designers learn to use what exists, or what they can steal. Playwrights Horizons started in a YMCA, where beds were in abundance. So, one stunning high-tech set was created out of bedsprings.

Breakfast with Les and Bess was designed by Dean Tschetter, who had done most of his work in television. "A key factor in selecting him was that he was able to get some scenery from the old 'Mickey Rooney Show,'" says Lee Kalcheim. "My play took place in a 1961 Central Park South apartment, and we had to show that the characters had a certain amount of wealth. So the walls and the doors came from old television scenery which Dean got. He was able to restructure them and build them into our set. Otherwise, the Hudson Guild couldn't have afforded them. Our budget was about three cents. We all had specific ideas about colors, but because you're not working for the Shuberts, you have to find these things. So a couch is found that's already covered in a right fabric and that's the way you go."

Since many small houses have raked seats and stages that are not raised, designers quickly learn that the stage floor becomes a major design element. A well-painted floor is a simple, inexpensive way of giving a set a sense of authenticity, even if the rest of the construction is made by suggestion and outline.

When reality is needed, the best place to look is at the theater itself. The lighting equipment—grids, instruments, cables—can be incorporated into the design. Fred Voelpel used the back windows of JRT in his design of a Manhattan loft for Mark Medoff's *The Halloween Bandit*. The circular staircase backstage at the Perry Street Theater gave Anne Bogart's *1951* a forbidding dimension. Government agents and FBI informers could watch the action from above in this musical about blacklisting.

The Anspacher Theatre is, perhaps, the most beautiful in the New York Public Theater complex. Yet it has two columns in the playing area that must be incorporated into the design. This was strikingly done by Bill Mikulewicz in his set for Thomas Babe's *A Prayer for My Daughter*. The play takes place in a police station, which needs to be ominous and overpowering, and those columns added just the right touch of size and power. Other designers have not coped with them as well. Yet, Joe Papp tells the story of the company's move to Broadway for a season of new American plays at the Broadhurst. The first in the series was Dennis Reardon's *The Leaf People*, and director Tom O'Horgan wanted to surround the action with natives; peering, watching, climbing trees. Designer John Conklin created an abstract jungle out of ropes, which actors could hang from, climb on, walk across, and of course, the ropes were supported by poles. When Papp saw the set he was astonished. "All these years, we've been complaining about the columns in the Anspacher. We move to Broadway and they add columns to the stage!"

One of the major assets that designers and directors have in houses like the Public, Cafe La MaMa, Theatre for the New City, and the original Manhattan Theater Club, is that there are several playing spaces to choose from, and the play can be set in the most suitable one. Circle Rep is a large house with flexible seating so that one production can be on a proscenium stage and the next in the round.

For props, furniture, special set pieces, New York has become such a center for film and television production that it has a community of rental houses that can supply anything. If the budget does not accommodate such costs, the larger nonprofit theaters often have extensive warehouses and will help out the smaller ones. Equity Library Theatre, since it does so many revivals, is a good source for period pieces, and the Public Theater, which has the largest supply, will lend anything not breakable.

Failing that, the designer goes to the cast, the theater's board of directors, the playwright's mother, his own apartment. David Trainer recalls that "the initial physical production of The Dining Room, upstairs at Playwrights—sets, lights, and costumes,—cost nine hundred dollars. Remak Ramsay lent several expensive props. There was a beautiful china centerpiece that cost thousands of dollars. I think it came from Andre's mother. That show always benefited by its associations. My mother's Polaroids made the set. Remak brought in a linen tablecloth. People had stuff in their bottom drawers."

Finally, there is always the abundance of the streets, courtesy of a constantly moving, constantly redecorating population. The problem is that something has to be grabbed at once or it will be gone in an hour. I once needed an old-fashioned commode for a set and spotted one, awaiting the Sanitation Department pickup, on my way to a dinner party. I had no choice but to ask my wife to give me a hand so that we could take it with us. The other guests never even blinked. They knew it meant I was in production.

Costume designers rarely get a chance to build an off-off-Broadway show from scratch. It is too expensive and time-consuming a process. So they become eagle-eyed shoppers, traveling the byroads of New York's bargain circuit; Orchard Street,

Union Square, the wonderful thrift shops. Most useful is Theatre Development Fund's Costume Collection. Housed in a warehouse near the Hudson River, the collection includes more than fifty thousand costumes that can be rented by nonprofit performing groups for nominal fees linked to the seating capacity of the house and the number of performances.

"The costumes come from all over," says Whitney Blausen, the collection's administrator.

Everything here has been donated by another producing organization or various client individuals. If you were to call me up and ask, I could tell you whether or not you could do a particular show out of the collection. Most customers are expected to come and pull their own costumes, and they do their dry cleaning and alterations and pay for the cost of shipping. But for companies who are too far away to come in, with sufficient advance notice, we're happy to pull a show for them. We don't want to disenfranchise people west of the Mississippi, and in a typical year, we have customers in about 35 states.*

Each designer, before taking on an assignment, should understand the theater's policy about crew and assistants. Larger nonprofit houses have resident technical crews and shops. Some can afford to send the designs out for construction by scene shops.

Smaller houses offer to pay a minimal fee for a carpenter, a costume designer's assistant, a wardrobe mistress, but it is often the designer's responsibility to find the person willing to do the job. The smallest theaters expect the designers to do all the construction themselves.

The New York design community is so well knit that help can usually be found, and designers who are not working are available to assist their friends. Besides, assisting is a good way to get known by theaters and directors.

The lighting and sound designers should be wary of getting seduced into jobs where they are expected to run the boards themselves. There is no way that these designers can do their jobs if they are not free to watch the show from the house during rehearsals and previews. When one runs a show from the booth,

*Leslie Bennetts, "Fezzes to Frog Costumes For Nation's Art Groups," *New York Times*, December 30, 1986.

with attention on mechanics and cues, it is a sure way of ending up
with a dissatisfied director and a poor reputation.

Additional production problems concern budget and schedules.
Off-off Broadway, there are two cardinal budget rules:

1. What there is is what you've got.
2. There is never enough.

Besides that, if there is enough money for nails and paint and to
pay the Costume Collection, if there is lumber left over from a
previous production, and lighting instruments, a board and cable
on hand, miracles can be wrought.

The greatest obstacles are generally poor planning, devious
producers, and self-deception. Good designs can be created on any
budget, as long as the designers know their limits from the outset.
Figures and time allowances which change in midstream are
disruptive. Once the production has a concept, the designer has a
picture, and the juices have started to flow, to run out of money in
the middle results in patch work, desperate decisions, and a
botched job. It is each designer's responsibility to make sure there
are clear lines of communication with the producer and to submit
a budget in writing so that there can be no claim of misunderstand-
ings later. It may do no good in the end, but the designer has
protected himself as much as possible.

Scheduling is the director's responsibility. Directing a show is
like running an army because there are so many people involved
with their individual concerns, so many chores with overlapping
schedules. This is particularly true off-off-Broadway, where there is
often no shop space and the set has to be built on stage, coordi-
nated around the rehearsals and the needs of the lighting and
sound designers. Accurate planning has to go into deciding what is
to be done, how much time each step requires, how much time
actors will need to adjust to the sets and lights and costumes, and
when is the right moment to introduce specific problems such as a
complex prop or period costumes that have to be incorporated in
the acting styles.

As with acting, one of the most serious enemies to creative
design work is anxiety. There are many people involved, many
demands, little time, and the threatening specter of public expo-

sure, so it is easy for the forces to collide. Proper planning and clear communication are the only ways to make sure that anxiety does not reach unmanageable heights. When designers know how much time and money they have, they incorporate these factors in their designs. If a director makes a commitment about stage time and schedule and then reduces it in the crunch, it will cost the director an enormous amount in the designer's respect and commitment, not to mention the final product.

For the director just starting out this can be a serious problem. The truth of the matter is that there are always new actors arriving on the scene. Shows can be cast, no matter how lousy the director's reputation is, no matter how many actors announce that they will never work for him again. But the community of designers is smaller and more selective. Designers can always get jobs assisting or constructing. Of course, they are eager to do their own things off-off-Broadway, and once they have established a good working relationship with a director, they will wish to work with him again. The director who does not protect his designers and fulfill his commitments to them, will find that his name is mud very quickly, and it will not be long before his shows look that way too.

When critics go to an off-off-Broadway theater and walk into the house to see a well-created pre-set, scenery that hints of interesting things to come, lighting that brings the eye to the stage, music in the background that clues the audience in to what they are going to see, they know they are in the hands of a professional director. It makes them lean a little more generously toward the play. Writers, directors, and actors should remember that and learn to be very nice to designers.

9

Casting

Directors generally agree that, second only to a good script, good casting is the most essential requirement of a successful production. Because it is so crucial, the process is filled with anxiety for all involved: actors who want the jobs, actors who are offered the jobs and do not know whether to accept, directors who want certain actors but have to make compromises, writers who want their fantasies fulfilled despite realities directors must face.

Broadway productions can take months to cast, postponing for the right stars, combing both coasts for talent and offering impressive salaries. Such luxuries of time and money are not available off-off-Broadway. Casting is done quickly, usually within two weeks of the first rehearsal, and choices are restricted to the talent available.

A well-known actor might be willing to step into an off-off-Broadway show scheduled imminently because there is nothing else on the horizon. If asked to commit a month in advance, she will be less likely to accept. If she does agree and something better comes along, she will drop out before rehearsals begin. Directors who cast too far in advance often end up casting twice.

Casting a new play, instead of a revival, adds to the problems. Actors have to be able to measure the writer's skill and promise. Talent agents are wary of sending actors to a project by an unknown. Directors and writers discover cracks appearing in their friendships. An unfamiliar play needs recognized actors to attract attention, so while directors are chasing "names," hungry young actors cannot get auditions.

Casting takes place on several levels. There is the open call, required by Equity, which offers every actor a chance to be seen. There is the reading by appointment scheduled for actors submitted by agents, known to the director, or plucked from the theater's picture file. There is the offer to actors of such repute that they do not need to audition.

The unknown actor hopes for a reading by appointment. Sometimes, he can achieve this if he is spectacular at the open call, but the best way to get a reading is through an agent. The best way to get an agent is to get seen in a production. However, this Catch-22 is not as hopeless as it may seem.

Actors' agents and casting directors are amazingly proficient about covering various showcase productions. Luckily for the young actor, the open call for the smaller showcase theaters offers more hope than the EPAs for the larger houses. Smaller houses get fewer submissions from agents. The competition from names is less intense. Since showcase theaters cannot afford casting directors, the actor can expect to audition for the actual director. Smaller showcases are generally not reviewed by the New York Times, but if the actor is seen in one, or in several, he might get an agent, and he might get seen by a casting director.

Casting calls for Equity showcases are posted at union headquarters and advertised in the trade papers (Show Business and Backstage). Every young actor, union member or not, should start by covering every open call for smaller houses, where there is some possibility of success.

Once the actor is cast and the show is running, Equity rules require that the company be informed of any VIPs who have attended. The actor should immediately send off his picture to this list and follow it up with phone calls. If his work impressed someone, he will be remembered.

Young actors often get together and produce their own "Scene Night." They rent a theater or a loft, print a flyer, prepare a program of scenes designed to show off their talents, and invite agents, casting directors, and others to attend. Pooling money and contacts sometimes makes this project pay off, although casting director Amy Introcaso says she covers every showcase she can get to, all of Broadway and off-Broadway, but does not go to Scene Nights. "I think they show the actors to a disadvantage most of the time because they are not directed, or they are directed by themselves. There never is enough time. The production values are poor. They are underrehearsed, so the actors look bad. When I see someone in a play, even a very inexpensive showcase, it is easier to figure out what they can do because you see them over the course of an evening."

Some of the larger theaters run general auditions throughout the year, offering actors an opportunity to be seen by the casting staff. The general audition does not aim to cast a specific production, but it enables the casting department to keep its picture file up to date.

At the Public Theater, it can take up to a year to get an appointment for a general audition, if an actor is lucky. Actress Roxanne Hart claimed, at an American Theatre Wing seminar, that she got her general audition at the Public by hounding them daily for months, making herself such a nuisance that they eventually succumbed. Pictures and résumés of actors who have written in for a general audition are circulated throughout the office. If any of the casting staff know the actor, or are impressed by his training or credits, or intrigued by his face or type, the actor is invited in.

Neither the Public nor Playwrights Horizons run EPAs for single productions. Instead, they run ten days of EPAs during the season in which any Equity member is given two minutes to do one monologue, and an actor who is impressive at an EPA will be invited back for a general audition.

At the Public, casting associate Brian Chavanne estimates that only about three percent of the actors seen at an EPA go on to the general auditions; however, Introcaso offers more hope.

"An example of someone getting started from an EPA was Michael Countryman. He came in on an EPA and was perfect for a part in Ted Tally's Terra Nova. It was a role that was particularly difficult to cast. The guy had to be big. There was something about the character that was real sad, and Michael's face had the right quality. I was the assistant at the time and had seen Michael in a showcase at Manhattan Punch Line. At the EPA, I remembered that I had seen him, so we brought him in to read for Gerald Gutierrez, the director, and it was one of the few times I saw Gerry stop an audition and direct an actor because his credits were so skimpy. We just didn't quite know if this was a fluke, but he ended up getting the part."

Since that breakthrough, Michael Countryman has gone on to work at the Manhattan Theater Club, Hudson Guild, and Ensemble Studio Theatre. He made his off-Broadway debut in Simon Gray's The Common Pursuit and is seen regularly on TV's "Kate and Allie."

Introcaso also points out that "EPAs for musicals are more

valuable for the young actor. I remember the actress who came in for an EPA at Playwrights, just when we were looking for a standby for the Broadway company of *Sunday in the Park with George*. She was sent straight from the EPA to a costume fitting and could not believe what was happening to her."

At a general audition, the actor is invited to do two contrasting monologues; the Public specifies that one should be classical and one contemporary. Success at the general audition means that the actor's picture gets placed in the active file from which unknowns might be called to audition for a part in an actual production.

A theater's picture file consists of actors who have worked in productions, actors known to someone on the staff, and actors who have done well at auditions but have not been cast. The unknown actor's goal is to get into the file; that is not accomplished merely by sending a photo through the mail. If nobody has seen the actor's work, the picture gets thrown out.

Young actors frequently complain that casting seems to be a closed shop and they cannot even wangle auditions for major productions. Directors only see people they know and the same ones get the parts over and over again. In fact, Equity has a Casting Council so that members' trials and tribulations can be discussed, but the situation is unlikely to change. Given the realities of off-off-Broadway, it is easy to see why directors stick to familiar faces; young actors have to have patience until they break into the golden circle.

A major benefit of the play development process for the director is the possibility of going into rehearsal with actors who have a history with the project, are committed to the script, and have had a chance to develop a relationship with the writer and the play.

It is an awful burden to conduct an artistic life like a series of one-night stands: going into each project with a set of strangers, rushing into intimacy and forcing openness and then, if success is achieved, only to have to start over with the next play, the next company.

In a *New York Times* interview, the popular director, John Tillinger describes the off-off-Broadway casting process:

No one knows the horror of working in New York. Just last week an actress perfect for her part was offered $80,000 for two weeks work in L.A.

What could I say to her, don't take it? It's not as though she could work at a decent salary for, say, forty weeks in the theater, and thus turn down that kind of money. That's all she's likely to make this year.

Every play involves mind-boggling compromises. You're lucky to get your third and fourth choices in some of the parts. The worst thing is when you beg a friend to take a part, saying you've got to help me out, so-and-so wasn't available, then so-and-so accepted but pulled out before the first rehearsal—his series got picked up—then so-and-so rehearsed for four days, only to get ten days on a movie in Indonesia. And that friend says I'll try even though I'm not really right for the part, and it means not going to L.A. for six weeks, and then that friend gets slaughtered in the reviews for not being right for the part.*

The situation is further complicated by the rush for "names." It seems odd that off-off-Broadway, which started as an alternative to commercial theater, should have fallen into the same star system trap, but it has. In recent years, Amanda Plummer, William Hurt, Sigourney Weaver, Molly Ringwald, Len Cariou, Bernadette Peters, Richard Dreyfuss, Robert DeNiro, Al Pacino, and Geraldine Page all appeared in New York's institutional theaters, and the scramble for such names is intense.

No career, no production, no theater can get off the ground without critical attention. Obviously, the papers have to cover the official Broadway and off-Broadway openings and the more important nonprofit houses. Beyond that, it is up to the individual reviewer's desires, and she is more likely to cover a showcase production if there is an actor in the cast whose work she admires, or if the director has received nice reviews elsewhere, or if one of the designers has impressive credits.

The names directors go after are not only stars in the commercial arena. There is competition for the respected Broadway character actor, the supporting actor on a cancelled series, the perpetual Broadway understudy who never gets to play the lead but is known to be brilliant by everybody in the business.

Directors want respected actors, but they need to avoid those who work so often they will not stay with the production. To this end, soap opera regulars are good bets. Most work on soaps a few days a week, so they are able to do showcases and they are

---

*Albert Innaurato, "A Playwright Decries an Era of 'Hit Flops,'" *New York Times*, July 20, 1986.

contracted to stay in town. The director will have to schedule around the soap rehearsals and must make sure the television producer approves of the actor taking on an outside assignment.

With soaps getting longer, more elaborate, and going on location, taping is not guaranteed to end at five o'clock. This is all right while a show is in rehearsal, but the off-off-Broadway production must get a guarantee that the actor will be available by curtain time during the run. Many soap producers, eager to keep their actors nourished by outside work, will agree and will honor the commitment at all costs. I have had an actress arrive from location by NBC helicopter in time for an East Village curtain.

Names not necessarily known beyond a few blocks in Manhattan are treated by off-off-Broadway like the Robert Redfords of the commercial world. And one of the reasons these actors do showcases is that they like to be treated that way. They do not audition, they have to be offered the role, and once a director does so, he does not offer it elsewhere until the actor responds. This is particularly true if the offer has been made through an agent. A director who gets caught in the embarrassing position of having made duplicate offers is in for a tough time casting future shows.

Approaching the name actor is usually more successful if it is done directly. The actors' unions—Equity, Screen Actors' Guild (SAG), American Federation of Television and Radio Artists (AFTRA)—will release phone numbers to legitimate casting offices and members. Sometimes, actors list home or service numbers as well as agents. *Players' Guide* is a mammoth catalogue of actors with photos and credits divided by type: leading man, leading woman, juveniles, ingenues, etc. Actors, from unknowns to stars, pay a fee to get their listings included, and the Guide is helpful in casting.

The lastest additions to casting offices are computer services, such as RoleCall and Base Line. Actors who pay to be listed can be identified by special talents and types. Current information is available as to where they are and what they are doing. These services are of value to film and television producers, since they provide information about who is on location and who is not; who is available for a few days work or a commercial which must shoot immediately. Brian Chavanne remembers casting an actor from RoleCall who played the flute because it was such a rare, specific talent that was needed.

Celebrity Service helps track down stars and identifies their agents. When the director of *Cuba and His Teddy Bear* requested Robert DeNiro for the lead, even Rosemarie Tichler, who has accomplished miracles in getting stars to work at the Public, thought he was crazy because of DeNiro's well-known inaccessibility. However, the casting department located DeNiro's attorney through Celebrity Service and tracked down the star; Mr. Papp himself eventually made the call. DeNiro surprised everyone by saying he would be delighted to see the script and, soon after receiving it, called back to say he was interested.

It is the responsibility of aspiring directors to build their own casting files. They should see as many shows as they can, keep programs for future reference, and make notes of talented actors' qualities, physical characteristics, and age range.

From these sources, directors identify the actors they wish to see. They, or casting directors, should make it understood over the phone whether an offer is being made or if the actor is to audition. There is a middle ground. The director can tell the actor about the part, can offer to supply him with a script to consider, and then suggest they get together for a cup of coffee. This is not an offer. The director will make the offer only after the meeting, but the actor is not asked to read, in deference to his reputation. This is a way to approach name actors, offering them some dignity, yet still checking them out before making a commitment.

David Trainer described the process in the casting of *The Dining Room*: "Before the first reading, Pete and I knew we wanted Charlie Kimbrough to play the father, and he did it and was wonderful. Of course, we asked him to do the production and he said, 'No.' Who knows why? Maybe he had a commercial to shoot. So, then we thought, 'Who are we going to get?' It was really important because, if there is a first among equals in that play, it is that part. Pete Gurney's wife's college roommate was Remak Ramsay's sister, and Pete knew Remak and I knew him distantly and had always thought he was one of the greatest actors I had ever seen onstage. So, we determined to ask Remak, but we had this question. He not only had to play crusty patriarchs and fathers, which we had no doubt that Remak could do, but he had to play children. Remak is six-foot-four-inches tall and he has a moustache. And he is a gentleman. But could Remak play a six-year-old boy at a birthday party? So, we sent the play to Remak, and my respect for Remak is boundless so I didn't want to say, 'Will you come in and audition?' That is not the point. The point is, 'We have a question. Do you have a question?' If we all have the same question, can we devise a way to answer this question to our mutual satisfaction? And I mean, mutual. Not, 'We are judging you,' or 'You are judging us.' We all knew and liked each other, but could Remak play a six-year-old? He read the play and loved it. He said he would be available to come in and talk to us. So he did, and it always devolves on the director to be the diplomat in these things. Directors run auditions, they do the talking, they do the steering, and I came around to this question of playing this kid because he has to play at least two children. He said, 'Well, how do you imagine it being done?' And I said, 'You don't do anything to play these children. You simply think like a child. You don't need to put a funny hat on. You don't need a sign that says, 'Now, I'm a baby.' It's written with the mental and emotional processes of a child. You simply act those processes. Does that make sense to you?' And he said, 'Yeah.' Now, here comes the heart-in-the-mouth moment. I said, 'Do you want to take a crack at it?' And he said, 'Yeah.'

"He opened the script and he read it and what was happening was testing. Was my theory a useful, workable theory? Could Remak, to his satisfaction, fulfill that? He's got the highest standards of anyone I know in the theater, so what he is thinking is, 'I've got to get up in public and do this. Can I be comfortable with it? What does it sound like?' Well, it sounded fabulous. It was stupendous. I remember looking at Pete Gurney and thinking, 'This is no problem.' And Remak began to think, 'This works.' And that was it.

"Now, that's what I think of as the model of what really goes on in auditions. Whenever I've worked on a show that has involved a famous person who says, 'I don't audition,' or 'Make me an offer' or 'Make sure the money is in escrow and then we'll talk,' I say, 'Forget it.' You're in big trouble because good people want the experience of dipping into that text, into that working relationship with a director. They want it for themselves. They're not proving anything to you. They know they're good. They want to know, 'Can I be good in this?' It is a mutual inquiry and, when done by people who like and respect each other, it's fun."

The subtleties involved in handling well-known actors cannot be overlooked. The actors need to know that the director knows the ropes. No matter how attractive the role, reputable actors are worried about getting involved in a production that will be an embarrassment. If the director handles the casting process professionally, the actor is more likely to accept.

Therefore, the director offers and he waits. And while he waits, he auditions lesser known actors from the picture file or those submitted by agents for other parts. And totally unknown actors keep calling for appointments. It's a time of stress and everybody complains.

My first play was produced at The Playwrights Unit. Now defunct, the theater was established by Edward Albee and Richard Barr out of the profits from *Who's Afraid of Virginia Woolf?* and it was one of the earliest, most adventurous workshops for emerging playwrights.

I was so thrilled, so wide-eyed and innocent, so unprepared for the trauma to come that I still get the shakes when I remember what happened.

After all the auditions, meetings with the director, juggling of possibilities, compromises, and disappointments, we finally got cast and went into rehearsal. In the first week, we lost one actor because she got a film job, another because she got colitis, and one who vanished after the first rehearsal and was never heard from again.

With that many defections, we had to postpone, and the director left because the new schedule collided with a previous commitment. I was assigned another director, who, of course, wanted to recast using actors with whom he had worked before.

Three days before we opened, an actor from the second company left for a regional theater job; she was replaced by someone waiting to learn if she had been cast in a show at the Chelsea Theater Center, a nonprofit house more important than ours. She took over our role with the understanding that, if she got the other, she too would drop out. We had no choice but to accept such suicidal terms, and to our relief, she was rejected by the Chelsea and we opened.

I could not imagine anyone doing good, calm, creative work amidst such constant upheaval, and longed for the day when I would be a Broadway playwright, when my actors would be well paid and signed to a contract that did not permit them to leave without a moment's notice.

As it happens, Edward Albee was casting his play *All Over* at the same time and we became privy to the glamorous comings and goings on the casting of that show. Here was a major American play by the hottest young writer of the moment, to be directed by Sir John Gielgud, on Broadway, fully financed and, as far as I could see, Edward Albee was going through the same wrenching experience I was at the opposite end of the professional spectrum.

According to the office gossip, every day some major star accepted a role, then turned it down because he would not work with someone else being considered, because schedules collided, because somebody's dog could not take the air travel. Scripts went out to the likes of Alfred Lunt and Lynn Fontanne, and the Albee team waited as breathlessly as we waited for our colitis victim's medical report. I distinctly remember the days on end when everyone was trembling in anticipation, awaiting a call from Switzerland from Lili Palmer, who eventually said no. And the unhappy faces when Deborah Kerr decided that she needed to vacation with her husband, so that if they wanted her, they would have to postpone.

Just as we opened my play with a cast of compromises and replacements, *All Over* ended with a cast far too young for the roles as written, much less lustrous than the names that had been bandied about, and there was even a major replacement required during rehearsals.

The difficulties in casting are not restricted to off-off-Broadway. They are the way of the theater, especially when it comes to new plays because nobody knows what is going to hit or miss. As possibilities increase, so do the director's expectations and the actors' terror. Broadway understudies are dubious about doing new plays off-off-Broadway and international film stars are dubious about doing them on Broadway. In the middle, the playwright is hit with the fact that the quality of his play is not the crucial element in anyone's decision. Actors express their anxieties by checking out what else is available, bickering about who else is in it, worrying over schedules and conflicts and whether they are committed to do a voice-over for a margarine commercial, which is where the real money lies.

Directors are people who, by nature, like to be bosses, relish authority, and need to feel in control. That is why commercial theater fosters a hierarchical, protective structure. Directors are surrounded by assistants and go-fers and are treated like gods. Why? It makes them better directors.

At the more prestigious institutional theaters, they are afforded this kind of treatment while casting. They have casting directors and their staffs to help out and advise; assistant directors and secretaries to make the phone calls; agents and actors who return those calls, want the jobs, and keep appointments.

But this is not the case for the young director at a showcase code theater, where there is no help, the phones are often tied up, agents are not eager to submit their top clients, actors of repute are dubious about taking the jobs, and even talented newcomers are balancing several offers.

The chaos of getting scripts out, answering calls, calmly awaiting acceptances, and making crucial decisions often gives young directors the jitters, and huge mistakes are made. They hate the feeling of being out of control and rush into decisions just to get the casting done. This is a deadly error, which can be avoided if the director defines the goals of each step. The purpose of the first audition is simply to weed out those who are unacceptable. Either an actor is wrong for the role because of size, age, type, hair color, dimensions, personality, or there is no evidence of training or talent. Anyone else—and these will be in the minority—should be called back.

Callbacks are required not because it is difficult to find the right actor, but because it is easy to cast the wrong one. They make it less likely for the director to fall in love with someone because it feels good to get something settled. The audition process renders a director so bleary that it is easy to jump at the first actor with a sign of life. The mind locks into a decision and the next person in the door, who may be better and more appropriate, does not have a chance. This rarely happens at a callback, where the list has been winnowed down, the director sees actors for the second time, and things seem slightly calmer.

"At a first audition, you want an intelligent reading," Lee Kalcheim explains. "Sometimes, actors start climbing the walls in auditions. They set the chairs out and they're doing all this blocking. If that goes on, you don't see the performance because you're too busy watching all the physical stuff. You want them to pick up the script and read it and have the content of the scene come out at you.

Then, you know they understand what this part is about. They get the rhythms and they hit their marks in the script. They let the play come out. I know it sounds like a playwright speaking, but directors want the same thing. The next thing you want to know is, can they take direction? Can they make adjustments? After that, you've got to bring them back, and if you want them to do more, you tell them."

All the director needs to discover at a first audition is whether the actor is physically right for one of the roles, whether his résumé lists some training and experience satisfactory to the requirements, and whether the actor knows how to stand, sit, and breathe. Amazingly, these standards will rule out fifty percent of the applicants.

The director then looks to see if the actor is, at all, in touch with his inner life. Is there a spark, a glow in the eye? Is there responsiveness? Is there intelligence? Is there wit? When the actor talks, when he reads, does he look at you? Does he listen? Does he seem to be affected by the material? Is there anything spontaneous in what is happening? Is there a human being here or are we faced with a plastic, dead-eyed, smiling, courteous doll? Such criteria eliminate a major number of actors who passed the first tests.

The director asks something different in the reading from those who are left. He gives a direction, asks for a change of intent or tone, points out something that he liked. Was there any response? Was there a flicker of understanding? Was there, perhaps, a glint of enjoyment in being guided? Did the reading change toward the right direction?

Anybody who passes these tests should be called back. The director has yet to deal with questions about the actor's emotional suitability for the role, his balance with the others who may be cast, the extent of his range, the quality of his talent, how close he comes to the writer's image.

The purpose of the first call is to cut down the pack to a manageable number. There will be time, at the callbacks, to make more serious decisions. If the director resists the temptation to rush the process, he can avoid catastrophes, and assemble a cast who will accomplish his intent.

Callbacks are also necessary as every role will require back-ups, therefore, the director cannot afford to stop looking too quickly. When all the auditions are over and the actors are offered the roles, there are bound to be conflicts of schedules and availability. After rehearsals begin, actors may drop out, and the wise director who has not thrown away his casting notes can quickly find a replacement. He has seen as many actors as possible, has seen the good ones twice, and has not settled on anyone without a list of alternatives.

There is a kind of director's panic that prohibits any final casting decisions. The director may keep changing his mind, redefining what he wants for the roles, bring in more and more actors, and alienate others already selected by auditioning them too many times (although the showcase code limits the allowed number of auditions to three). He may take so long to make decisions that he loses the actors he wants by the time he makes the offers. By sending out confusing signals to actors, worrying the writer, and overburdening the staff, he jeopardizes the whole project. When this situation arises, the producer or the casting director must step in and help the director clarify his thoughts, althought this kind of indecisiveness does not bode well for the future of the production.

One of the best pieces of advice a casting director ever offered me was at such a crisis point. I could not find the actor of my dreams. I had seen dozens and was growing more confused because each one had something but no one had it all. Some looked right for the role but could not play it. Some had the talent but were too young or too handsome or too skinny or too fat. With time running out and the pressure building, the casting director pushed me in the right direction by saying, "Go for talent, not for type." In a crunch, when nobody is perfect, the thing to do is select the very best actor available and never mind what he looks like. At a certain point, decisions must be made, and avoiding them only damages the director's ability to get on with the job.

This incident offers a clue to what a good casting director does.

1. An effective casting director knows the ins and outs of the casting procedure and Equity rules
2. Runs the EPAs and passes on any spectacular talents who have appeared
3. Sets up the appointments for the actors the director wishes to have read, and calls in people he thinks should be added to the list

4. Knows how to contact the names the director wishes to make offers to
5. Researches the history of actors under consideration
6. Has established relationships with agents and frequently gets recommendations from them
7. Keeps track of reactions and comments
8. Gets a sense of the director's tastes so he can bring in more people
9. Follows up the readings with offers or courteous thank-yous, and files away the good people who have not been cast for future reference
10. Holds the director's hand
11. Reports back to the producer about how things are going
12. In a subtle way, pushes the director towards the people he himself likes.

Rosemarie Tichler says her role at auditions is to serve as "a consultant. If the director misses an actor, to say, 'I've seen his work. Let's take another look.' If we know something about the actor that the director wants and is not getting, to say something about that." On the show I did at the Public, Rosemarie was like a den mother for all—writers, actors, and me—sitting in on auditions, beaming with approval, leaning over every once in a while to comment. Once I gave a talented actor a direction and he changed his reading in a new and funny way. I roared but Rosemarie leaned over. "He's very good but, you know, he's not giving you what you asked for." It was a perceptive insight that I could have missed on my own. She also clued me into the way Papp would respond to a particular quality, an important factor since he approved of all casting in the final stage. And when she liked the same actor I did, it made me all the more confident.

Good casting directors are of immense value to directors—and to actors.

The fly in the ointment in casting a production may turn out to be a writer who leans too heavily toward the literal, the correct, the logical. The same way he can be a burden at design meetings because he wishes to see on the stage only what was in his head, the writer may limit the possibilities in casting by approving actors because of their superficial verisimilitude to the images that started the play.

Marshall Mason, at another of the educational Dramatists Guild symposiums, said:

Authors most often will accept an actor's audition piece, saying, "Oh, that surface thing I see is what I want in my play." Sometimes, if you cast on the basis of that surface thing, that's all you'll get. The director, with perhaps a more perceptive eye as to the actor's process, can sometime see a hidden, inner quality that is much more important to the part and that can enhance the play in a way that the author might not have recognized.*

This is a particular problem if the writer has fallen in love with actors who have done the readings. This happened to Lee Kalcheim on the casting of Breakfast with Les and Bess. Actors James Broderick and Charlotte Moore had done several of the readings and then, "just before we were ready to go," says Kalcheim, "Jimmy died, and no matter who came to read, I kept hearing his voice, so no one was good enough. I wanted Charlotte Moore to do it but she had worked at the Hudson Guild Theatre three or four times, and her agent said, 'You're becoming known as Miss Hudson Guild, so she said no. Casting became very difficult, unfortunately for any other actors, because a playwright hears a character the way he wants to hear it, and if you don't pass in front of them with that . . . well, several people that we wanted couldn't do it. I was never one hundred percent for Keith Charles until the rehearsals started, mostly because of my memory of Jimmy. And I think Keith would be the first to admit he was tentative himself. He hadn't had a part this size in a while. I had never seen him do anything, and I just didn't think he had that size. But, as rehearsals went on, he grew into it. Now, the irony is, when I hear the role, I hear Keith."

However, as Israel Horovitz said at an American Theatre Wing seminar, "Once a play is cast, eighty percent of the interpretation is done. A clever playwright, if he has only a limited time available, gets involved in the casting." Writers should attend all auditions, make their thoughts known, and try to define what they are seeking for each role. Once this is clearly defined, they can let the director decide which actors will best fill those needs. It is the director who has to work with the actor. It is the director who knows how to differentiate between an actor's ability to audition well and his ability to develop that reading into a multifaceted performance.

*Otis L. Geurnsey, Jr., ed., Broadway Song and Story (New York: Dodd, Mead and Company, 1985), p. 354.

David Trainer explains, "I try to get the author's concerns, the casting director's concerns, and I watch the final auditions with not only my concerns, but the concerns of my colleagues. I try to work with the actors to demonstrate that those concerns are groundless or, in fact, are not. You do that by asking actors to make adjustments—'That was good, but what if you play it, rather than being afraid of your grandfather, try and force your grandfather to . . .' Sometimes, they are not adjustments you would make in production, but they are an attempt to illuminate some facet of an actor's method and talent that is not readily apparent."

Theatrical tradition, and the Dramatists Guild Broadway contracts, give the writer veto power in casting; moreover, no director wants to suffer through four weeks of rehearsal with an unhappy writer. Both director and writer have power in the casting process, and it is important that each be content with the final choices. The step-by-step natural growth of play development almost promises that director and writer will see eye to eye over casting, and if not, the writer has usually developed enough trust to go along with the director's decision.

At the Public Theater, according to Rosemarie Tichler, "The writer has approval, the director has approval, and the producer has approval. Mr. Papp comes in when the writer and director have made their first choice. He sees those people he doesn't know or he says 'yes' about those he does.

"The writer/director relationship has to be strong if the play is going to work. If that doesn't work, there's going to be a wedge and I don't want to be that wedge. When I'm in a situation, which is very rare, where the playwright might know more than the director, if I think the director is throwing away more actors than I think he should be, I would form an alliance with the playwright or I would call in Mr. Papp. When there is that kind of tension between director and writer, the actors most certainly feel it and it never makes for comfortable auditions. The structure is not sound and it's always a mess. I've never seen it fail. You know it very early in casting. There's going to be a showdown at some point. You may get past it before you go into rehearsal, but there's going to be a showdown."

Actors who understand the ins and outs of casting walk into an audition with a tremendous psychological advantage. They must face a complex cast of characters, struggling in a web of tensions, who are probably more confused than the actors are. If an actor's manner lets them know that he understands the role, can play it well, and can solve their problems, everyone in the room will sit up and take notice.

A mistake actors often make in auditions is to assume the director is confident, decisive, and judgmental, with his mind set, eager to reject anybody wrong. Actors incorrectly see themselves as needy and helpless, and imagine that their job is to squirm into some preconceived picture. Nothing could be further from the truth—and more harmful to the actor.

"A play that is going to work out is a partnership between the actors, the director, and the author," explains David Trainer. "My definition of a director is, 'An enzyme who creates a chemical union between the acting and the writing and then dissolves.' You should not go to the theater and see directing. If you do, it's like seeing the lights, something is wrong. But the director has to find those people with whom he can effect that union. I know, from an actor's point of view, an audition is, 'They're judging me.' From my point of view, it's always, 'Do I want to do it with this person? Are we going to hit it off?' "

Actors have to remember that the director is tired and worried. He has been sitting in a musty audition room, growing less and less sure of what he wants, more and more concerned about the script. He feels the writer and producer breathing down his neck, he is depressed because he just got rejected by a star. The director needs to be reassured, and the actor can be a breath of fresh air in this miserable situation.

An astute actor knows this and uses it. She tunes in to the director's needs and does not wait to be told what to do. Instead, she makes the effort to reach out by starting the conversation and supplying the energy. At an initial call, if an actor reveals a bit of personality and comes across with confidence, the director will be intrigued.

Most directors confess that they can make up their minds about an actor by the time she sits down in the audition chair, and they go through the reading as a courtesy. It does not matter if the actor is entirely wrong for the role, or if her conception of how to play it is off the wall; the actor who brings decisiveness into the room will be heard, and even if she is not cast, she will be remembered.

Why, then, do so many actors walk into an audition with nothing to say, waiting to be told what to do? They smile limply, nod at everyone, sit with their hands clutched around the script, and wait for someone else to start the conversation.

Even if the actor has been given only two pages of the script to study in the hall, why not say to the playwright, "Boy, this is an interesting script. I don't know what the story is about because they didn't give me the whole play, but there is something you can feel in this little scene, something in the dialogue that bounces off the page!"

Or perhaps turns to the director. "Hey, this is a lovely theater. The space is so intimate and comfortable. I bet it's a joy to play here. I've never seen anything here but I'll have to come down. What's running now?"

If the actor finds something in the situation that honestly excites him, he can walk into the room and talk about it. He might end with a question for the director or writer to answer, and he is off and running.

He has caught their attention. He has relieved some of their anxiety. He has found a way to reveal something about himself. If an actor has any talent and is at all right for the role—and if the director knows what he is doing—this actor will be called back.

Once an actor manages to get a reading for a part in a new play, he must do one thing which is not necessary when reading for a revival: ask to read the script!

The casting director might react as if the actor were causing trouble, though. Rosemarie Tichler says that the Public "is one of the few theaters where scripts are provided. It's policy. We want actors to be the best prepared they can be." At smaller houses, there are never enough script copies and the casting director is, at that moment, busy getting them out to the names, many of whom will not have the courtesy to return them when they turn down the role. The casting director does not want the added problem of getting scripts to every unknown who is reading. Although a young actor may be intimidated, he should stick to his guns. The writer and director will appreciate the fact that the actor's reading has been so informed, that he has something intelligent to say about the play, that he took the trouble to read the script.

Given the nature of many modern scripts, actors may be unable to find a logic in the play, even after reading it. Without a director to guide them, it may be difficult to understand the story and decide what to do with the character. Rosemarie Tichler advises "If you really don't understand it, you have to go with any impulse you have. Most directors don't want to give an actor any direction before they've seen the actor do something. Then, the director will say, 'Think of it this way.' If you are really stuck, I would say, 'What's going on?' but you are better off if you can ask a specific question."

Struggling with an incomprehensible script and an unclear role is often the burden of the newcomer because such scripts and parts get the most turndowns from known actors. Rosemarie noted that "the casting director will often explain to them, go after them, try to make them see what they are not seeing. I urge them to read it again and think of it another way."

Despite her efforts, twenty-two actors turned down Christopher Durang's *The Marriage of Bette and Boo*, later a big hit. A scheduled production of Thomas Babe's *Father and Sons* had to be cancelled because so many actors rejected roles. "Wally Shawn's early plays got lots of turndowns," says Rosemarie. "No one got it. No one thought they were funny. Since *Aunt Dan and Lemon*, they know he is a serious man."

The tough scripts usually give the unknown a break, and actors who are prepared to tackle the problems are already a step ahead of the others. "It's good for actors to try to look at plays, work at textual analysis," Rosemarie adds. "I can spot an actor who makes choices. That often is related to a real looking and examination of texts. When we hear the words, something should be happening, some choice should be made. If there's a moment here and the actor is walking by it or walking through it, you wonder about the actor's intelligence. The first thing the actor has to do is break down the script so he knows where something has to happen. In casting, there is a lot of discovery of what the play is about. Just recently, casting replacements for *Drood*, somebody created a moment that we'd never seen. The show's been running for years and this actor made a discovery in one minute of the text."

Pamela Berlin says, "The hardest role for us to cast was Gillian [in *To Gillian on Her 37th Birthday*] because the character was so elusive. Especially so, at that time, in the script. Later on, she got clarified, but when we were auditioning, it was as much my confusion and the writer's confusion about what we wanted in the role that made it difficult. We weren't sure, and I had it in my mind that if someone came in and made it her role, I wanted to be able to say, 'That's it! I never thought about it that way!'

"We saw lots and lots of people. Some were very physical,

athletic, active, and they made really wild and bold choices. Some did not do that at all; they basically sat down and read it. It was probably more helpful to see people up and moving because that's who the character is. Cheryl McFadden came in with a flock of other people, and we saw her three times.

"Eventually, it was between Cheryl and another actress, two very different ladies. We were still unclear about who and what we were looking for, but as she came back, she got simpler, which was nice, and that is probably what won us; that it became simpler and truer. It was very easy in that role, especially when you see that strange language on the page, to get mannered or to get into a lot of game playing without substance. Cheryl started getting to the heart of what was going on between those two people when she came back."

Actors reading a new script often erroneously look for the surface, intellectual level. They either get intimidated because they cannot find it or give a flat reading. At an audition for a new script, an actor need not play the words. He need not play the logic. He need not play the punctuation. The director wants him to bring a spark of life to the page. If it is the wrong spark, that is okay. Once it exists, the director will take the time to tell the actor how to shape it, and then they are both on their way.

"You find something, anything, even if it has nothing to do with anything on the page," according to Susan Merson. "If the director is smart, he'll see that you have the ability to make a choice. Be clear about who you are, even if it may be totally wrong. I've seen actors fail in an audition situation because they try to do too much work. If you do too much, you get caught in the middle process of creating a character. That's not what an audition is about. At an audition, you want to sparkle in your best way. All of us have certain strengths. We laugh well or we come at characters with vulnerability well. If you can find those elements in the character you are reading for, go for it, because that's what's going to show you off best."

Here is some advice for actors auditioning for new plays:

1. Actors should look in the script for their characters' "wants." It does not matter if the actors discover the right ones, as long as they find ones that are strong and clear; ones that have an urgency about them.

2. Actors must be able to personalize those wants, to connect

them to something in their own lives that will unleash memories and feelings. It has to be something actors feel is important to them.

3. If, after a quick reading of the script, actors can zero in on urgent wants that connect with something in their own experience, they should focus on their memories and let their psyches go to work. At this point, it is all right if they wander from the logic of the script.

4. Rather than searching for the character in descriptions or intellectual analysis, what actors should look for on the page is a rhythm, a voice. They should try to get the characters' sounds into their heads, the same way they would listen to a recording to get a quick fix on a dialect. One of the signs of a talented playwright is that each character sounds differently. The reader knows who is talking without checking the names above speeches. If actors can connect to the rhythm of their characters in scripts like that, without understanding anything else, they are on their way to a good audition.

5. Actors should look for as many transitions in the audition scene as possible. Where does the scene swerve? Where does something new happen in the middle of a speech; better yet, in the middle of a sentence? Where does the character get a new idea or change his mind? Transitions make a reading interesting and allow the actor to play many notes on his instrument.

6. Good actors physicalize. Some actors want to stand and move at an audition; some do not. The director, however, can spot a leg moving in the character's rhythm. Actors can play with the pages in their hands, move their shoulders and their heads. They allow the character to affect their bodies and energy flows through every muscle.

7. After actors have connected to their characters, personalized them, found a rhythm on the page, pinpointed the transitions, they should let the scene happen to them. This was the case with Sandy Dennis during that long-ago exercise with Herbert Berghof (see chapter 5); she had not decided in advance to end up at my feet, but she found an impulse and had the courage to follow it wherever it led.

8. Smart actors find the light. It does no good to do brilliant work in the shadows. There is generally little enough light available, but actors can scan the stage and get themselves into it. It is reassuring to the director when an actor does so, and certainly helps the reading.

The final step of casting, the final decision, is made behind closed doors. It is based on who is available, who looks good next to whom, who brings out what in the others, who reminds the writer of his mother (and whether that's good or bad).

Harold Clurman writes:

A prime factor in casting, one too often overlooked, is that the process should not concentrate solely on individual parts but on the nature of the company as a whole. One might cast a play with actors, each one individually "right," yet not acceptable in conjunction with the others. This goes beyond the obvious matching of ages, homogeneity in family relationships, the height or weight of actors who play scenes together. An excellent actor may simply not "mix" with others equally proficient. I do not refer to personal incompatibility and the ensuing temperamental clashes, but to the requirement for unity of texture which a production must possess if it is to signify more than a disparate assemblage of talents.

The unity I speak of has to do with social and cultural background, the ways in which the actors have been trained, their techniques and artistic ideals. Combining actors, even when all are qualified for their particular assignments, without their possessing something in common in all these respects may have the same disquieting effect as a real tree placed on the stage among painted ones: it becomes difficult to ascertain which causes the greater disharmony, the real or the artificial.*

In casting decisions, the actor has no power and must not berate himself if he does not get the job. It is one of the most difficult disappointments to handle; to be called back once, and then twice, to connect with the role, to sense success—and then be rejected. The experience can be terribly destructive if the actor does not understand some of the reasons the decision went against him.

As actors go through the perpetual rounds of auditions and rejections, they have got to find a way to survive with spirits intact. They must make sense out of painful situations. It is helpful to learn as much about the casting process as possible, to recognize that there are a number of aspects about the final choices that have nothing to do with talent.

When faced with this awful disappointment, reaching the brink and still losing the role, actors must take heart in the fact that they were seen, they impressed someone, and they will be remembered.

*Harold Clurman, On Directing (New York: Collier Books, Macmillan, Inc., 1974), p. 72.

10

The Rehearsal Process

Mike Nichols once said, "Directing is like making love. You never see anybody else do it. So you're never sure you're doing it right."[*]

During a lecture at the Actors Studio, Lee Strasberg divided the rehearsal process into stages. It is crucial, he said, for the director to define the goals of each stage so that the actors are not straining for something more. If they fulfill the requirements of one stage, the work will evolve naturally into the next.

The first stage is reading. The company sits around the table, discusses the script, analyzes the characters, breaks the play down into beats. This is all intellectual, and the director does not expect the actors to work for more than a logical understanding.

After that, the actors improvise to explore their relationships and personalize the situations. Staging emerges out of the beats defined around the table and these explorations. Staging is slow and painstaking at first because the actors are tenuously finding their characters, relationships, physical lives. If the director allows them to work carefully at first, he can quicken the pace later. Once the actors know who they are and what they are doing, once they have defined their "actions" in each scene, the work will flow more smoothly.

The third stage involves the absorption of mechanics. It takes four or five rehearsals of each scene, after blocking, for the actors to make it their own. At the first rehearsal, which is off book, all the director asks is that the actors struggle for their lines. They cannot act and concentrate on mechanics at the same time. If the analysis was right in stage one, if the blocking emerged organically in stage two, if the actors are allowed to absorb it all in stage three, they will start to relax and let things happen.

Stage four involves piecing it together. As each moment emerges

* Quoted in "All About ADI," American Directors Institute brochure, 1986.

from stage three, it is connected to another; beat by beat, scene by scene, act by act. If the actors are rushed into "results" before they are ready, the director is muddying the waters and nothing but tension will emerge.

Stage five is run-throughs. The actors find the arc of the play; the way it grows, the way their characters change. The director watches to see if the story comes through, if the scenes balance and build, if the pace is right. Then, he allows the performances to grow and thrive on their own. If he has done his work well, it will happen.

During Strasberg's lecture, actor Doris Roberts leaned over and whispered, "It seems so simple and clear, yet, in all my years in the theater, I've never had a director who worked that way!"

Theater people gossip about the idiosyncrasies of directors at rehearsals.

Marshall Mason stages in short (European) scenes, often spending an entire day on half a page. He requires that the actors arrive at the first blocking rehearsal with the particular scene memorized, and they work with every prop from the start. This does not mean rehearsal props, either. Mason wants the actual champagne bottle, the actual ice bucket, the actual cork if the actor is required to pop and pour in performance.

Alan Schneider directed *Who's Afraid of Virginia Woolf?* on the stage of the Billy Rose Theater in the complete set, with every Scotch bottle, every glass, every ice cube in place from the first rehearsal. And he did it in fourteen days.

Mike Nichols did the first production of *Barefoot in the Park* for the Bucks County Playhouse in one week of rehearsal.

Jerome Robbins demanded, and got, eight weeks of rehearsal—double the usual four weeks—for *Fiddler on the Roof*.

The Al Pacino production of *Richard III* rehearsed for twelve weeks. I asked one of the cast members if the extra time had helped. He thought for a moment, then said, "Naw . . ."

Jack Garfein keeps actors around the table, discussing and analyzing for so long they are ready to jump out of their seats. He claims it is better for the staging if they go at it like hungry animals.

Richard Foreman says he learned to direct from acting in high school productions. Since his drama club teacher always pre-blocked, that is the way he still does it.

Helen Hanft, who has done so many plays at La MaMa Experimental Theatre Club she has been dubbed "Queen of Off-off-Broadway," was in David Rabe's In the Boom Boom Room at the Public Theater, directed by a newcomer plucked by Joe Papp from a college teaching job. The director never got the cast together for discussions. Instead, the stage manager handed out the director's comments on slips of paper, neatly folded and labeled. When Helen got her handful, she said to the stage manager, "Tell him I prefer directors who talk. You see, I never went to college."

Harold Prince is so used to directing big noisy musicals that he even directs straight plays with a whistle hanging around his neck. When he wants to change something, he stops the actors with a piercing blow. Prince works at such a high energy level that he tires quickly and leaves the rehearsal hall after half a day, turning over the company to his trusted associate, Ruth Mitchell, with the admonition, "Ruthie, drill 'em."

Marc Daniels, the top notch TV sitcom director ("I Love Lucy," "Alice," "Flo") directed Norman Lessing's 36 for JRT. I was involved in the preproduction meetings and the early work on the script. Then, when he went into rehearsal, I told Marc to call when he wished me to see a run-through. I expected to hear from him in three weeks or so. Six days later, I got a call! As was to be expected, the run-through was awful. The acting was mechanical. The cast was miserable. I believed everything I had ever heard about the rushed work of television. But, from then on, Daniels used every moment to improve, define, and perfect the delivery of each and every laugh line. He told the actors when to turn their heads, when to take a breath, when to attack, and when to let it simmer. He was such a perfectionist that he called actors with notes about details in the middle of the night. One actor insists he got called with a note after the show had closed. In the end, the play was the most polished, sharpest, funniest success we ever had. Critics loved it. Audiences loved it. Even the actors loved it—once rehearsals were over.

Glenn Jordan, who started off-off-Broadway before going on to television and film, claims his directing technique was simple: "Hire good people and get out of their way."

Laurence Olivier writes, "It is not a director's job to teach actors how to act. It's his job to make the most of the talent they already have: to make actors feel relaxed and happy in their work."*

---

*Laurence Olivier, On Acting (New York: Simon and Schuster, 1986), pp. 122–3.

Andre Gregory believes that if a New York director wants to have control over his art he has two choices: He can be Mike Nichols and hire the best actors, the best designers, work under the best conditions money can buy, or he can turn his back on professional theater to work with amateurs and students in a self-created situation. Between these two extremes, lies compromise and misery.

It is true that the secret of directing off-off-Broadway is compromise. The actors are not paid a living wage, in many instances they support themselves by bartending or waitressing, or if they are lucky, doing voice-overs. If an actor gets a film audition that conflicts with rehearsal, he will go to the audition. If he gets the job, he will leave the show overnight.

Flexible directors are able to stay calm, focus on what needs to be done, do good work, and get the curtain up. If they insist upon totalitarian rule, on actors who will sit around waiting to be used, on rehearsals that move strictly in a logical, linear manner, and on schedules that depend on spur-of-the-moment inspiration, they will end up frustrated, and actors will leave.

The aim is to schedule rehearsals so actors are used when they are called and never stand around waiting to work. If the schedule is broken down by scenes and covers several days in advance, the actors have a chance to book their other appointments around rehearsals. If they are required to be off book at a certain point, that should be noted on the schedule. The first time they work with props should be noted. The more prepared the actors are, the better they will work. The sooner they get onstage after arriving, the less energy will be wasted in the corridor.

Some companies can go faster than others; so can some scenes; so can some stages in the process. A lot depends on the individual actors and the mix in the cast, the needs of the script, and the rhythms of the director. But if the actors learn that they will work when they are called and that they will be finished when the director has said they would be, they will show up on time: prepared, focused, and ready to work.

Since schedules are built around the actors' availability, directors might work on the beginning of act 1 on Monday, the end on Tuesday, act 2 on Wednesday, and then return to act 1 on Thursday. Plays are directed like movies, in tiny scenes out of sequence, moment by moment. Therefore, directors need to have a solid handle on the script to be able to guide the actors into the day's work with a picture of what went before and what will happen after.

The first few read-throughs are crucial and must be scheduled so that everyone can attend. Since the scene work is done in such a piecemeal fashion, this is the only time the company can get a clear picture of the whole. Very often, it is the only time all the actors will meet one another before the final week's run-throughs.

It is helpful if the company's day off is a weekday and rehearsals are scheduled for Saturday and Sunday, since there is often less outside pressure on the cast over weekends. These rehearsals offer the director a chance to put things together and rehearse in sequence so the company can begin to get a sense of the scene, the act, then the play.

During the week, actors like to have their days free for auditions, so rehearsals should start in the late afternoon and go until early evening. They should not end too late at night because many theaters are located in treacherous neighborhoods and actors are not happy if they have to go home in fear.

Even with a carefully considered, accurate schedule, there will be last minute conflicts, upsetting the best laid plans. The world of advertising agencies and commercial casting offices is filled with terrified executives and delayed decisions. An actor may get a call at six in the evening for a full day on a commercial at eight the following morning. When that happens, the actor will report to the stage manager that she cannot show up for rehearsal.

Since there are no understudies in off-off-Broadway, the director will have to continue on schedule, working around the missing actor, or with the stage manager standing in. If that is impossible, and the director has prepared a breakdown of the script indicating which characters are needed in every scene, he will know at a glance what else he can do with the people on hand. It would create chaos to revise the schedule at the last moment and expect actors to adjust their other commitments. It would be costly to lose the day. The director must be flexible enough to do what he can with whomever he has, even if it means jumping ahead to work on material unconnected with what was done on the preceding day.

Equity allows the company the option of rehearsing six days a week at five hours per day, or five days at six hours each. Generally, there are advantages in the six-day schedule since the rehearsals are shorter and actors, after a full day at another job, may have a limited concentration span. In addition, the work builds momentum through the week, each day spilling over into the next.

The day off breaks the cycle, however, and the rehearsal that follows it is often slow going. Most directors do not start anything new at the first rehearsal after a day off. Rather, this rehearsal is used to recharge the motor, which will then speed up on its own as the week progresses.

Union rules call for breaks of either five minutes each hour or ten minutes every two hours. The choice is the director's, depending on the intensity and energy of the company, how well the work is going, and the stage of rehearsal the play is in.

One of the functions of directors has always been to reassure, comfort, and encourage writers to do their best work possible. As directors turn to offer the same kind of parenting to the actors, writers may feel abandoned and excluded. This is one of the most painful parts of being a playwright. There is neither comfort nor cure, and every writer feels it. But if writers can understand why the rehearsal code of behavior requires that they stay silent and communicate with the actors only through the director, they will feel better and more positive about the process.

Actors need to feel comfortable and safe. It is a highly unusual kind of life that requires one to get off the subway, walk into a rehearsal room, and in front of relative strangers, reveal oneself. Actors' emotions are their tools; in order to use them well, they need to know that someone is watching and protecting them. That person is the director, and in the process of rehearsal, the actor comes to depend on him like a parent.

Actors frequently joke by calling the director "Daddy" or "our father." As the work gets better, as they reveal more, as the risks grow, they will cling to him even more. Only in this way can actors return to the emotional accessibility of childhood necessary for good work. They can experiment, explore, follow their intuitions, make mistakes, and put it all back together again, as long as they feel there is a loving, objective eye who will protect them from making fools of themselves in public.

This role cannot be jointly handled. Actors cannot look to both the director and writer for approval. They cannot be caught between conflicting responses. They cannot handle this kind of complex, personal, transferential relationship with two parental figures. If the writer interposes himself between the actors and director, he is doing harm to the work.

In addition, every actor fantasizes that the writer has all the answers. This is an error, but even the assumption does damage. There is a period in rehearsal when the actor feels as if she is drowning in confusion and anxiety. It would be a pleasure to turn to the writer and find out how to do this scene. But the actor is only short-circuiting her own creative process by looking to the play-wright for such an answer.

Mark Blum expresses the actor's point of view when he says, "In the actual rehearsing of the play, when something doesn't work, I like to have the freedom to say what I'm feeling. If the playwright is not there, I can say, 'I just don't get this line. Where am I going? How do I get there?' and to have me and the other actors in the scene and the director assume that it's my problem, that I just haven't found it. We don't have to tell the playwright yet because probably I will find it. But, if we search around and scramble in the dirt and come up for air and we realize that we've found the real journey here and this line is an impediment to it, or it's wrong or crazy or it has too many words in it, we know exactly how to phrase that, because we've explored it and spent an hour on it. Whereas if the first time the thought occurs to you, you have to explain it to the playwright, you won't be able to explain it right.

"I did *Little Footsteps* at Playwrights Horizons and the playwright, Ted Tally, lived across the street. He would come in at the beginning of the rehearsal. It's nice to feel that the playwright is in it with you, he's part of the family. He'd drink some coffee and have a doughnut, talk about some of the thoughts he had about the play, and ask what you thought of this scene and what about that. Then, maybe, he'd stay around for a while and then he'd go home. He'd do some rewrites, then maybe he'd come back around lunchtime to see how you were doing. He was always around, but he wasn't there in the room all the time, glaring at you with those eyes that can kill."

Comfort between actors and directors is engendered because there is a sense that they are discovering together; that neither knows exactly what the result should be and neither is judging the other. The writer speaks with such authority, whether he merits it or not, that he lessens the possibility of bringing other options to the stage.

Consequently, it is imperative that writers, when they attend rehearsals, sit at the back of the rehearsal space, and make themselves inconspicuous. After rehearsal they can meet with the director to go over what they would like to see changed.

It is not necessary for writers to be present at every rehearsal. Obviously, they have to sit in on the first reading, but while the mechanics of staging are being worked out, while the actors are exploring and experimenting, their attendance might prove to be more of a hindrance than a help. Many writers come to the first reading, then return once a week, and as the work heads toward run-throughs, attend more frequently. Changes in the script can always be made, and are more helpfully made, at this point.

Lee Kalcheim, creator of *Les and Bess*, describes the process from the writer's point of view: "The actors have an enormous amount of input. They have it even when they don't say anything; simply by getting up there and doing the part. It crystallizes the problems. If a scene wanders, they have to wander. You actually see them going backward and forward. Les has a long monologue in the second act when he comes home drunk and is appealing to Bess to get their marriage together. It wasn't direct enough and I remember a lot of rewriting on that, rearranging things so there was a clarity to it.

"When we started to work on the second act and got a run on it, we saw that the actor was hitting his mark and then taking two steps back, and the scene was getting bent out of shape because the speech kept wandering. What I wanted him to do was to start in low gear, then work up to medium gear, then go into high gear and, bang, he hits her with it. Barnet [the director] said, 'Look, you say this. Then, you keep coming back and repeating it. You don't have to say it four times.' Your first instinct is to say, 'Oh, no, I need that.' Then, you cut it and it's better. The actor gets better. It's cleaner and he gets there.

"I also had to hone and shape for the actress who was listening. Holland Taylor had practically nothing to say in the scene. I mean, her husband is coming at her and she is a feisty woman. It seemed difficult for her to believe that she wouldn't respond. And I said, 'This is the one time, and it is a very special time in your life, when this is coming from this man's heart and he is not to be interrupted because he is getting to you and you are grieving.' And defining it for her made me go home and look at it and cut and shape it. I had to keep the good moments in there and make that definition work."

There are theater legends galore about the kind of rewriting that goes on in rehearsal: entire acts thrown out, new characters added, others discarded, endings changed, scenes resequenced, comedies turned into dramas. It is one of the aims of the play development process that such extensive revision be unnecessary late in the game. Once a script has gone through so many readings and rewrites, it is hoped that at least the basic structure is solid.

If not, everyone is in trouble. The commercial theater is equipped to handle massive change, and there are all those dramatic tales of everyone staying up all night in Boston hotel rooms, wrenching a hit out of a bomb. A Broadway production gets more rehearsal time, perhaps a preopening tour, and previews in New York. If that is not enough, previews are extended and the opening is delayed. It costs money, but it can be done.

This is not true in nonprofit theater, where budgets are small and schedules are tight. If a theater runs on a subscription basis, tickets are sold in advance, and delays can cause major problems. Some houses, like the Public or Playwrights Horizons, can keep a production in previews while they fix and change; or they will close it in previews, go back into rehearsal, and open for the critics at a later date.

Mark Blum tells of just such a scenario in the development of Ralph Pape's *Say Goodnight, Gracie*: "There was a workshop at Playwright Horizons. We performed for a few weeks there and then took off for a couple of months and Ralph rewrote. We rehearsed another full period of three weeks for a production at the 78th Street Theater Lab, then previewed for five or six weeks, and by the time the play opened for critics at 78th Street, it was totally rewritten. Then, it moved to the Actors Playhouse on Sheridan Square.

"It was a play about five people whose anxieties are so enormous that they colored every single moment and everything they said and, yet, they were never mentioned. Ralph, as a writer, was never really in touch with that subtext. It was there because it was in his psyche and in his talent and he put it in every line subconsciously. Therefore, in the course of rehearsing the play and performing it at

Playwrights, when we would get to points in the play that would feel odd, we wouldn't always know why they would feel odd. You'd say, 'I don't know why but I don't want to say that line now.' Usually, a writer would say, 'That line is there so you would say it there. That's the way the play is written.' But we were fortunate to have an environment in which we could stop for an hour and say, 'Can we talk about why I don't feel like saying that line now?' And what eventually we would come to was that the line was true to the character but often not true to that moment of the character.

"There was no plot in the play. It's about a bunch of people getting ready to go to their high school reunion, and they sit around the apartment and joke about old times and old TV shows, all the while smoking pot, and eventually descending into a mire of reminiscence and drug-induced pain and falling asleep and not going to the reunion because they can't get out the door. It's without intermission or time change or scene changes. It starts and you're on stage for two hours and then it's over. It's a journey which five people take together and the real path of the journey is not in the lines at all.

"So each of us actors began to discover what each of our journeys was, and what the group journey was, and how each person takes the journey, and the little detours that each takes along the way. As we began to discover that and become more clearly focused on that, it became easier for Ralph to see where his writing was right and where it was missing."

It is rare for young writers to be afforded such luxury, and given all the other limitations, it is usually impossible for anyone to work well with a script that needs such extensive revision. If the director is still focused on rewrites, the actors will not get the attention they need. Hysteria will run rampant. Tempers will flare. Actors will leave. The purpose of the entire play development process is to prevent this from happening.

Changes that involve integrating the actors with the script must be made in rehearsal. Just as the actors must be comfortable with their costumes, they must be comfortable with their words. It does not resolve the problem for anyone—director, designer or writer— to brush off actors' complaints.

If an actor has trouble with a line, if he always stumbles on it, fails to remember it, if it stops his inner flow at every rehearsal, something must be done. Either the director must explore the moment in depth to find out where the actor's connections break, or the line must be changed. It does no good for the writer to insist that the line is right and the actor should just say it, for the director to assume that the problem will vanish or for them to declare jointly that the actor has a mental block. It is the actor up there, on the stage, making this script work; if there is a moment, or a scene, or a line that stops him dead, it will affect everyone onstage with him.

The same is true if there are mechanical problems: a discrepancy between the lines and the blocking so the actor does not have enough time (or has too much time) to get where he has to be; an important speech which must be delivered while pouring coffee; a line describing the co-star as "fragile" when she is six feet tall. It is true if the actor's rhythms and the writer's rhythms collide at a certain point, or if the actor feels the choice of words are not true to his character. The writer must not only accommodate the actor's needs; he must come to recognize that the actor knows as much, if not more, about this character they are jointly creating.

Oftentimes, actors' perpetual complaints stem from their own anxiety. That anxiety must be dealt with; it will not go away on its own. Generally, with a little hand-holding and reassurance, and a good night's sleep, the actor will get over the crisis and it will be smooth sailing thereafter. Most actors, somewhere in the rehearsal process, will grow terrified and will express it in a complaint about the script or their costumes. The experienced director can spot what is happening and handle it. The experienced actor gets over it.

Lee Kalcheim talks about his leads, Keith Charles and Holland Taylor: "Everyone has anxiety. During the second rehearsal, Holland was going around saying, 'Where will the ashtrays be?' We said, 'Where will the what be? What are you worried about that for?' That's the normal kind of silliness. At the beginning, I think, Keith was a little scared, and there were some problems between him and Barnet. The first day of rehearsal, there was real trouble because Keith talked a lot, questioned the script a lot, and we had to ask ourselves, 'Do we fire him if he's going to take up all this time?' Then, Barnet took him aside, I think rightfully so, and said, 'Hey, this is a terrific part. It's the best part you've ever had. Are you up for it or are you going to chicken out? You want to do it or you don't want to do it.' And Keith swallowed hard and said, 'Okay.' I think he finally acknowledged that he was scared. Once that broke, he was wonderful. He grew and grew and he was great. It was a gutsy move for a director to make. Barnet was taking a chance because we could have lost him; he could have walked. I don't know whether I would have taken that risk."

Most experienced directors are aware that there are loonies: actors who get tied up in their own angst and grow further from reality as rehearsals proceed, whose anxieties cannot be relieved by such straight-from-the-shoulder talk. Problems balloon. As one complaint gets resolved, another starts growing. Tears flow. Paranoia surfaces. Time is wasted. Hatred spreads through the company.

Ironically, the loonies are often attractive, talented, give wonderful auditions, and seem perfectly sane offstage. It all comes as a huge surprise as the tension begins to build. However, once a director has been through the horror of working with this type of actor, he learns to spot the signals early. He will confront the situation as soon as it appears, and if that does not work, will move quickly to protect the designers, the writer, the rest of the company.

Given that there happen to be such burdensome actors around, and that writers always suspect that any complaint about the script is coming from one, still actors must, at first, be granted the shadow of the doubt.

On the other hand, neither directors nor actors are writers. Actors always sneer when writers try to demonstrate how a line should be read. Writers do not know how to act, and if a bunch of writers were on stage, any play, even A Streetcar Named Desire—or especially Streetcar—would die. The same is true when actors try to rewrite. Writers deal with structure, counterpoint, texture, resonance; many qualities which the actor, in his absorption with his own role, may not appreciate or understand. Directors and actors often appear to think that the art of writing is simply creating lines that are comfortable for the actor to say. Writers respond by saying that the actor's comfort is limited by the range of his life experiences, which might be different from the character's.

This conflict between what the director and the actor need in the way of words to get the show moving and the fact that the writer wants the words to do more, supplies much tension to the work process. Some of this is healthy and useful. Those who have been involved in the play development process develop respect for the writer's craft and come to recognize that the writer's perception is different from their own.

Lee Kalcheim, again: "There was a crucial point when Barnet wanted to cut what I thought was an essential scene out of the first act [of *Les and Bess*]. It was a confrontation, which was really the basic confrontation of the play, and I think he thought it tipped it too soon, that it laid the play on the line too soon. My feeling was, it's a rehearsal, so we took it out and I looked at it and I thought, it's death if we take that out.

"What happened was that the first act ended and the play was too soft. You want to leave at the end of the first act and say 'There's my conflict. This is what I'm coming back for.' And I said, 'I've got to put my central character into some kind of crunch here so that we know what his dilemma is.' So we put the scene back in.

"That was the way we worked together. We'd be at rehearsal and he'd look across the aisle at me and run his finger across his throat, meaning 'That should be cut,' and I'd just hold up my hand and say, 'Wait.' You've got to try these things—that's the rehearsal process. I was perfectly willing to try the first act without that scene because, otherwise, how was I going to decide? He could have been right. So you watch it once or twice, and then, in my soul, I said, 'This is just wrong.' "

Writers work from memory, from images so old they float free from sources, from snatches of overheard conversation, from mysterious inspiration. A lot of this is difficult to defend in the midst of a tense rehearsal, and it is easy to give in under attack. The writer often finds out later that it was just those unexplainable moments which were crucial to his play.

The actor's job is to help define those moments, not automatically discard them. The actor should try to find the reality in the spots causing trouble, not reduce everything to the comfortable and familiar. Not only does that harm the play, it confines the actor.

Pamela Berlin says that in rehearsals for *To Gillian on Her 37th Birthday*, "The scenes that got examined closely were the scenes between David and Gillian, trying to define the nature of that relationship. It was a very complicated relationship and the feelings were very complicated. He misses her and he is angry with her. We had to get that anger into the scenes and strike a balance between the playfulness—she is playing with him, toying with him, trying to get him to return to the world—and the seriousness of what she is doing. We spent a lot of time in rehearsal on that balance because it was underwritten and we had to search for what was there. The writing was very spare and the language of the play is beautiful. But it gets tricky, especially in those scenes between David and Gillian because they spoke in shorthand and the actors had to fill in the dots."

The writer wants to hang onto the resonance in the dialogue, but the actor fights for the specific and the real. Sometimes, one wins; sometimes, the other. Most often, there is compromise. One thing is certain: A solution requires respect from both parties for what the other does. The actor questions, keeps trying, and always gives the script a chance. The writer, understanding why the actor needs to know, searches for answers the actor can use and does not dismiss his difficulties.

As actors work on each individual beat and struggle with the moment-to-moment problems, they are trying to find the overall story line—both for the play as a whole, and for their characters. Getting a hold on the story line is often the most perplexing problem facing actors doing new plays.

"Some plays are more surefire successes because the story is more clearly defined," says Mark Blum. "In many of Neil Simon's plays, not only the main stories but each actor's individual story is very clearly delineated and, therefore, if you get technically proficient actors, those plays work. That is not true of plays by all young writers. Gracie has never been successful in any of its other productions anywhere because it is such a difficult, buried play. Key Exchange is deceptive because people read it and think it's like Neil Simon, but it isn't. And that is why it has been unhappily surprising to producers who have tried to do it in Los Angeles and Dallas and Toronto. The lines are being said well but, somehow, the story is different.

"To me, the real story in the play is the development of the friendship between the two men. They meet as very different people, both resistant to the other's way of looking at the world; yet, somehow fascinated by it. During the course of the play, they come to appreciate and share more of their perceptions. Finally, when both of their romantic relationships fall apart, my character relates to being single in a misogynous way, as his friend has always bragged he did, and the friend relates in a fragile way, the way I have always told him I have related to things. In the last scene, there is a recognition that somehow we have merged and there is a tremendous bond.

"None of this is ever said but that's the central story. Certainly, from my point of view that is the story because I am not in the other story. But, another thing that we discovered in rehearsal is that there is a bond between me and the other man's girlfriend which is never spoken. My character and Brooke Adams's character have only one moment alone, when she tells him about her mother having cancer. It is a moment of tenderness, friendship, and caring, but what was never alluded to in that moment, which is central to the play, is that these two could be lovers. In order for the three characters to bond together, which has to happen if that play is to make sense, the potential for that relationship has to be there. We only found it because we explored that in rehearsal. Brooke and I found something in each other in that tiny scene and it played through the whole rest of the play."

The actors' discoveries, limitations, and personalities will affect the writer's work in rehearsal. David Trainer describes a rewrite done during rehearsals of The Dining Room: "There was a scene that did not work in rehearsal. I restaged it and redirected it and did it as many different ways as I could on the assumption that I was at fault. That's what you have to do—assume that the text is right. Also, it is easier, at that stage, to redirect than it is to rewrite. But, at the end of two weeks, I came to the reluctant but clear conclusion that the scene was wrong.

"Pete and I sat down and talked about what the scene had to do. The Dining Room progresses from morning to evening, even though it is across fifty years, so the scene had to take place in midmorning and it had to have two women. The women had to be Ann McDonough, who is younger, playing the older woman, and Lois de Banzie, who is older, playing the younger woman. We set out eight or ten terms, like auto mechanics taking apart an engine. The carburetor has to go here and the exhaust has to go there. Pete and I got it exactly defined and the new scene was written overnight— the dancing school scene. Pete was never crazy about it, but it's a safe place in the play; twenty to twenty-five minutes in. It's a gentle scene and it works, which the one we replaced didn't. There are moments when you can do almost anything you want so long as you don't throw away what you have accomplished already. This was one of those times."

When a playwright has all the ground rules laid out and is writing for specific actors at a specific point in the play, the process is different from the writing he did from scratch at the kitchen table before production. The work that is done on a script in rehearsal is directly related to the actors involved.

Trainer continues, "The strengths and weaknesses of those two actors were taken into account. Annie plays style wonderfully well, so the character acquired a certain flair. Lois can be sort of lumpy, so the daughter became somewhat lumpy. It was written to the strengths of the women, and that added color to a scene that was not substantially textured."

The tensions involved in the rehearsal process require that a strict code of behavior be observed. Mark Blum says, "Most directors will try to be a buffer between the actors and the playwright. There is more diplomacy in the situation if the director and the writer have a one-to-one private relationship where they sit in an office and talk about things. When rehearsals are going on, the director is working with the actors. If there is a playwright sitting in the rehearsal room, along with four other actors and designers and stage managers, and the actor, at that point, says, 'Marvin, I can't say these lines. They stink,'—even if they do, he has created a bad situation because the playwright has heard his play criticized in front of other people and he has to defend himself. Occasionally, an actor and a writer may be able to collaborate privately, but in my experience it is more beneficial if the actor and the director discuss it, then the director and the playwright discuss it, and then it comes back."

Writers ought to turn in properly typed revised pages. If the changes are important and have caused conflict, it is a mistake to ask the actors to just write the new lines into their scripts. In the process of crossing out and writing, the new lines will be questioned before the actors have had a chance to work on them and the dispute will start all over again. And if the newly typed pages do not have punched holes for easy insertion into the script, the actors are more likely to question the wisdom of the rewrite.

This is especially true in making cuts. If an actor loses a big speech or a treasured moment and is required to X it out with his own pencil, he is being asked to stab himself in the heart. The page should be retyped with the speech deleted so the stage manager can hand it out with no attendant drama.

Codes of theatrical behavior such as these are ignored at everyone's peril. Because emotions are so raw, theater people have developed a litany of rules and superstitions which keeps tensions under control.

The director always says, "Could we take it from the top, please?" "Could we do that again, please?" "Once more, please." The stage manager says, "Places, please."

Even the laughable habit of calling one another "darling" stems from the constant need for reassurance and affection. This tradition of courtesy is a bow to the sensitivity and delicacy of the work, and as silly as it may seem to the outsider, when tempers flare and tears flow, the fact that everyone says "please" and "thank you" and "darling" often saves the day.

Once the script problems have been resolved and the actors are starting to work off book, it is the writer's time to complain.

Many college actors, who have never had a writer breathing down their necks, have never learned to memorize verbatim. They take it as their right to play around with the "thes" "ands" or "buts," changing tenses, revising sentence structure. They insert a word of their own because it makes more sense at first and they keep saying it that way in rehearsal. If no one corrects them because the error is so small, it will become embedded in the brain, and they have no idea they are not saying the words the way the playwright wrote them.

Such sloppiness drives the playwright up the wall, and for good reason. He has toiled over each word, and every change, minor though it may be, is like a fingernail on a blackboard. We are not talking here about major changes that require some discussion. We are talking about lazy learning habits; a stage manager who is not doing his job; an undisciplined rehearsal structure.

Actors who mislearn lines often add words and make things more difficult for themselves. They break up the rhythms of the script, so the distorted line becomes hard to remember. Thought and sentence structure grow convoluted. The director and writer have worked through the script to make the dialogue simple and direct, to make things easier for the actor, to give him space to breathe and think. Then actors get hold of the scripts and end up with complicated sentences and too many words to handle.

Most young actors are too easy on themselves. When they run lines at home, their mates and friends are too loving to correct every little error. They do not learn the line correctly from the first, so there is always a nagging doubt about it, which results in the errors multiplying. When their work is flowing in rehearsal, they do not want to be stopped for minor corrections. The dead writer would never know the difference, but the live writer may be sitting in the last row.

The problem lies in the stage manager's lap. It is he who sits on book when the actors are on their feet, and runs line rehearsals and gives line notes. When the stage manager is on book, he only gives lines when the actor requests one. As Strasberg said, if the point of the rehearsal is for the actor to relate and discover, that is not the time to stop him because he has changed an "and" to a "but." However, he should get a note from the stage manager about it afterward.

When the actors are on their feet, stage managers are working to serve them. Their eyes are glued to the script, following it line by line, never getting distracted by the fascinating process onstage. When an actor loses a line in the heat of the action, it may mean that something new is happening emotionally. If he calls for a line and there is a scurrying of pages from the stage manager's table, his concentration has been shot and he has lost the chance to discover what was there to be had.

Sitting on book is a painstaking, boring job; hard on the eyes and numbing to the brain. But it is crucial to the creative process. Some amateur stage managers do not take it seriously enough. It is the directors' responsibility, when working with young, untrained stage managers, to explain what is required so that the job can be done well; to split it between the stage manager and an assistant so no one has to handle it for too many hours at a stretch.

While sitting on book, the stage manager notes any line changes that the actor makes repeatedly and he hands out the line notes after rehearsal. They serve to let the actor know where he is going off, and he is requested to look over the incorrect passages at home.

However, the most effective way to correct such errors is with a line rehearsal, which does not focus on the creative needs of the actor but rather on the script. The actors sit in a circle to run lines and the stage manager corrects every mistake as it occurs. The director and writer stay away because this is boring drill work, embarrassing for the actor to do before authority figures. It is the best way to get the lines down correctly and generally the actors are grateful for the help.

If the writer is writhing in his seat over the way the lines are twisted, it is not necessary for him to explode, curse the actors, or make a speech about how hard it was for him to write these words. He must insist to his director that line rehearsals be scheduled. Directors often have to be pushed into doing line rehearsals because of the time they take from other needs, but if the writer calmly insists, they will be scheduled.

Mark Blum says, "I always intend to say the words the way they're written. In the process of learning lines and in rehearsal, sometimes, you screw it up and say it a different way. Or you consciously rephrase it to get a hook on it. Maybe the moment is right and the wording is wrong or the rhythm is wrong. And, sometimes, in the process of saying it the wrong way, you come up with a way that feels better. You want to ask the playwright for that. But I'd just as soon not have the playwright there, hearing me say it twelve different ways. Probably, I'll end up saying it the way he wrote it anyway, but I must, at least, be able to focus on what is bothering me.

"If it's a comedy, in the course of screwing around in rehearsal, I might say something funny. Chances are twenty times I won't, but one time I will, and the director laughs and says 'What did you say that time? Let's write that down.' Some playwrights love that.

"Some playwrights are wedded deeply to the text as written, word by word. And there are some writers, like David Mamet, whose words are written to be said the way they are written and, if you say them differently, you are screwing around with one of the major reasons he is a good writer. With some writers, the rhythm of their words and their syllables are not the primary talent. With Mamet, the reason the line is there in the first place is because it has six syllables in it. It had to be that way.

"Some writers tend to overwrite, and they'll be cutting during rehearsal anyway. Ted Tally will say, 'Listen, I wrote this line here because I couldn't figure out what the right line was. I'll write a better one later, but use this for now.' If you have a situation like that, you feel free. The playwright understands he's got some things that are just temporarily there and so do I. We've got four weeks and we'll get there. Some playwrights are more sanguine about that kind of process than others."

We have discussed actor's panic, designer's panic, and writer's panic. The worst panic, however, is director's panic. When that hits, the production is really in trouble. If any of the others go off the deep end, it is the director's task to spot the crisis, analyze it, and figure out how to handle it. When the captain has deserted the ship, there is no one to serve that function. Nobody knows what is wrong. Everyone feels lost, and the terror spreads.

Director's panic happens when the director loses faith in his own instincts, in the actors' work, in the script. He has grown terrified and overwhelmed by the producer, or the critics, or the work to be done. He becomes indecisive and uncommunicative. He no longer listens or hears. He is unresponsive to the actors. He does not see what happens on stage. When the actors ask questions, he does not answer. His eyes go dead.

Generally, there is no way of repairing the damage or reversing the downward spiral. The company can never regain the necessary trust in the director, even if he manages to come out of this state. If the director is not fired at this point, the production will be doomed.

The only positive thing that can be said about this fate is that once the young director has experienced such panic, he commits to memory what the signals were and never lets it happen again. Or he leaves the business in terror. It is like a fatal disease: you either develop an immunity so it cannot strike again, or you are dead.

Here are some clues to avoiding the syndrome and, possibly, pulling out of it. There is nothing like going through it once for learning how to cope with it, but these few helpful pointers might make sense at a crucial moment.

1. Directors should always focus on the goals of this day's rehearsal, and this day's alone. If they fall into the trap of looking ahead at everything to be done, the situation can become overwhelming. Before they go into the rehearsal room, they should define what they wish to accomplish. If they achieve that, they should be pleased and start planning the next day. In fact, if they manage to get 50 percent of what they planned done, they should be pleased. A great deal of time that appears to be wasted in

rehearsal will pay off later. All the laughter, breaks, tangents, wrong directions, talking out of problems, may seem to block progress, but real work is going on. If half of each rehearsal produces obvious results and half produces nothing, the apparently unproductive half may pay off later.

2. Directors' inner time clocks are important to scheduling. There are directors who are daytime people; there are those who function best at night. Obviously, it is best to rehearse when the director is at a peak. If a director starts at high energy and then peters out, new material should be scheduled for the beginning of rehearsal; the final hours being saved for drill work. If a director takes a while to warm up to get going, the procedure should be reversed. If a director is totally wiped out after a five hour rehearsal, meetings with designers, the writer, and the stage manager, should be scheduled before rehearsal starts. Everyone should be told what the director's needs are and how he works so they know what to expect, when to come for help and when to leave him alone.

3. Directors should always use the day off as it was intended. In the midst of everything to be done, there is always the temptation to schedule extra work, see actors privately, have production meetings on the company day off. Directors need a day of rest too, to think things over, replenish the creative juices. Sometimes, the slide into panic can be halted by the one day of stepping aside and reviewing the situation.

4. Directors should not be afraid to hide behind the stage manager. Protecting the director is one of the stage manager's functions. He should handle the actors' rehearsal conflicts, the designers' needs, the producer's demand for paperwork. Once directors get the ball going in every court, they should save themselves for where they are indispensable: rehearsals.

5. Directors should always be aware of their subliminal feelings toward the actors. If they find themselves browbeating one actor all the time, threatened by another, attracted to a third, they have to stay on top of these emotions and exclude them from the work. All kinds of unconscious signals, past experiences, neurotic tendencies come into play in the complex relationship between actors and directors. Extraneous, uncontrolled impulses are the directors' responsibility to analyze and discard.

6. When the worst happens and they start sliding into terror, the

only way to climb out is by listening. Directors should listen to actors' questions, writers' complaints, stage managers' problems. Directors in panic shrug everything off, find everyone too demanding. They get so overwhelmed by their own needs they cannot cope with anyone else's, so they stop hearing and handle none.

7. This final suggestion comes out of deep personal experience. When emerging from late night rehearsals, going home becomes a large and costly problem. It is generally resolved by members of the company sharing cabs. Directors should not join them. The few times I have been trapped in a cab with actors have been unbearable. Rehearsal is over. I want to slump out of responsibility. Yet, many actors can never get enough attention and approval.

"What did you think of that turn I took in act 1 today?"

"Did you notice I was doing something new with my voice?"

"Did you catch that look I gave her? Wasn't that terrific?"

Because I am tired, because I now want someone to take care of me, I am suddenly tempted to discard everything I know about the actor-director relationship, to throw theatrical courtesy to the winds, and sock each and every one of these demanding infants in the mouth!

Better for the work to take my life in my hands and go home on the subway, alone.

11

Anxiety Alley

Many productions, even those that have done well in the rehearsal process, fall apart in the final stage; run-throughs, technical rehearsals, dress rehearsals, previews—Anxiety Alley. If the first ingredient of success is a good script, and the second is good casting, the third is the company's ability to handle anxiety.

"It seems almost inevitable, yet you forget everytime you get there," says Pamela Berlin. "With *Gillian*, it was the weekend of the third week and we were getting ready to go into tech. It was the first time we had a run-through for Curt Dempster, artistic director of EST, and one or two others. Afterward, there were a lot of notes. Michael and I went home and worked on the script, mainly editing, until about three or four in the morning. It was that scary, scary time when you think the show is an utter disaster, and you are trying desperately to do something to fix it, and you don't know how you're going to get through the next day of rehearsal because everything feels so monumental. You have so much work to do and you'll never be able to do it all and you're going to lose the actors' confidence and faith when you walk in and give them all these changes. Somehow, you pull yourself together and you walk in the next day and you start working and, surprise, you get a lot of good work done in a short amount of time and it's all to the good. There seems to be one day like that in every production of a new play."

In Anxiety Alley, the terrors mount. The obstacles become enormous. Emotions explode. Normal people turn into monsters. Just when the actors should be coming into their own, when the play should be making sense, when all the pieces should be falling together, the situation can fall apart.

When this happens, the damage is devastating. It is not only that the actors do not move forward; they move backward. They are not yet secure enough in what they are doing. The work is not yet "in the bones." If tension enters before this happens, they grow desperate to recapture what was wonderful in rehearsal the week before. They stop discovering. Instead, they strain; they push; they manufacture feelings. The director desperately tries to figure out what is wrong.

"There are instances when I've got the wrong play," says David Trainer. "It's wrong. I'm wrong. Something's wrong. Then, it is a question of what do I know. What can I do to help myself, to help this play, and that's instructive and fun too, in it's way. Fun, if you use a broad definition of the word; like being highjacked is probably fun. You've had an experience—and you got to go to Beirut. But it's not fun while you are in the midst of it."

When tech complications are added, directors might be trying to solve some lighting problem, so the actors feel deserted, which increases their terror. Writers sense that something is wrong and grow afraid it is their script. They cannot get the directors' attention so they hysterically make drastic cuts, or write new pages, or decide on tiny word changes that drive the actors crazy.

Costumes are not ready when they should be or do not fit when they arrive. Or, just when the actor needs a run-through to make sense of the whole, precious time is wasted running sound cues; not because the sound is so complex but because the kid on the tape machine has never done it before. Many smaller theaters cannot afford headsets, so tech work, which is complex and tense enough, is noisy and chaotic.

If the theater has no shop, the set designer is fighting for stage time to finish construction and painting. The crew works around rehearsals into the early hours of the morning. Impatience and anger are exposed. This is the time when actors get other job offers out of the blue and leave, when assistant stage managers decide they have had enough of the glamour of the theater and disappear.

The stage is coated with sawdust. Actors get splinters from unfinished furniture. Costumes get torn on nails. Cable, instruments, tools lie about for anybody to trip over. There are so many strangers wandering in and out that everything not nailed down gets stolen.

In this period, rehearsals are no longer scheduled around the needs of the actors; the needs of the production come first, and everyone is expected at every rehearsal. One cannot work around an actor at a run-through. It does no good for the stage manager to walk through the part, offering the other actors no familiar rhythms, no energy, no emotional connections. The entire cast must be at every rehearsal and must hang around for notes at the end. Although this is expected on Broadway or on a movie set, it may become unbearable when the actors are not paid, when they work at an office all day, when they watch rehearsal for the first time and begin to doubt the success of the venture.

Off-off-Broadway depends on the faith and confidence of the participants. When that can be nourished during the difficult final days, miracles can be achieved. When optimism begins to sour, problems multiply, tension builds, disaster looms.

Anxiety Alley starts the day the flyers arrive from the printer. Off-off-Broadway productions do little advertising. Some papers and magazines run free listings, and the theater sends flyers to its mailing list. The majority of the flyers are supplied to the members of the company, who, it is hoped, will bring in a large chunk of the audience.

To the actors, the flyer is a reminder to the casting world that they are alive. The actors pounce on the flyers and, from that moment on, can be spotted in the hallways addressing, stamping, circling their names, and gossiping about who is certain to come.

In commercial theater, there are always going to be reviews. As frightening as that inevitable exposure is, it is easier to handle than the possibility that one's work will go unnoticed. It is this terror that pushes the gossip and fantasy action in the hallway to dangerous proportions.

The smaller the venture, the higher the level of desperation. Somebody is always boasting that a famous casting director is sure to show. There is constant chatter about which reviewer would be most responsive to the script, which producer has a dark Broadway house available. Each actor sends cute notes to aunts and cousins, rekindling an infantile need for affection and response. This may have been where the desire to get onstage came from initially, but professionals have distanced themselves from it and the regression does not help these anxious hours.

This is when the director should be building a cocoon of privacy around the work so that the actors can find their confidence and the performance can begin to flourish. It is a crucial period, and if directors sense that the hallway gossip is becoming manic, they have a responsibility to stop the action and bring the focus back to the work.

Beginning actors, and certainly beginning writers, fall into the trap because they so desperately want recognition. Directors must point out that excessive fantasy is an expression of anxiety that increases the problem, instead of solves it, and that spreads through the company like an epidemic.

By this time, actors have conquered the mechanics. Their concern about remembering lines and blocking are over, and they are discovering a sense of place on the set. The props and costumes, as they come in, help them find a physical reality. They begin to forget that they are on a stage, that they are being observed. They grow involved with their fellow actors, truly playing the story. Everything that they have been directed to do becomes organic because they can finally let their inner lives take over. What happens onstage is no longer mechanical, no longer tentative, no longer controlled by the brain but by the emotions.

Strangely enough, when this happens, actors also acquire increasingly more objective control. Robert Lewis, renowned teacher and director, describes this development:

Now we come to the last rehearsal process before we get to the run-throughs, which is the "smoothing out" of all the externals. By now let us say everyone is playing fine but this fellow is in front of that one, or this grouping doesn't look right and you need to change a few positions, or somebody's voice has to be adjusted one way or another. All the external problems can now be worked with nicely and smoothened out because you've got your form, inside and out, set. And if you, the actors, as well as the director, have done the proper preparation before, you will find it is possible for you to execute all sorts of things you could never have imagined possible earlier in rehearsal. You'll find, for example, you can be looking away from your sweetheart, instead of at her, at the moment you realize she doesn't love you, if for some reason you have to be looking that way. It can be a reason quite apart from anything you could have imagined. It could have something to do with proposed lighting or scenery. Or let us say that the director suddenly feels it is more exciting for you not to be looking right at her at that moment. The point is you now know so much about it that the director can safely say, "Although you have been previously looking at her in this moment, I would like you now to play the moment looking away from her." And you can do it because you understand enough about it to realize the scene might be better for technical reasons that way, or more exciting, and to find a reason to do it like that. In other words, it is now possible for you, if you have prepared the earlier stages properly, to justify almost anything that is asked of you in the final staging.*

Just as there was a moment in the play development process when the play became the director's, and no longer the writer's, now, during run-throughs, the play becomes the actor's.

The auditorium is quiet and houselights are dimmed to help the actor's concentration. The work is not interrupted, it is discussed afterward in notes. The actors are beginning to sense what is right and wrong on their own. They act from their impulses instead of for the director's approval, and a good director will allow them to do so.

During the early stages of rehearsal, actors want the director to stop them the minute they go wrong. If beat A goes off, it does not help if the director allows the scene to proceed, hoping the work will straighten itself out. A wrong beat A will only lead to a worse beat B, overburdened by the tiny corner of the actor's brain which is now wondering what is wrong and why the director offers no help.

Actors are like children learning to walk; first they make tiny swimming motions, then they crawl, then they take those few tentative steps and need to know that someone will catch them if they fall. But when their bodies announce that they can do it on their own, they want to be free to race up and down mountains.

A wise director senses when the company is ready for run-throughs. Forced into them too early, actors will push and strain for performances. Held back too long, they will grow overcautious and frustrated. There is a moment when the director will step aside and, come what may, allow the actors to experience the full arc of the play from beginning to end.

This moment is like every other step in this final stage; as the actor approaches independence and completion, it is accompanied by terror. First run-throughs are legendary nightmares. The actor comes face to face with the fact that this wonderful, protected

---

* Robert Lewis, *Method—or Madness:* (New York, Toronto and Hollywood: Samuel French, Inc., 1958), pp. 145–50.

rehearsal period will come to an end, and he is going to be out there alone.

The emergence of the stage manager as an alternative, but less overpowering, parent figure will help the company through this time of tension.

Once the company is in run-throughs, it is the stage manager who controls rehearsals. He starts them, calls places, calls cues, sets props and costumes. Many directors move to the back of the house, and it is the stage manager who sits up close, on book; the new captain of the ship is at his post alone. The actors are eager for this transfer of authority. In the first weeks, they turned to the director with every question and complaint; now, they naturally go to the stage manager. He becomes their ally, and the director, an observer.

It is a mistake for the director to cling to power at this stage. If he undercuts his stage manager, demeans him, rushes him, expects rehearsal to go at his own pace instead of the stage manager's, he is blocking an important transfer of dependency that is beneficial to the actors' freedom, and he will be resented the way an overprotective parent is.

However, off-off-Broadway directors must prepare their stage managers, who are likely to be novices, for what is expected of them. When handled well, this transition allows the actors to grow, the director to withdraw, the stage manager to assume the control needed to run the show. And the rehearsal process enters the final stage with a minimum of anxiety.

Sometimes directors may withdraw too quickly. Tired of taking care of the actors, overburdened by technical problems, eager for the cast to assume responsibility, they begin to feel anxious themselves. Instead of growing more alert as the play goes into its final stages, they become numb, stop seeing, and let problems slide.

If a director's notes after a run-through are too few, too vague, or too confusing, the company is likely to get nervous. The actor can accept the fact that he is going to perform this play for strangers and critics, but the director remains a presence through the constant flow of notes. They serve to keep the anxiety at bay, as well as to improve the work.

Notes can define for the actors how they behave under stress so they can spot the warning signals. Some go too fast, some slow down. Some actors forget to breathe, some take no transitions. Some shout, some whisper. A bad performance can be a learning experience if directors can pinpoint how and when the actors can hop off the roller coaster of tension, even if they have just started on it. Directors should be able to supply actors with moments of clarity and definition that serve as buoys in treacherous waters. Once an actor reaches one of these moments, no matter how lost she has been up to then, she should be able to refocus and head in the right direction.

In addition to the individual performances, directors make sure that the essential through-line is communicable to an audience. It is at this point that they go back to the basics, which often get lost in the moment-to-moment work. What is this play about? Who is the hero? What is his conflict? How does the experience change him? Every performance now has to be defined within this structure.

Pacing becomes crucial. As actors grow more confident they will naturally go faster. However, they are used to the rehearsal rhythms and, in their anxiety, may cling to pauses that they needed earlier, but no longer do.

Directors will often call a pacing rehearsal. The actors sit in a circle and go over their lines, as in a line rehearsal, except they run their lines in the same rhythms and with the same pauses as they do in performance. If the director stops at every pause and asks for a reason, the actor will recognize the ones he is taking only out of habit and will be able to eliminate them. Having these pointed out specifically is more helpful than a note to "pick up the pace." And the actors find that removing unnecessary pauses frees them to interact more spontaneously.

The director must be prepared for the fact that every new element sets the actors' work back temporarily. After the actor absorbs the mechanics, grows used to the flow of the play, and begins to enjoy his freedom from the director's control, he approaches a performance level. Then, something new is introduced: props, the set, lighting, costumes, the move from rehearsal hall to stage. With each new element, the performance takes a step backward. One can see the actor spending the rehearsal adjusting to new elements until they are absorbed into the flow of the work and he is free to move ahead. It is a two steps forward, one step backward process, and the director must allow that to happen.

*   *   *

When the show goes into run-throughs, the writer should attend every rehearsal. The final shape of the play emerges and the director needs her there to share reactions and ideas. The writer might also find she has a lot of work to do.

"I remember our being in the theater," says Pamela Berlin, of *Gillian*. "I was working with Allen Hughes on the lights, which were very complicated, and Michael was holed up in the dressing room with a typewriter, making changes and running out and showing me something and running back into the dressing room, and we'd go back to the tech."

The production dramaturg reenters the picture at this stage to serve as a sounding board for the director and writer. Since he knows the script, the writer's intent, and the director's concept, the dramaturg can offer informed, objective measurement of what has been achieved and what is lacking. The good dramaturg now no longer only comments on the script, but offers notes on the acting, direction, and design as they fit into the whole.

Many directors suffer an acute sense of loneliness because all the responsibility is on their shoulders. Writers and dramaturgs must therefore be supportive of directors and aware of their needs. Directors must now deal with the reactions of onlookers: designers, staff, invited guests, and most frightening of all, the theater's producer or artistic director.

Pamela Berlin says, "EST has these gypsy run-throughs when Curt and the staff and certain members come in and watch the play, and it is always a day you dread and loathe. Curt and these others disappear into his office and talk about the play, and Curt gets some feedback and then he comes and talks to you. Even though I've been through many of these and I've always hated them and I grouse about them, they usually are helpful—for the actors, too, in terms of getting a sense of what is working and what's not with an audience."

The artistic director's input can be invaluable, and if unavailable, will be sorely missed. Mark Blum was in Martin Sherman's *Messiah*, a critical failure at the Manhattan Theater Club, and he explains, "David Leveaux was a young, bright, charismatic director who had never worked at that theater before. He and the playwright had done the play successfully in England, and they felt rather more isolated and independent at the Manhattan Theater Club than other directors feel. Lynne Meadow, the artistic director, was on maternity leave, so she wasn't there. I've done another play at the Manhattan Theater Club and there was very strong input from her. In this case, I am sure there was pressure from the dramaturg and others to change stuff but the playwright never rewrote a word that I know about."

Directors frequently find themselves assaulted by opinions during run-throughs; however, while the reactions of the observers are valuable, it is still too early to act on every evaluation. Writers and dramaturgs can assist directors by sorting through reactions, discussing them, analyzing them, and then helping to decide which to worry about and which to ignore.

Good producers have a solid connection with their audience's sensibility. They have an uncanny ability to look at the stage with the eyes of the ticket buyer and predict what the audience reaction will be. But this does not mean that they can accurately propose a solution. David Trainer says, about Andre Bishop's role during work on *The Dining Room*, "I remember going to Andre and saying that Pete and I had a disagreement about something, and Andre said, 'The artists must solve this for themselves. The producer can't.' Andre understands that you have to create an environment in which the people like and respect each other and care so that the work will come together, but he cannot come in as a deus ex machina and sort things out. He never told us, 'Do this' 'Do that' or 'David's right or wrong.' He said, 'You guys go and argue.' This was very useful because he put us back on our own devices rather than thinking some higher authority is going to solve this. There was one scene which I insisted Pete rewrite, and Andre always felt it was funnier the old way. He understood why I said that it needed to be rewritten. I felt it was a trivial approach to a problem and made the characters one dimensional. If Pete wrote it another way, it would probably be less funny but more substantial, and Pete bought it. Andre kept saying it was funny, but I said it was funny at the expense of the characters. Those laughs count against you. Who knows? Was I right or wrong? Anyway, the change got made and Andre said, 'It was funnier the old way.' And it was. But nobody knows what's right. We're trying to fulfill the true purposes of the play, but we are groping."

Producers usually are not as intimately involved in the play development process as are the director and writer and dramaturg. They cannot look at the stage with the same knowledge of mechanics and inner workings the others can. They see the whole, but not the parts. The producer will say, "This scene is a bore. Pick up the pace." His evaluation is accurate, but not his solution. The scene may be a bore because nothing is happening between the actors, because one note is being played for too long. Perhaps the actors need to go slower, to discover the curves in the scene, to make new discoveries, and then the scene will not be a bore. The producer will say, "Act 2 is too long. Cut this scene." Act 2 may be too long and that has to be resolved, but if the director jumps to make the cut, it may be in error.

Pacing and length are the most common problems at this stage, but, time and again, though there have been tales of huge reductions in playing time as the actors relax, not a single cut may have been made. At the earliest run-throughs, actors are still thinking their way through the play. Many go slowly on purpose. Many are cautious and frightened. Little by little, the patterns grow smooth. Reactions become natural and more spontaneous. The actors begin to "cook." It happens to one and spreads to the others. Pauses get dropped. Pace picks up.

The stage manager times each run-through, and in the burgeoning production, one can spot the progress on his daily chart. It is a natural process and it is unnecessary for the director to cut scenes as a result of pressure from the producer, or to push the actors to go faster, when there are signs that it is happening on its own.

What the director and writer look for are the beats that fail to speed up or go easier for the actor. This means that there is something happening in that specific moment that is, perhaps, illogical or unclear. A line is taking the actor off on a sidetrack, is stopping the motor of the play for him, and, sometimes, he does not even know it. If there is always an unnecessary pause, a dead spot, if the pace suddenly slows down and takes several beats to get back to where it should be, the problem has been spotted. It is that line, that beat, which must be cleaned up, and miraculously, when it has been, the actors are free to let the work flow again. Clearing up those little glitches has an astonishing effect on the pace and the timing.

Emily Mann tells of such an experience during previews of the Broadway production of Execution of Justice. The show was too long by twenty minutes, and the producer pushed for a particular scene to be cut. When she did get the show down to the proper length and had actually pared off the twenty minutes, the producer said, "See, I told you that scene had to go!" Actually, it was still there. She had only cut two or three lines.

It is often sadly true that the technical facilities and experience of the tech personnel are not up to the level of the writing and acting in the off-off-Broadway arena. Everything has to be done in the crunch of too little money, time, space, help, and materials. Crews are recruited at the last moment, if they can be had at all, and they are usually kids doing it for fun or, at best, to learn. Tech week is stressful and hectic enough at a major regional theater with every resource at its command; at a tiny off-off-Broadway house, it can stop the actor's process in its tracks.

However, all will not be lost if the director prepares the cast and advises them that, for the next few rehearsals, she will be concerned only with how they look, how they are lit, so that all the wonderful work they have done will not be lost in shadows. She can tell them that she will not be watching the acting at all, that she will give no acting notes and, suddenly, the actors will feel freed. Many an actor has created wonderful new work, relaxed fully, and brought his performance up a level at the techs because he was not fighting the process.

During this last frantic week of rehearsal, the director may ask the writer to freeze the script temporarily. The actors have an extraordinary amount of new information to absorb and should be allowed to grow comfortable with the script as it stands until they have gotten over the hump of the first public preview. Once the anxiety level has been reduced, the director and writer can resume making changes, if necessary.

Theater legend has it that a bad dress rehearsal bodes well for opening night, and there is some truth to it. Just as there is a moment when actors must get off book or they will not proceed to the next level, or when they are ready to move from scene work into a run-through, there is a moment when the actor is ready for response. Laurence Olivier describes this state as he approached his first performance as Richard III:

As an actor approaches a first night the sense of excitement is extraordinary. As with a bullfighter, everything is geared towards the moment of truth with his audience. One second of mistiming and it's over. One slip and they'll have you. Every waking minute the seconds are ticking away on your automatic time clock. You have gone into the countdown. As the last week approaches, anything that gets in the way of your train of thought is an irritation. An outside conversation (outside of the production, that is) is not welcome. Everything is homing in towards the raising of the curtain and if you've got it right—or think you've got it right—you are not overconfident, but looking forward to the challenge. I could smell the play and couldn't wait to have it wrapped round me like a cloak. Waking in the morning, showering, shaving, it was there: the twinge in the gut, the knowledge that something was about to happen. I had no way of knowing it would be a success—there is no way of knowing that—but I knew in my head that I had almost completed the jigsaw.*

By the time the dress rehearsal rolls around, the director and writer are tired of laughing at the same bits over and over. Designers are involved with their own areas of responsibility. The costumer sees every wrong hemline and is far too busy taking notes to laugh. But the actors know there are people out there, and the lack of response makes them strain. The bad dress rehearsal can be a sign of the actor's extreme readiness for an audience.

An open dress rehearsal can resolve the problem, but it is a risky practice off-off-Broadway. The tech people are always behind schedule. Wet paint abounds. The lighting designer is still playing with levels. The house is filled with tools, lumber, paint buckets, and food cartons. The seats are covered with sawdust. The producer does not want to pay for a cleanup until opening day, so if an audience is invited to the dress, precious time will be lost as the director and writer have to clean up the mess.

All told, the open dress is a luxury that off-off-Broadway cannot offer the actors, no matter how much they may want or need it. Therefore, the production most ready to open is also most likely to go off at dress. The actors are all dressed up with nowhere to go, but the director who is forewarned knows that all will be well on the following night.

Incorporating the audience into the production is like incorporating any other element; first it throws the company and creates anxiety. Gradually, the actors learn to use the audience response as

* Laurence Olivier, *On Acting* (New York: Simon and Schuster, 1986), pp. 122–3.

they came to use the costumes, sets, props, and lights, and the performances grow another notch. It takes time, and progress is not always steadily upward. The first public preview can be so charged with nervousness that the stage is filled with electricty, only to be followed by a downer the following night when exhaustion sets in. By the end of the first week, the director can begin to get a clear picture of how the show works. By the first weekend, when houses are better than they were midweek, the actors seem to be more confident; then, the day off comes around. Many off-off-Broadway productions only play Thursday through Sunday; the three-day gap frequently sets the company back once again. Confidence has to be rebuilt. Familiarity and security only come with playing the show night after night.

"It takes forever," says Susan Merson, "to go through all the director's notes, the producer's notes, the stage manager's notes, the other actors' panics, until you, yourself, begin to connect to the character in a very elemental way. About a year into the run of *Vanities*, I knew Mary better than anybody in the world because I had played her so long. And when she became mine, really in the third act, it was like an out-of-body experience. I would sail out over the audience every night."

In the minimum showcase code run of twelve performances, frequently stretched over three or four weekends to get the best possible houses, the process is frustrating and actors have a difficult time reaching the security of a full performance. The irony is that by the time the actors have grown used to the on-again-off-again schedule and are finally beginning to peak, the show usually has to close. Only once this peak is reached can the director and writer depend on what they see onstage. They can no longer blame a bad night on nerves. They no longer have to deal with performances that change radically from night to night. They can then analyze the script problems and start to fix, but in most showcase runs, by then, the experience is over.

Productions with longer runs offer more opportunity for repairs, particularly because there are more performances weekly. The actors have a chance to get the motor going. Momentum takes over and progress is made as the playing week progresses. Still, many weeks of playing are required before the day off is not a setback.

Warm-ups before previews can help bring the company back to prime performance level. Each director has his own kind of exercise to offer: yoga, chants, and rolling around the floor are some examples. More traditional is the line rehearsal, enabling the actors to think through the entire show, playing each beat in miniature. This is an effective way of regrooving the channels in the brain and consolidating the company after a day off. A more elaborate technique is the speed-through, in which the company goes through the entire show on their feet, lines and blocking by rote. It is a simple way of regrounding the company in the mechanics so that when the curtain goes up they can let the work flow.

Equity rules allow for rehearsal during previews so script changes may be made and problems worked out. If changes are given in postperformance notes without scheduling a rehearsal, one can see a flicker of panic in the actor's eye the following night as he approaches the moment: "Is this where that cut comes and what the hell is it?" The actor needs the rehearsal to absorb the change so that it settles into the bottom layer of his brain along with the other mechanics.

Directors often expect actors to make all kinds of adjustments onstage in front of the preview audience, and this can be a source of conflict with the company. There is the backstage legend of the star who was asked to add a picture hat to her costume during previews. She agreed but asked for a rehearsal so she could work with the hat a bit. The director sneered at her concern. She could experiment with it just as well in the following night's performance, he said. "Certainly," she answered sweetly, "but does the hat know the lines?"

Actor Pierre Epstein was in the Broadway production of Enter Laughing, the comedy hit by Joseph Stein that made Alan Arkin a star. Pierre tells this story: "We were out of town and everyone was convinced the show was a bomb. Reviews were bad, the box office was down, audience response was tepid. There were one or two scenes with big laughs, but even they weren't working. The show was too long. There were too many dead spots, too many plot complications. Alan was giving this brilliant performance but the production was not centered around him enough and the bad stuff was killing the good. More than that, we were all depressed and sure we were going to close and that must have been coming across the footlights. Well, the script was based on Carl Reiner's autobiographical book and it was terribly important to him that it succeed.

So he flew in from the coast and arrived like a breath of fresh air; tanned and confident and ready to work. Joe Stein and the director were stretched out in the lobby, exhausted and defeated, but Reiner started snipping and changing, cutting this line, that bit. At first, we thought he was crazy. Here we had this huge bomb on our hands and he's making tiny cuts. But every day we were inundated with them; line cuts, rewrites, changes in blocking. Then, two scenes had been so pared down that he could combine them into one. Scenes got resequenced. The little changes led to the big ones. He simply would not stop, and everyone's spirits lifted. It wasn't planned. I don't think he ever knew where he was headed, but eventually, he had reduced the script from three acts to two, and it just so happened that act 1 ended with Alan's first big socko laugh scene, sending the audience out happy at intermission, and act 2 ended with his other big scene, sending them home even happier. So we came into New York with a star and a show that was a smash."

Plays in previews are not generally fixed with one startling inspiration or one drastic overhaul. (Although playwright Albert Innaurato did just that with his Coming of Age in Soho, which started performances at the Public Theater with a woman in the lead and opened for the press with her gone from the play and a subsidiary male character rewritten as the hero. In order to achieve this, however, the production shut down during previews to give the company time to rehearse what was practically a new script). Mostly the changes are small and specific. First, one moment gets fixed, which in turn changes another. The director and writer follow the audience reaction like hunting dogs after a quarry.

Company notes during previews have a different tone than notes after run-throughs. Everyone is involved and every problem is shared. Everyone has a different sense of the audience. Everyone has heard from friends in the house. Lee Kalcheim says that, during previews of Breakfast with Les and Bess, "One of the large problems was that Holland Taylor had a hard time being nasty. Her character, Bess, had to be tough and what would happen is that she would go out after a performance and her friends would say, 'Oh, you're so tough and nasty.' So, she'd come back the next night and be sweet. It killed the play because there was no tension anymore. The play needs someone who is tough and nasty, and her husband is fighting to get back that person he fell in love with. If there's no wall there, there's no fight. So Barnet had a big showdown with her finally and said, 'Look, this is just not going to work that way.' It was hard. I understand how actresses want to be liked. They want to play likable people, but I think she was getting bad signals from friends. When it was finally resolved, it was fine. But up to then, it was dicey because she was different every night, and when she was sweet, the play was not working."

Directors have to sort through the audience input and decide what to respect, what to discard, and then, once a wrong moment has been spotted, to ascertain whether it is the script, the acting, the costumes, or the lighting that is throwing off the audience.

"Judgments and criticisms on these occasions are not always misguided," writes director Harold Clurman,

but the atmosphere in which they occur is overwrought. There is fierce, nerve-racking pressure—financial, egotistical and, worst of all, corporate. Everybody gets into the act: show biz mentors, husbands, wives, boy and girl friends, other actors, other directors, other writers—experts all! It is my invariable practice to warn everyone concerned with the production against giving credence to these well-wishers and, if possible, not to listen to them at all.

It is panic time, and the director must keep his own counsel. There is no arrogance in this: he must realize that he knows the play and its problems better than anyone else. He should and will heed advice thoughtfully offered by people whose theatre knowledge or instincts he respects. But he must resist even the playwright and the producer if he believes them in error.*

On the other hand, David Trainer describes the previews of The Dining Room: "When we were in previews, we saw how careful Pete was about laying out the ground rules. The first scene, you see two people in this room and then there's another scene and you see a few more people and they talk about this room and it's a different room they are talking about. What he's done in the first two scenes is laid it down that this room is going to be many rooms and that is the first rule of the play. The third scene, actors from the first and second scene reappear as different characters. That's the second rule of the play, which is this room stands for all rooms and these actors stand for all people. Pete is a supreme believer in the rules.

* Harold Clurman, On Directing (New York: Collier Books, 1974), pp. 136–7.

You do everything according to the rules and it is foolproof. Anyone who directs it differently is nuts, because it works.

"Well, when you start previewing, for the first week or so, you are learning to communicate the nature of the event to the audience. It's not a rational or an articulate process, but it happens in every play. You learn to serve it up right, and we were concerned in the previews that the first five to eight minutes of the play defeat the whole thing, and I told Pete that the first really sustained piece of drama is the breakfast scene. I said 'Let's get to that. Cut one of these other scenes.' This was one of our major disagreements. He said, 'Absolutely not, David. It violates the rules. It won't work. We'll get there faster but it doesn't lay out the rules of the play.' Directors can sometimes be too expeditious, and I said, 'C'mon, c'mon, c'mon. The scene doesn't work. Get it out of there. Then we get to the good stuff a minute faster.' He said, 'Look!' and the foot came down hard. He fine-tuned the first scene, but he wouldn't cut it, and he was right and I was wrong.

"That's the thing in previews. You wonder do we have to direct better, do we have to write better? Should we just be patient and come back tomorrow morning and do the same thing and pray that it gets better naturally? In this case, the writer was right. Just leave it alone.

"Another thing we learned in previews was to play the actions very strongly. There was one preview when we thought we were dead. There was no laughter, no life, nothing. Everybody looks to themselves and thinks, 'The play is a disaster' or 'the production is a disaster.' The actors thought they were a disaster. Everyone thought, 'I've failed. This thing won't work.' Wendy Wasserstein was there and she thought it was wonderful. We're all at a funeral and she's saying. 'Oh, it's wonderful. It's great!' But she said to Andre, 'You know, the thing is, you can't play polite material politely.' And Andre passed this very perceptive comment on, and I said, 'Gotcha. Thank you, Wendy.' I went into rehearsal the next day and it took me forty-five minutes to do what I had to do. I said, 'Remember what your objectives are and you need to play them very strongly. Anytime you fall off the action, it is the equivalent of that lockjaw approach. It becomes an illustration.' Then, we rehearsed little bits of scenes. 'You've got to really hit that line. You've got to hit the verb of that line and really make the action clear.' All the wires tightened up. The machine worked, and we never had a problem with that. It was an important lesson. There's no story involved. There is no plot—like who stole the gun—that keeps you going no matter how lax the performance becomes. It has to be tight, and tightness in the theater has to be projected. So, we went back to every scene and we said, 'You want this. You want that and you want it badly.' "

A good deal depends on the director's ability to instill his company with confidence and a sense of community. I once asked an actor to overhaul totally our concept of his character between a matinee and an evening preview because the audience was responding so negatively to him. The other actors suggested things they could do onstage to help. The costume designer went out and bought him a more attractive shirt to wear and, that evening, we turned the tide. It was partly due to an accurate analysis of the problem, to the actor's ability to respond, and no doubt about it, to the fact that everybody pulled together in the crunch and helped maintain his confidence. The most difficult part of fixing a show is that so much is done in public. But it cannot happen any other way and the company must resist becoming overwhelmed by embarrassment and a sense of failure.

Then, at last, the critics come. Only, sometimes, off-off-Broadway, they don't. The New York papers, local and national magazines, and television programs only cover the Broadway openings on a regular basis. It depends on the prestige of the theater, how busy the reviewers are, whether a press agent is handling the production, or whether one of the names on a flyer is impressive. Maybe one paper comes, maybe several do. Some come at the beginning of the run, some not until the final weekend. Or, the reviewer comes early and his editor holds up the review until there is space, so it does not appear until the final weekend. The system is so unpredictable that the tension extends over the entire run. The gala Broadway opening night of a bygone era was certainly anxiety-producing, but, at least, the company could prepare for it psychologically, could stack the house with friends, wait up for the reviews in the morning's first paper, and, when it was over, it was over.

We had a big opening night at JRT when we did Arthur Miller's musical, Up from Paradise. A Miller premiere rated first-class critical coverage, and they all came, en masse, on the official opening night. Such a showing is designed for the big Broadway house where an army of critics can be spread throughout the orchestra, but in our one hundred–seat house, they took up three rows straight across, all with pens and pads, on the alert. It was like playing to the Berlin wall, and the rest of the audience was so intimidated that nobody dared to laugh. Every time John Simon's pen scratched across his pad, the entire row behind him leaned forward to read what he'd written.

In other words, you don't want them to come too early because you are not ready; you don't want them to come at the end of the run, when the review will do no good at the box office; you don't want them to straggle in one at a time and thereby stretch the tension out over the entire run; you don't want them to come all at once because that is so overwhelming in a tiny house.

But, most of all, you don't want them not to come.

The question is never as simple as "Is the review good, or is it bad?" First of all, it is important to be mindful of which paper the review is in. Some papers have more clout with the theatrical establishment than others, some with the younger ticket buyers, some with the older ones. The second question is, "Who wrote the review, is it an important reviewer or a second stringer, and if a second stringer killed it did someone more important elsewhere disagree?"

Furthermore, the review's impact will depend on the day of the week on which it appears. To be well reviewed by Frank Rich on page 3 of the Weekend section of the Friday New York Times is as good as it gets. A review in the Times on Saturday or Sunday has nowhere near as much impact. A review in the back of the section is not as good as one up front; top of the page is better than the bottom; with a photo is better than without.

Only then, does one wonder about the content of the review. If it is good, is it a "money" review, the kind that makes the reader want to rush for the phone to order tickets? If it is not so good, is there one quote that will make it seem like a rave in an ad? Many good reviews are, in fact, off-putting to the theatergoer, and many mediocre reviews make the reader want to see the show anyway. "The Times didn't like On Golden Pond," says Earl Graham. The play was moved to Broadway anyway because, according to Graham, the commercial powers-that-be knew that "all the stock theaters, all the amateur theaters were going to do this play to death. The play closed in five nights on Broadway, but demands for the stock and amateur rights were pouring in. Then, another producer opened it in a smaller house. Then, it was taken out on a first-class tour. In terms of the stock and amateur rights, it was one of the biggest successes to come along in the last couple of years. Then, the movie was sold to Jane Fonda, and the rest is history." William Finn says that Frank Rich's New York Times review of March of the Falsettos was so good, "it could have been written by my mother," but it is rare that the creators of a show feel that sure of how the reader will react. If anxiety has been the handmaiden in every step of the process so far, the same is true about the reading of the reviews.

"When the reviews [of The Dining Room] came out," says David Trainer "they needed interpretation. When I read the Times, I had no idea if it was good or bad. There was one wonderful quote, but we all retired to bed without knowing. Andre [the artistic director] said, 'We'll know in the morning if the phones ring.' Well, in the morning, the phones began to ring.

"The subsequent reviews were weekly. It was an impact that accumulated over time. An amazing thing happened. Time, New York Magazine, The New Yorker—each week, a different major publication had a good review, so that rather than, bang, everybody comes out one morning and that's it, it filtered out. Every place you turned, you picked up another magazine and there was another good review of The Dining Room. And, in this tiny theater, it began to build rapidly."

If the review is a bad one, everyone feels as if his life has gone down the drain. "When you're in rehearsal," says Mark Blum, "you live in a little insulated world of that rehearsal. You work every day with a small group of people and you trust each other. You have some initial belief in the project and then you become lost in that world and, although people gradually come into that world, the theater's staff, the artistic director, and the designers, and you hear feedback from them, slowly and gently, you don't really ever know anything until it's too late. You've already done it and the reviews are out.

"Doing a new play is like jumping out of an airplane with a parachute. Once you've jumped you've got to pull the thing and land where you land. Sometimes, the parachute doesn't work quite right and you end up being stupid. One of the hardest things about being an actor in New York is that, if you're going to have any fun and take any risks, you're occasionally going to be bad and people are going to make fun of you in public. People are going to write bad things about you in the paper that your parents are going to read. You know, that this is a talentless, stupid, bad actor, and that's unfortunate because nobody can be right all the time."

After a set of particularly bad reviews for a JRT production, the actors were seated around a table in the bar across the street, consoling one another, and one of the members of the cast, Austin Pendleton, said, "You are not a professional in this town until the New York Times comes and, the next day, for all the world to see, the critic says the show was a bomb and it was all your fault."

After that trauma, you pick yourself up, dust yourself off, and try again.

12

When a Show Moves

As soon as an off-off-Broadway production has been declared a hit, the possibility arises of transferring the show to a commercial theater, either on Broadway or off, for an unlimited run. Such a move means larger houses, higher ticket prices, more advertising, higher salaries for actors, increased royalties for director and writer, and a percentage of the take for the original showcase producer. In some cases, the off-off-Broadway house raises the money to make the move on its own; in most cases, a new producer from the commercial arena is brought into the venture.

"Once the reviews came out," says Lee Kalcheim, of *Breakfast with Les and Bess*, "my agent got on the phone and Barnet got on the phone and the Hudson Guild got on the phone. The theater, contractually, had the option to move it on their own, but they didn't have the wherewithall to do it."

This is so often the case that the standard contractual clause granting the off-off-Broadway house the first option to move the show or to co-produce it, is questioned by agents.

"If the showcase theater is in the business of commercial production, like Joe Papp, then that makes sense," says Earl Graham. "If not, then I have to say when they ask for that right in the first place, 'We're giving you a piece of the action so you are getting recompensed for your work. What is the purpose of your being involved in the move? You want to barter this play?' In one case, the attorney said, 'What if the producer wants our sets and costumes?' He can't have them without buying them, so they can negotiate a price. That has nothing to do with the author's contract. Moreover, he'd have to work out something with the designers. Anything that the theater has contributed cannot be used without permission. I have no problem with that, but I have to suspect why the theater would want the right to co-produce the play commercially when they are not commercial producers. The contract spells out the percentages the theater will get from the future of the play. I don't see the point of giving them anything more."

Of course, the reason is that the off-off-Broadway house can make more money if it can control the show in its commercial reincarnation. There is a big difference between co-producing and getting a percentage of the writer's royalties, even, as was the case with Gillian, where, according to Pamela Berlin, the new producers "basically bought EST out with a nice fat check." The Manhattan Theater Club gave up a great deal of potential profit when Ain't Misbehavin' was turned over to other producers and MTC was only given a percentage. "We figured we were young. We would learn and do it differently next time," says Lynne Meadow. "But how many times does an Ain't Misbehavin' come along?"

"The way Playwrights Horizons moves shows," says David Trainer, "is that board members put up the money. A woman named Anne Wilder financed the move of Sister Mary, and a woman named Edith Ehrman loaned Playwrights fifty thousand dollars for The Dining Room. If the play failed, that money would revert to a gift. If the play succeeded, she would be paid up to the amount of her loan, with no interest and no additional profits. Well, The Dining Room moved to the Astor Place Theatre, and the money was back in Edith's hands so fast, it didn't know where it had been. It may have taken more than a month, but not much. The set had to be rebuilt, but the tables and the rugs and the props were the same. The rest of the budget was for advertising, increased salaries. The Dining Room financially was always a lean and productive business enterprise."

In addition to the financial concerns of moving a show, new partners will bring new options and new pressures.

"Producers started coming down in droves," says Lee Kalcheim, about Breakfast with Les and Bess, "and there were offers. One was from a very good producer to move it to Broadway, but he wanted to shut it down and recast it with stars. Then, there were offers for off-Broadway. One producer wanted to take the package as fast as he could and put it in another theater. I wanted to compromise. I wanted to move to Broadway with these people. 'The reviews have just come out,' I argued. 'Frank Rich has said these people are wonderful. What the hell do you need stars for? How are stars born, anyhow?' But the producer felt that unless you put a star up on the marquee, people won't come. No matter how many examples I gave them of plays that had opened with no stars, they were called exceptions.

"I struggled with that dilemma and, ultimately, I didn't want to go through another opening. I didn't want to close, bring in new people, and then sit with all that tension thinking, 'Will the critics say the first cast was so wonderful and it doesn't look as good as it did?' So, I finally said, 'I think this cast is wonderful and I want to move it as it is. We'll go off-Broadway, and if it does well there, we can move into a Broadway house.'

"The irony was that, in January 1980, there were plenty of Broadway houses available, but none off-Broadway. I couldn't believe it. The show was optioned and we had to wait through January, then February. Still, there were no theaters and we were beginning to lose actors. Tommy Nolan's wife was eight-and-a-half-months pregnant and her family lives in Utah. I'm saying, 'Don't leave town. We're going to move this,' so he hung around and hung around and finally decided that they were going to drive back home, and they got halfway to Utah, and she gave birth.

"It wasn't the producer's fault. There just weren't any theaters available. We looked. We went down to the Provincetown Play-house, but it was too small. Every day you're waiting for the phone to ring, you're hoping someone's play will close. Then, to put the icing on the cake, one of the two producers involved didn't have the money. If we had found a theater the next day, he didn't have the money to go in there anyway. So, another producer called and said, 'I have a theater.' We made a partnership with him and then his theater fell through.

"Out of the blue, the Lambs Theatre became available and was offered to us. We had lost Tommy Nolan, and Amy Wright had gone into something else, but we galvanized ourselves and every-thing happened very quickly. Now, the problem was that there had been a layoff between January and May. We had lost the momen-tum. We had to republicize and get the critics back. They finally came, and it ran eight or nine months.

"If I had to do it again, I probably would opt to go to Broadway. I didn't have the guts then. I was exhausted and didn't want to close down, look for stars, wait a year. I liked these actors and felt a sense of loyalty to them. With hindsight, knowing how the theater operates now, I should have taken the chance. I didn't realize until

I saw Dick Van Dyke do it in the PBS version. Now, Keith Charles was absolutely wonderful, but Dick was wonderful, too, and Dick's a star. People would have come to see Dick Van Dyke do it on Broadway, but they would not have come to see Keith Charles. I think it's wrong, but that's the way it works."

Generally, if the move is to be to Broadway, the new producers not only want to bring in stars, they want to replace the director with a name.

Pamela Berlin says, "There was serious interest from three different places, and two were less interested in taking me. One wanted to chuck the whole cast, as well as me, and start over again. I did not have a contract with EST, so it was up to Michael [the playwright], who said, 'I'm not doing it again unless Pam directs it.' There was nothing on paper. It was all Michael."

According to Lee Kalcheim, "One of the producers who wanted to move Les and Bess to Broadway wanted to get rid of Barnet. I said, 'I am not going to do that. You're wrong.' "

Controlling the choice of cast and director is another advantage an off-off-Broadway company has when it moves the show on its own. Amy Introcaso claims that Playwrights Horizons has never dropped an actor or director in a commercial move. "Sometimes, they don't come. Michael Gross was in Geniuses and he went off to do "Family Ties," but if a show is a hit, we think it's because of the playwright and the director and those actors who are in it."

When a cast replacement is required, says Introcaso, "There is always the problem that everyone remembers the performance that the other guy gave. I tend to look for replacements who are not exactly like the original actor. It's better to get a different type so that the other actors and the playwright and director do not think this is someone who is just not as good. If you get someone who is slightly different, you get a different reaction."

And the actor stepping in always feels the pressure. Mark Blum took over for David Marshall Grant when Table Settings moved, and he says, "James Lapine gave me the shape of the speeches in a way that I couldn't understand. I didn't hear the music of it, and the comedy was in the music. I could only take it by rote as he was giving it to me, and I thought, 'Oh, oh, I am in trouble here because we are only a week away and I'm not hearing this at all.' I was only reproducing it as it was being given to me and I was panicking.

"I had a very heated private conversation with Lapine. I said,

'Look, I don't feel that I am giving you anything of mine. It seems that all I am capable of doing to satisfy the needs of the play is to reproduce rhythms that you have in your head, but that I'm not hearing in my own head.' Jim said, 'I do want what you have but we're on a very short time schedule here. This piece is very musical and I have the music in my head.' His feeling was that if I sang the song simply by the notes, that the rhythm would fill me with the life of it, which eventually was true. But it was a different way of working than I had ever done before, and there was the added complication that the writer was the director.

"I would have liked the amount of time that everybody else had so that I really would have had my own rhythms working for me by the time we came to lock things in. But here I was, everyone else was staged and their voices were connected and I was trying to get into the flow of a play that already existed, and it was important that I get there fast. Eventually, since I did the play for a long time, I felt like it became very much my own part, and very much infused with my own voice."

An important consideration in making a successful move is finding the right space, particularly if the move is to Broadway.

Christopher Durang was brought up on television comedy and had his first play produced at the Yale Cabaret. His humor is sly, quick, savage, and it works best when the actor is within winking distance of the audience. His work and his talent have been molded by the space of the new theater.

Two of his early plays, *A History of the American Film* and *Beyond Therapy* were successes off-off-Broadway and in regional theaters, and both were brought to Broadway with lots of advance hoopla. In each case, the designers filled the stage with elaborate sets. In *Beyond Therapy*, the set changes took so long, they played havoc with the essential rhythm of the script. In *A History of the American Film*, the actors had to broaden the humor in order not to be dwarfed by the space. Both Broadway productions were failures.

Shirley Lauro's *Open Admissions* started out in the Ensemble Studio Theatre's annual one act play marathon. The script was tight, tense, explosive, and brilliant. It was a two-character, one-set play, and in the confrontation which occurred between the two people, the audience found out everything it needed to know about their pasts, their families, their struggles, the city, the world in which this was taking place. The compression imposed on the piece by the tiny space is what made the play work.

With rave reviews, the play was optioned for Broadway and the writer was told to expand. The eventual production had more sets, more scenes, more people, more explanations, more words, and much less success. The play had been a miniature gem, created out of the writer's sense of city life and the way tightness of space and lack of time builds to a frustrating horror. By expanding the play to a length that destroyed its rhythm, for a space that diminished its tension, the writer lost her play.

Similar fates awaited *Angels Fall*, *The Human Comedy*, *King of the Shnorrers*, *Leader of the Pack*, *Passione*: all successes in their original spaces, all failures when moved to Broadway.

This is the reason many productions now resist this move to Broadway and prefer an off-Broadway house. Marsha Norman's *Getting Out* premiered at the Actors Theatre of Louisville and opened in New York at the Phoenix Theatre. When it was transferred to commercial auspices, the producers wisely chose an off-Broadway, instead of a Broadway house, the exquisite Theatre DeLys (now the Lucille Lortel Theatre) in Greenwich Village. The decision to retain the intimacy necessary for the play paid off with a long, healthy run.

Even financially, staying small makes sense. These days, a large chunk of a production's income comes from subsidiary rights: regional, stock, amateur, touring productions after the New York run. *Breakfast with Les and Bess* has been optioned for a television series. *March of the Falsettos* was produced in England. It is often wiser to stay small; get good reviews; have a lengthy, prestigious New York run; and then reap the profits from the subsidiary rights, than to make the riskier move to Broadway, lay an egg, and severely damage all future possibilities for the play and the production.

However, space problems can be as acute off-Broadway as they are on. *To Gillian on Her 37th Birthday* moved from EST to off-Broadway's Circle In The Square. "We lost a lot in moving," says Pamela Berlin. "The production was as good, if not better, but the space was a big detriment. The space at EST was a problem but there was something magical about creating a spacious beach in a claustrophobic little room and having the audience believe it. Circle In The Square may have been the right theater for *American Buffalo*, but it was not right for *Gillian*. There is a lot of beauty in the play and there is not a lot of beauty in that space, nor any that you can create. It's three-quarters round so people are sitting across from one another, they can see each other. We lost the surrounding sky. We had everything down at one end and the actors were playing in a long bowling alley. They were a mile apart, instead of being three feet apart, which is what they had been before. With that show, in which the physical life set the tone and the closeness established the intimacy, with a script that was not all there, when the space was wrong, it affected the actors and a great deal got lost."

After the off-Broadway success of The Dining Room, it was produced at Washington's Kennedy Center, with a completely new cast, including Barry Nelson and Frances Sternhagen. But, in this case, the change in the size of the house had a positive impact on the play. "We opened in a theater with 78 seats," says Trainer. "It moved downstairs at Playwrights, where there were 150. The Astor Place had 299. When it got to the Kennedy Center, it played to 1,100 and, there, the response was BOOM and the same every night. You have a sufficient cross-section of humanity so that it becomes predictable. If you do something sort of like you did it last night, there are enough people that the mix is going to go BOOM. In a small theater, if there are three people who don't think it's funny, they can affect a whole section of the audience.

"My experience of plays is that they vary a lot from night to night, but a well-rehearsed play always delivers the payoff. The actors know where they've got to go, but how they get there varies a lot, and there is always that extra part, which is the audience. The audience begins to respond in a certain way and you can't help but deal with it."

A move to a larger house often requires major adjustments on the actors' behalf. Marshall Mason discusses the move of As Is from Circle Rep to Broadway's 750-seat Lyceum Theatre:

The actors were playing it downtown for eight weeks, so they weren't too thrown by anything when we moved. The first day of rehearsal up here they were clowning around. They were secure enough, in other words, to take it lightly. But the biggest problem is always volume, especially after you've played a 160-seat theater. Mark Myers plays right down front, and every night I go back and give him another note saying, "Even bigger." It's hard sometimes for an actor to imagine that they've got to be that loud because they get so used to playing the scene right next to you. Fortunately, this theater is not like other theaters I've played where you really have to belt it out. You can be pretty conversational in here and still be heard. But the hardest thing was finding the right level—how to be loud enough, retain the intimacy, and not play out front all the time. The problem was to get them to open out a little more. I'd say, "Hey, you're on Broadway, it's okay. All the audience is out here, they're not in the wings." I've encouraged them to open out a little, which has been the hardest part.*

A Broadway move often requires major design changes in the set. While both Breakfast with Les and Bess and The Dining Room had to be rebuilt to fit onto their new off-Broadway stages, As Is required serious rethinking of the set.

One of the elements that was important to the design of As Is downtown, was that I wanted the stage to be a classical stage, to have a sort of Greek feeling about it. So we came up with the idea of the columns and the fact that the stage was really, literally, a stage. In the Circle Rep stage, since it's a black box, it was simple. We just built a little stage and put it like an island in the middle. But getting that same effect on Broadway is difficult because you have a proscenium here, and the feeling of a stage floating in the middle of a stage was not so easy to accomplish. What we did first, in order to achieve that, was to rake the stage.

David Potts, our designer, also said, "I think it's very important that we retain the same proportion because we've got the proportion that we want, the proper human scale for the drama." We didn't want to make them into O'Neill characters by having the set very much bigger and the people small. At the same time, downtown the columns just went up as far as the ceiling and then stopped. I said, "David, why don't we finish them off and make them into arches." So that's how the arches came about. It finishes the columns architecturally, so your eye is satisfied as you look to the top. But at the same time, we kept the light grid down at the thirteen feet, six inches level, which maintains the former scale.

I made the bed larger. The bed downtown was a couch unit which transformed into the bed. I told the designer, "I don't want the literalism of a hospital bed. The play is poetry, we are addressing issues of life and death; it's not a clinical play." I wanted the furniture to reflect that kind of universal quality. So we had a couch that was wooden and then during the scene change that couch became the bed. When we moved uptown, we had the luxury of being able to have a separate couch and a separate bed,

---

* James Furlong, ed., "Mason Discusses His Work," Journal of the Society of Stage Directors and Choreographers, (Summer 1986).

but I retained the same look for them. I made the bed six inches longer and four inches wider because after we opened downtown, I started looking it over and thought, "Oh, that bed, boy, it's awfully small." I made it just a little bit larger so that the audience wouldn't think about how small it was. The couch was just a big old piece of plywood downtown and I said to David, "Let's make it bigger." Those were the luxuries we couldn't do downtown, not because of the expense, but because of storage space.

I believe we were budgeted—including television advertising and, what do you call it? cushion—for $500,000. I think that the move was done for about half that and the rest was for advertising and cushion.*

The move of Breakfast with Les and Bess cost, according to Lee Kalcheim, "around $300,000 and it was underbudgeted. That got it on but there was very little in reserve. It didn't allow enough for advertising.

"We rehearsed for two weeks. We were terribly afraid the layoff would hurt, but it didn't. Something had happened. The actors were better. It was fresh. We had to do some recasting, which was hard, and then, of course, we had made some changes. The actors knew that some work had been done on the script and that was helpful.

"Of course to an audience, there may seem no changes at all, but to the actors, changes require some rethinking. Yet, I felt it had more timbre when they came back. The laying off of it seemed to help. At the first rehearsal, they were just jumping in and they seemed better than ever.

"Basically, I think it was a better play than it had been at the Hudson Guild, and we opened and the response was by and large the same. We had to republicize it and get the critics back to get people to come, but the audience response was good. They laughed in the right places. The difference between playing for an audience of 120 and one of 300 is not that great—maybe the laughs are bigger because there are more people.

"In terms of the transfer, the rehearsal experience and the work on the play was all wonderful; the hard part was the practical problems, finding the right producer and the right theater."

David Trainer also found that re-rehearsing The Dining Room for the transfer was not a problem. "It was a well-rehearsed show, so the

---

* "Mason Discusses His Work."

actors knew what they were supposed to be doing. It was a bigger stage, so timing was affected, but these were top pros. It took them another thirty seconds. You have to walk on stage another foot, big deal.

"Then we started previewing and the first night at the Astor Place was incredibly smooth. The second night there were problems in adjusting to the new space, but the first night is going to be great because everyone cares about the outcome. Andre Bishop told me that. He was saying, 'You've got to be there. You just can't move it in one night and go away.' We were all learning how to do this. Nobody knew and we were helping each other through. We were a happy group of people. First of all, there's nothing like success to make people happy. But also, it was a very affectionate group; not without tension, because when you are dealing with a cast there are always tensions but, basically, we had a great time.

"Sometimes, first productions can obscure a play so no one ever sees what's there. I am trying not to praise myself but I think this first production of The Dining Room was true to the play so that the production was successful. I benefited from that personally as well, but the play benefited too because it was seen and understood. It has been done around the world and people who were going to do it came to the Astor Place and saw it, and no matter where they did it, they learned from that original production.

"One of the things I've found the more plays I direct is that there is less to directing than meets the eye. It is having the sense of knowing where the heat and the life of the play is and then clearing away the debris that surrounds it. It's great fun. When I read a play and it's got a life that I respond to, I feel, 'Let's go. Let's clear all the garbage away and get this out there.'

"Some plays just work. Who knows? If you could predict, you'd be a magician. But I'll say this about The Dining Room: whatever incidental tensions and pressures there were, and they were great, the life was always there. We always came back to that simple thing. This play works. It's going to get us through. We just have to keep on."

13

Survival Tactics

We started this book with a glance at those wonderful, attractive, talented kids who descend on New York City full of optimism and good cheer. Unfortunately, within a very few years, most of them are sour and disappointed, and their talent has been bent out of shape. Talent must be encouraged. It must be used. It must have response. It must be protected. But the person most responsible for providing that protection is the artist himself and he can do that by honing his sense of reality into a shield.

Anyone entering the theater filled with fantasy is in for constant hurt. That hurt seeps into the system and shrivels the talent. Every young theater artist must be prepared not to internalize rejection, so that the inner life stays healthy and usable.

Play development depends on collaboration that can only be achieved when there is honest interaction, responsiveness, and mutual respect. When artists enter the rehearsal hall with other agenda—a hunger for stardom, paranoia, power needs, fear of failure—the play is sure to die. Working on a new script is intimately connected to the tensions of the world in which it happens. The young actor, director, or writer has to learn how to survive in that world so he will walk into rehearsal with an open mind and heart. He must hang his deprivations in the hallway with his hat.

The artist who is jaded and tired, who wallows in old wounds, who is suspicious and unreachable, cannot be a part of the play development process. Everybody has tales of woe about how they lost parts unfairly; how the script was ruined by an inept director; how the actor who did the reading got gypped out of the production; how the bad reviews were caused by a fluke. Theater people learn to roll from disaster to disaster, from one unproductive reading to the next, but, somehow, their passion and commitment stays alive. Their aim is not stardom, but survival.

The actor who stays in a small town, works for a corporation like IBM and pours his heart out for the community theater at night, the director who teaches and does three student productions a year, the writer who works at his desk after the kids have been put to bed—these people have an easier time of it. They keep the dream unsoiled and their impulses fresh. They continue to get joy out of their work. This is hard to do in New York, where dreams become a public commodity—batted around and handled and compromised by every producer, director, agent, and wheeler-dealer on the street.

The problem might be that New York is too full of projects, fantasy, prospects. College actors, getting off the bus, are hot property because they are new. Talented kids may find the scene easier to crack than they ever thought it would be. If they are twenty-two and look seventeen, they are eminently castable. Teen-agers are needed for casting in commercials and soaps, as film extras, on videos, and on the stage.

Two years later, however, they cannot play those parts anymore, certainly not before the camera's unrelenting eye. They are no longer teens. They are not yet ready for the next castable category—rising exec, young parent. The work stops and it has nothing to do with talent. It has to do with "the look": whether it fits into a category, whether it is fresh or overexposed. They have to wait until they are definable again.

Their phones stop ringing. They wonder if they are broken. Their agents do not return their calls. They go to EPAs and see hundreds, no thousands, of faces like their own. They cannot get appointments for auditions. Six months ago, their books were filled. Now, there is nothing to do all day.

It gets worse. The theater world circulates around work. When they are in a show, actors have no time for anything else, certainly not family or civilian friends. The experience they share with other cast members is so intense, no other relationship can compete. There is so much to talk about. The dream gets richer because it is shared. Their lives are wonderful because they belong. There is that wonderful opening night party. Sometimes, there is a closing night party, although it is never as wonderful.

When they are not working, there are fewer calls. Everybody

else, it seems, is working. Everybody has found a new family. Those that are left behind have nothing as interesting to talk about. They cannot even go see a play because they get consumed by jealousy.

When I was a young writer, I met a colleague on the street. He was doing much better than I was; winning grants, getting produced. Still, he told me, he was depressed. (In Manhattan, you have these surprisingly intimate conversations on street corners.) He told me he was thinking of leaving the city and going back home to write.

"Why, for crying out loud?" I asked. "You're doing so well!"

"Somebody's always doing better," he said. "In New York, everyone feels like a failure."

How does one survive in a system where the pay is low and erratic; where there is no daily schedule to rely upon; no annual promotions to define value; no job titles to keep parents informed of progress; where close friends are competitors; where there is no credit for past successes; where ninety percent of every day is spent looking for a job?

Coping with these reality problems often requires artists to wrap themselves in protective armor. The irony is that it is the availability of dreams and hopes, of feelings and sensitivities, of secrets and needs, that are the tools of the trade. Nobody wants to see an actor onstage whose defenses are all he can offer, or one who communicates desperate need. Nobody will produce the writer's play if it is filled with self-pity and misery.

How does one stay open and vulnerable in a way that is needed in the rehearsal hall, yet protect oneself from the onslaught that awaits, outside the door?

Everyone who has been on it knows about the murderous merry-go-round: fantasy; anxiety; failure; depression; bitterness. Those who survive learn to grow armed against it. Still, the newcomer arrives; unprepared, unwarned, undefended, and goes for a ride.

Theater people keep themselves afloat with fantasy. They feed on it, hand it out to others. Producers pass it to directors, directors to actors, actors to friends.

The higher the level of fantasy in any project, the more the level of anxiety rises because the stakes are huge and exposure is public. Yet, anxiety is the greatest enemy to creative work, and it increases the chance of failure. Fear of failure increases the anxiety.

When failure does come, the fantasy crashes. Because there are so few outside supports, this leads to depression and isolation. Self-pity follows, along with paralysis, bitterness, desperation, and everything that sours the work.

Once that happens, a dead end has been reached. Protecting oneself against this cycle is the most important part of surviving in the theater—more important than good head shots, having a nose job, or finding an agent. Working on new scripts cannot be separated from this essential struggle.

As I have traveled the bumpy road of my career, I have picked up a few helpful hints that might be of value.

YOU ARE AFTER A LIFE, NOT JUST A CAREER.   A career in New York theater is a tough way to run a life. The disaster rate is very high. People turn into drunks, into crazies, into addicts. This is not because they are neurotic or weak-willed or losers. The structure of the life itself offers no supports. There is so much time spent waiting, alone, out of work. The competition is intense. The expectations are huge. The failure is mortifying. If you have to dive into this world, you have to—and the joys are intense—but you must be aware of the traps. You must face facts and be armed with weapons: a way to earn a living, outside interests, other areas that will feed your self-esteem, family and friends, an inner sense of structure, a hold on reality.

CREATE A SUPPORT SYSTEM THAT WILL GET YOU THROUGH THE LOWS.   The measure of strength in your life is not how it feeds your success, but how it gets you through the failures. Brain surgeons do not get reviewed in the New York Times, but young playwrights and actors on their first outings do. In this business, failure is inevitable and everyone is going to hear about it. Even more frequent and equally damaging are the dry periods. Writers get blocked. A director's confidence gets so shaken by a bomb that it takes two years to get back his touch. Actors have faces that are out of sync with their qualities. There are some twenty-year-old actors with the bearing, the tone, the feel of a forty-year-old. They will get a lot of work eventually, but it is going to be a long, twenty-year wait. You must have supports while you tough it out. Don't lose touch with your family and outside friends. Don't turn your back on intimate relationships because you are so devoted to your career. Find a lover, get married, have kids. If fame is going to strike, you can have it all. When it is not striking, these are the people who will help you hang in there until it does.

IF YOU FIND A CREATIVE HOME, STICK WITH IT.   Every artist wants a home, everyone needs one. It is where you will do your best work, and if you are doing good work, the world will find you. Look at how many successful careers developed out of long-term relationships of writers with directors, actors with companies, directors with designers: Marshall Mason and Lanford Wilson and Circle Rep, John Malkovitch and Steppenwolf Theatre Company, Jerry Zaks and Christopher Durang. It takes a long time, a lot of trust, intimacy, and a history to do good work. Protect yourself against the one-shot method of off-off-Broadway production by finding a home. Once you have found one, do not turn your back and go running to the better offer, the bigger name, the next step up, as soon as it falls into your lap. Think it over. You might be losing more than you are gaining.

CREATE A PROJECT OF YOUR OWN.   Anne Meara once told me that she and Jerry Stiller developed their stand-up comedy act because "it was the only way of escaping the anonymity of being New York actors." They made a name for themselves in clubs, became stars on television, started doing summer tours because of their name value and, now, have come full cycle and are the respected stage and film actors they set out to become. Susan Merson toured her one-woman show to high school gyms, Hadassah meetings, ladies' luncheons, and for years, it paid the rent between jobs. It was Pat Carroll who cast herself as Gertrude Stein, who originated her one-woman show, who commissioned the script. Actors, directors, and writers should use their free time to create projects they can do anywhere with a stool and a lightbulb. Outside of Manhattan, there are spaces to be filled and audiences hungry for live theater. If you have a project that you can carry on your back, it can be sold, and you will have some control over your creative life.

LEARN TO HANDLE YOUR ANXIETY.   I have learned a great deal about my work from playing tennis. When I am on the court, relaxed and happy, concentrating on the process, not competing, not being judged, not aware that I am being watched from the sidelines, it is amazing what I can do. Relaxation and pleasure allow the blood to flow through the veins. The nerve endings send messages to the muscles and the body figures things out on its own. Movement flows. Intuition flourishes. Impulses are clear. New ideas emerge. Execution is effortless. The next day, if I am uptight, frightened, inhibited, and eager to please, I cannot hit the ball.

Working in theater is similar. You cannot force it. You cannot worry it. There is only so much you can be taught. Art is controlled by the psyche and the nerve endings, not by conscious control, not by good intent, not by gritted teeth. If you have found a way to relax—yoga, breathing, gossip, prayer—use it. If you have found a place and a community in which you are comfortable, where you have a sense of privacy and protection, you will do your best, however good that is. If you have not learned to handle your anxiety, it will become a paralyzing force and no one will be able to see through it.

IF THE FATES TAKE YOU IN ANOTHER DIRECTION, DON'T FIGHT THEM.   I once hired an actor for a small role and also to serve as assistant stage manager. He was a terrific ASM; efficient, dependable, responsible, thorough. On my next show, I offered him the job of stage manager but he turned me down. "If directors start thinking of you as a stage manager," he said, "you don't get any more acting jobs." I think he was making a mistake.

Getting a reputation as a good stage manager will, first of all, help pay the rent because stage managers can always find jobs. The talented ones move from the smaller houses to the bigger houses to the Public Theater with the speed of lightning. It is a good way to meet directors and writers and stay in the thick of things. And who knows where it will lead? The stage manager of that first show I did at the Albee-Barr Playwrights' Unit was Lindsay Law, who is now executive producer of the renowned American Playhouse series on Public Television. He moved from stage managing off-Broadway, to stage managing on television, to producing.

A second career can help if you are in a period when you are waiting-it-out. You have a way of hanging in there. Writers should direct. Actors should write. Directors should produce. If you end up successful in a way you had not expected to be, remember that it was never your success in one field that caused your failure in the other.

If the theater world offers you a way to achieve validation and payment, take it. You will not get better at what you want to do by banging your head against a stone wall.

JOIN THE ADMINISTRATORS. Institutional theater is controlled by administrators, and many creative people have developed good skills in order to further their careers. Gordon Davidson, Jon Jory, Marshall Mason and Lynne Meadow all run their theaters, as well as direct. Robyn Goodman, co-director of the Second Stage, is an actor. Her partner, Carole Rothman, directs. David Mamet got his plays produced by starting the St. Nicholas Theater Company in Chicago.

Many writers serve as literary managers. The pay for these jobs is usually slim, but it guarantees you a shot at what you really want to do. If you are a writer and there is a small theater you wish to work with, offer to sort through the pile of unread manuscripts. You will soon be literary adviser. An actor should offer to file the eight-by-ten glossies. She might end up casting director. If you have an administrative talent, cash it in to get where you want to go.

IF YOU DO NOT JOIN THE ADMINISTRATORS, WATCH THEM AT WORK. In institutional theater, it is the artistic director who is the real star, and his funding sources—the philanthropists, grant givers, foundation heads, and boards of directors—are the most significant audience. The people who have pushed their theaters into the big leagues— Gordon Davidson, Zelda Fichandler, George C. White—are brilliant at handling the money people, wheeling and dealing with the tycoons. This is often difficult for artists to do.

Writers have to cope with artistic directors who love them when they are eighteen-year-old "emerging talents," but are not so happy when they are twenty-five-year olds who wish to be treated like adult professionals. Actors are expected to be dangled like orna-ments at benefit galas. Directors have to take notes from community leaders with high moral standards. Theater supporters can be in it for reasons which make the artists cringe. The air is often ripe with condescension. Talented administrators let it roll off their backs. They get what they want out of the money world, smile when being infantilized, and still retain their self-esteem. Watch what they do and learn how they do it.

New Dramatists has a fancy board of directors consisting of

powerhouse theatrical attorneys and agents, big-time producers, Broadway playwrights of another era, and rich old ladies. The charter requires that four member-playwrights also serve on the Board; one year, I was one of these. We four approached those meetings in a Park Avenue boardroom with terror and fascination. We huddled together at one end of the table. Whenever something patronizing was said about writers, we muffled our hurt and bit our tongues.

The executive director, at the time, was Kathleen Norris, a classy lady who knew how to kiss cheeks with panache, flirt and gossip when required, but still fiercely protected her writers. Once, Kathleen was reviewing the upcoming schedule at a meeting and, as she often did, was exhorting the board members to come to the readings.

"Kathleen, darling," said one famed woman producer, "if you held your readings in the afternoon, we'd come. Schedule some weekday matinees for us. In the evenings, my dear, we go to the theater."

Eight sets of knuckles at my end of the table turned white. It was difficult to hear that and not feel belittled. But Kathleen didn't miss a beat.

"My dear, you are forgetting something," she responded sweetly. "You see, we are the theater."

Index